CROWN
&CASTLE

First published 1978
The O'Brien Press
11 Clare Street, Dublin 2, Ireland

© Copyright reserved
ISBN 0 905140 11 7

Jacket design: Michael O'Brien
Binding: J. F. Newman Ltd.
Typesetting: Redsetter Ltd.
Printed by Folens Printing Co. Ltd.

CROWN & CASTLE

BRITISH RULE IN IRELAND 1800-1830

Edward Brynn

THE O'BRIEN PRESS
11 CLARE ST DUBLIN 2

CONTENTS

Introduction

The Viceregal Lodge, Phoenix Park, Dublin

INTRODUCTION

Since World War II Ireland's history has been illuminated by an impressive series of new studies on demography, administration and economic development. Once biography dominated Irish historical scholarship; this is not so much the case now. Inevitably, many of these newer studies are monographic and they constitute the literature through which specialists in the field of Irish history address one another.[1] The appearance of books and articles on subjects of narrow compass presages increased efforts to expose the nooks and crannies of Ireland's past to intense and sometimes disorienting scrutiny. From all this will emerge a corpus of historical literature equal in its own compass to that of nations which have long sustained a vigorous and highly sophisticated tradition of historical scholarship.

In all this, considerable emphasis has been placed upon the full century separating the Act of Union from the advent of World War I in 1914. The difficult theme of administrative history has been particularly well served by Professor R. B. McDowell of Trinity College.[2] Irish politics has been given a Namierite interpretation in E. M. Johnston's *Great Britain and Ireland, 1760-1800,* written in 1963. A very high level of scholarship has been reached in Charles Townshend's recent study of *The British Campaign and Ireland 1919-1921: The Development of Political and Military Policies.* R. D. Collison Black's *Economic Thought and the Irish Question, 1817-1870* and K. H. Connell's studies on Irish demography have established new standards in those areas. Ecclesiastical and educational developments during the nineteenth century have also attracted their share of gifted students.

As each new contribution to Irish history sees the light of day it becomes more incumbent on those who seek to make their own mark to reconcile their contribution to the larger framework already in place. This is especially the case in the nineteenth century, where perennially attractive themes such as Catholic emancipation, the great famine, and agitation to repeal the Act of Union continue to feature prominently. In this case an effort is made to draw together a number of theses, some of which have already been studied in isolation, and to marry them to those individuals who early in the last century were charged with the responsibility for sustaining British power in a troubled and often fractious land. By viewing the administrative dynamic in the context of some of the British viceroys themselves it is hoped that this monograph will appeal to a readership at once interested in the development of Irish political institutions and at the same time discouraged by studies which present large amounts of administrative detail. By treating several themes as they interacted with one of the nation's most important institutions, this small contribution to the corpus of Irish historical literature may suggest new dimensions for study in a period particularly important in terms of Ireland's emergence as a modern nation-state.

The half century stretching from the revival of an independent Irish parliament in 1782 to the enactment of Catholic emancipation in 1829 featured a quickening of the pace of Irish history. Nationalist sentiment sharpened, and for a brief moment Catholics and Protestants alike dreamed of a secular state able to command the loyalty of all economic, social, and denominational elements within the island. Late in the eighteenth century the Irish economic picture brightened, and a new confidence in the nation's prospects was reflected in the reconstruction of Dublin and several provincial centres. Leaders worthy of the nation's new confidence took their place at the helm of public affairs and the literary achievement, impressive even in darker times, challenged England itself for the right to shape the course of the English language.

The happy flow of events was distracted by war on the continent, rebellion at home, extinction of the independent legislature, and collapse of an ecumenical approach to the religious problem. Collapse of the age of Charlemont and Grattan, nonetheless, was followed soon enough by the emergence of that of O'Connell. Hopes and fears stirred. The process of defining

7

Ireland's future resumed, even if almost every element was changed. Social conflict sharpened as depressed classes waxed militant. Britain's enemies hoped to exploit discontent, and every concession at Westminster seemed only to whet the nationalists' appetite. Hope alternated with despair, and for many Ireland's sense of historical purpose seemed to have been sacrificed on the altar of fratricidal struggle.

On other fronts, however, a new Ireland began to emerge in the early decades of the nineteenth century. Among the most important ingredients of this change was administrative reform and the emergence of a new middle class. Reform of Ireland's ancient instruments of government was destined to prepare the way for a more interventionist age in the interpretation of administrative responsibilities. The new middle class would challenge the tastes and indeed the viability of the old landlord-tenant relationship. Out of all this would come a new social and political fabric which, despite further rebellion, economic change, and alienation from Britain, would carry most of the island to the days of the Republic.

Every age can be held up as a watershed of one sort or another. Without forcing this conviction beyond tolerable limits, this small study pursues the idea that the first three decades of the nineteenth century saw the gradual emergence of modern Ireland in its essential respects. In part the change was administrative and in part popular tastes began to dictate to the entrenched aristocracy. Old ways of doing things tried to resist the tide of innovation. For a moment Ireland ceased to produce writers of the first rank and instead seemed to devote attention to the immediate and painful questions of tithe reform, Catholic relief, famine, and endemic rural unrest.

Superintending, or at least watching, all these developments in the early nineteenth century was the Lord Lieutenant as representative of the Crown in Ireland. There is a tendency among historians to dismiss this ancient office as little more than an anachronism, a reminder of the distant past when English rule in Ireland depended largely upon the vigor and enterprise of a single individual. In fact, as McDowell has observed, even in the nineteenth century "Irish conditions encouraged or compelled the state to exert itself vigorously on a more extensive front than in contemporary England," and a control feature herein was the viceroy. Without advancing pretensions on behalf of the Lord Lieutenant such as one can find in his patent, this study will take advantage of the continued existence of the office after the Act of Union to provide a perspective on change and continuity in Ireland during the first third of the nineteenth century. It is hoped that an administrative analysis leavened by biographical studies of the viceroys themselves will attract the interest of those readers for whom institutional history is sometimes tedious and at other times perplexing. More important, by focusing on Ireland's chief executives it may be possible to suggest several dimensions to the phenomenon of modernisation in Ireland which heretofore have not received the attention they perhaps deserve.

The administrative apparatus centred on Dublin Castle at the outset of the nineteenth century was small, almost intimate. Those departments — there were almost two dozen of them — which were not housed inside the castle walls were often close enough to be nearly considered so. This intimacy and proximity suggested to one chief secretary that Ireland's official functions were "conducted only by continuous conversation". Coupled with this and in part stemming from it was the tendency in Ireland to take a strictly pragmatic approach to new problems as they came to Dublin's attention. This pragmatism encouraged a spirit of innovation which quite frequently meant that Ireland took the lead in devising new procedures and policies for meeting the needs of a society in the process (however slow and uneven) of modernisation. It also encouraged reliance upon strong personalities, and this element will feature prominently in the following pages. Administrative change and the impress of certain personalities were ultimately reflected in a substantial rationalisation of Irish government; in the space of thirty years all but four of Ireland's departments were abolished or amalgamated. In this sense the pace of change was almost revolutionary, and this study will examine the role of the viceroy in this process.

It would be a mistake to see governmental change in early nineteenth century Ireland as simply or even primarily an exercise in bureaucratic rationalisation, however. Attitudes which had served to sustain the traditional order of things were in flux, and in many cases this change was reflected in successive viceroys' social engagements and in their efforts to manipulate public opinion. Much of this activity strikes the modern observer as frivolous or pointless, but in the context of a society still distinctly traditional and in some respects almost tribal, the ritual of official life was quite as important as the substance of it. Again the viceroy was looked to as the barometer of future

9

political weather, and much as in the case of monarchs of old his every move was given' significance. Intended or not, such symbolism lay at the heart of the Irish polity, as goes far to explain why the viceregal system survived in Ireland long after its purely administrative value was widely discounted.

This study is distinguished from many efforts in administrative history by the emphasis placed on the use of private rather than public correspondence. Of these private collections the richest are those belonging to Hardwicke and Wellesley. The Hardwicke papers were the subject of some interest at the beginning of the century when historians mined them to confirm stories of naked patronage abuses attending passage of the Act of Union. The Wellesley papers are more voluminous but those relating to Ireland have not been extensively used until recently. The papers of the Duke of Richmond housed in the National Library of Ireland constitute a smaller but useful source. Many other manuscript collections, some obscure and some prominent, have also been consulted. Several monographs and a good many longer books suggest to what extent this effort is indebted to the fine work of other scholars.

At first glance the footnotes will appear rather too extensive for a book of this size. Any effort to present history to a general audience must see a sacrifice of many details. In terms of scholarship this is sometimes a most painful process, and yet without consolidation general themes are often submerged in the wealth of detail connected to every event. The footnotes will assist the reader who wishes to pursue one or other subjects further than is possible here.

Many friends and acquaintances contributed generously of their talent and time in the preparation of this manuscript. I am indebted in particular to the staffs of the National Library of Ireland, the Royal Irish Academy, the Library of Congress, and the United States Air Force Academy. Much of the writing took place in the somewhat improbable setting of South Asia while on assignment in the Foreign Service of the United States. In a very real if indirect way I am indebted to Professor R. B. McDowell of the Department of Modern History at Trinity College. He has demonstrated to a sceptical generation that the history of institutions and ideas, set in the context of administrative analysis, could be made interesting as well as informative. My mother, Mrs. Walter Brynn, contributed her secretarial and editorial expertise in each of several drafts. My wife Jane supplied the necessary patience and encouragement which only one also in love with history and Ireland can muster. The interpretations and the errors are left to me.

TABLE I

MEMBERS OF BRITISH MINISTRIES WITH EFFECT IN IRISH GOVERNMENT 1800-1806

First Lord of the Treasury (Prime Minister)	Secretary of State for the Home Department	Lord Lieutenant	Chief Secretary to the Lord Lieutenant
WILLIAM PITT Dec. 1783–Mar. 1801	WILLIAM HENRY CAVENDISH CAVENDISH-BENTINCK, Duke of Portland July 1794–July 1801	CHARLES CORNWALLIS, Earl Cornwallis June 1798–April 1801	ROBERT STEWART, Viscount Castlereagh Nov. 1798–May 1801
HENRY ADDINGTON Mar. 1801–May 1804	THOMAS PELHAM, Viscount Pelham July 1801–August 1803	PHILIP YORKE, Earl of Hardwicke April 1801–Mar. 1806	CHARLES ABBOT May 1801–Feb. 1802
WILLIAM PITT May 1804–Jan. 1806	CHARLES PHILIP YORKE August 1803–May 1804		WILLIAM WICKHAM Feb. 1802–Feb. 1804
	ROBERT BANKS JENKINSON Baron Hawkesbury May 1804–Feb. 1806		SIR EVAN NEPEAN Feb. 1804–Mar. 1805
			NICHOLAS VANSITTART Mar. 1805–Sept. 1805
			CHARLES LONG Sept. 1805–Mar. 1806

TABLE II

MEMBERS OF BRITISH MINISTRIES WITH EFFECT IN IRISH GOVERNMENT 1806-1812

First Lord of the Treasury (Prime Minister)	Secretary of State for the Home Department	Lord Lieutenant	Chief Secretary to the Lord Lieutenant
WILLIAM GRENVILLE, Baron Grenville *Feb. 1806–Mar. 1807*	GEORGE JOHN SPENCER Earl Spencer *Feb. 1806–Mar. 1807*	JOHN RUSSELL Duke of Bedford *Feb. 1806–Mar. 1807*	WILLIAM ELLIOTT *Mar. 1806–April 1807*
WILLIAM HENRY CAVENDISH CAVENDISH-BENTINCK, Duke of Portland *Mar. 1807–Oct. 1809*	ROBERT BANKS JENKINSON Baron Hawkesbury and Earl of Liverpool *Mar. 1807–Nov. 1809*	CHARLES LENNOX Duke of Richmond and Lennox *April 1807–June 1813*	SIR ARTHUR WELLESLEY *April 1807–April 1809*
SPENCER PERCEVAL *Oct. 1809–May 1812*	RICHARD RYDER *Nov. 1809–June 1812*		WILLIAM WELLESLEY-POLE *Oct. 1809–Aug. 1812*

13

TABLE III   MEMBERS OF BRITISH MINISTRIES WITH EFFECT IN IRISH GOVERNMENT 1812-1827

First Lord of the Treasury (Prime Minister)	Secretary of State for the Home Department	Lord Lieutenant	Chief Secretary to the Lord Lieutenant
ROBERT BANKS JENKINSON, Earl of Liverpool June 1812–April 1827	HENRY ADDINGTON Viscount Sidmouth June 1812–Jan. 1822	CHARLES LENNOX Duke of Richmond and Lennox April 1807–June 1813	ROBERT PEEL Aug. 1812–Aug. 1818
GEORGE CANNING April 1827–Aug. 1827	ROBERT PEEL Jan. 1822–April 1827	CHARLES WHITWORTH Viscount and Earl Whitworth June 1813–Oct. 1817	CHARLES GRANT Aug. 1818–Dec. 1821
FREDERICK JOHN ROBINSON, Viscount Goderich Aug. 1827–Dec. 1827	WILLIAM STURGES BOURNE April 1827	CHARLES CHETWYND, Earl Talbot Oct. 1817–Dec. 1821	HENRY GOULBURN Dec. 1821–April 1827
	HENRY PETTY FITZMAURICE Marquess of Lansdowne July 1827–Jan. 1828	RICHARD COLLEY WELLESLEY, Marquess Wellesley Dec. 1821–Dec. 1827	WILLIAM LAMB April 1827–June 1828

TABLE IV MEMBERS OF BRITISH MINISTRIES WITH EFFECT IN IRISH GOVERNMENT 1827-1830

First Lord of the Treasury (Prime Minister)	Secretary of State for the Home Department	Lord Lieutenant	Chief Secretary to the Lord Lieutenant
ARTHUR WELLESLEY, Duke of Wellington Jan. 1828–Nov. 1830	ROBERT PEEL, Jan. 1828–Nov. 1830	HENRY WILLIAM PAGET, Marquess of Anglesey, Feb. 1828–Jan. 1829	WILLIAM LAMB, April 1827–June 1828
CHARLES GREY, Earl Grey Nov. 1830–July 1934	WILLIAM LAMB, Viscount Melbourne Nov. 1830–July 1834	HUGH PERCY, Duke of Northumberland, Jan. 1829–Dec. 1830	FRANCIS LEVESON GOWER June 1828–July 1830
		HENRY WILLIAM PAGET, Marquess of Anglesey, Dec. 1830–Oct. 1833	SIR HENRY HARDINGE July 1830–Nov. 1830
			EDWARD GEOFFREY SMITH-STANLEY, Nov. 1830–Mar. 1833

15

TABLE V PRINCIPAL OFFICERS OF THE IRISH GOVERNMENT 1800–1812

Lord Lieutenant	Lord Chancellor	Chancellor of the Exchequer	Attorney General	Solicitor General
CHARLES CORNWALLIS, Earl Cornwallis June 1798–April 1801	JOHN FITZGIBBON, Earl of Clare 1789–1802	ISAAC CORRY Jan.1799–Aug. 1804	JOHN TOLER July 1798–Dec. 1800	JOHN STEWART July 1798–Dec. 1800
			JOHN STEWART Dec. 1800–May 1803	WILLIAM CUSACK SMITH Dec. 1800–Jan. 1802
PHILIP YORKE, Earl of Hardwicke April 1801–Mar. 1806	JOHN MITFORD, Baron Redesdale May 1804–Feb.1806	JOHN FOSTER Aug. 1804–Feb. 1806	STANDISH O'GRADY May 1803–Oct. 1805	JAMES McCLELLAND Jan. 1802–Nov. 1803
				WILLIAM CONYNGHAM-PLUNKET May 1804–Oct. 1805
JOHN RUSSELL, Duke of Bedford Mar. 1806–Apr. 1807	GEORGE PONSONBY Feb. 1806–Mar. 1807	JOHN NEWPORT Feb. 1806–Mar. 1807	WILLIAM CONYNGHAM-PLUNKET Oct. 1805–Mar. 1807	CHARLES KENDALL BUSHE Oct. 1805–Jan. 1822
CHARLES LENNOX, Duke of Richmond and Lennox April 1807–June 1813	THOMAS MANNERS-SUTTON, Baron Manners Mar. 1807–Apr. 1827	JOHN FOSTER Mar. 1807–Oct. 1809	WILLIAM SAURIN Mar. 1807–Jan. 1822	
		WILLIAM WELLESLEY-POLE Oct. 1809–July 1812		
		VESEY FITZGERALD July 1812–Oct. 1813		

TABLE VI   PRINCIPAL OFFICERS OF THE IRISH GOVERNMENT 1813–1830

Lord Lieutenant	Lord Chancellor	Attorney General	Solicitor General
CHARLES WHITWORTH Viscount and Earl Whitworth *June 1813–Aug. 1818*	THOMAS MANNERS-SUTTON Baron Manners *Mar. 1807–Apr. 1827*	WILLIAM SAURIN *Mar. 1807–Jan. 1822*	CHARLES KENDALL BUSHE *Oct. 1805–Jan. 1822*
CHARLES CHETWYND, Earl Talbot *Oct. 1818–Dec. 1821*	SIR ANTHONY HART *Apr. 1827–Oct. 1830*	WILLIAM CONYNGHAM PLUNKET *Jan. 1822–Apr. 1827*	HENRY JOY *Jan. 1827–Apr. 1827*
RICHARD COLLEY WELLESLEY, Marquess Wellesley *Dec. 1821–Dec. 1827*	WILLIAM CONYNGHAM PLUNKET *Dec. 1830–Nov. 1834*	HENRY JOY *Apr. 1827–Nov. 1830*	JOHN DOUGHERTY *Apr. 1827–Nov. 1834*
WILLIAM HENRY PAGET, Marquess of Anglesey *Feb. 1828–Jan. 1829*			
HUGH PERCY, Duke of Northumberland *Jan. 1829–Dec. 1830*			

TABLE VII   OFFICE OF THE CHIEF SECRETARY AND SUBORDINATE
POSITIONS 1800–1830

Chief Secretary	Undersecretary for Civil Affairs	Undersecretary for Military Affairs
ROBERT STEWART Viscount Castlereagh *Nov. 1798–May 1801*	EDWARD COOKE *1789–Oct. 1801*	WILLIAM ELLIOT *To May 1801*
CHARLES ABBOT *May 1801–Feb. 1802*	ALEXANDER MARSDEN *Oct. 1801–Sept. 1806*	E. B. LITTLEHALES *May 1801–1819*
WILLIAM WICKHAM *Feb. 1802–Feb. 1804*	JAMES TRAIL *Sept. 1806–Mar. 1807*	
SIR EVAN NEPEAN *Feb. 1804–Mar. 1805*	SIR CHARLES SAXTON *Sept. 1808–Oct. 1812*	
NICHOLAS VANSITTART *Mar. 1805–Sept. 1805*	WILLIAM GREGORY *Oct. 1812–Nov. 1830*	
CHARLES LONG *Sept. 1805–Mar. 1806*		
WILLIAM ELLIOT *Mar. 1806–Apr. 1817*		
SIR ARTHUR WELLESLEY *Apr. 1807–Apr. 1809*		
ROBERT DUNDAS *Apr. 1809–Oct. 1809*		
WILLIAM WELLESLEY-POLE *Oct. 1809–Aug. 1812*		
ROBERT PEEL *Aug. 1812–Aug. 1818*		
CHARLES GRANT *Aug. 1818–Dec. 1821*		
HENRY GOULBURN *Dec. 1821–April 1827*		
WILLIAM LAMB *Apr. 1827–June 1828*		
FRANCIS LEVESON GOWER *June 1828–July 1830*		
SIR HENRY HARDINGE *July 1830–Nov. 1830*		

18

Philip Yorke, Earl of Hardwicke
Lord Lieutenant
April 1801–March 1806

Chapter 1
In Dublin Castle

Ireland is too great to be unconnected with us, and too near to be dependent on a foreign state, and too little to be independent...

C. T. Grenville to the Duke of Richmond (1784)

THE VICEREGAL HERITAGE

FOR EIGHT CENTURIES the English Crown maintained a surrogate executive in Ireland. The office of viceroy was often altered, each time to reflect current realities of the Anglo-Irish connection. This study concerns itself with the last major metamorphosis, the shift towards direct rule from London in the wake of the Act of Union.

The tendency towards concentration of executive power in London's hands in part shaped Irish nationalist agitation for repeal of the union during the nineteenth century. At the same time, an administrative revolution touching on the Church of Ireland, the bureaucracy of Dublin Castle and instruments of law and order all contributed to a restructuring of the Anglo-Irish connection. In its new form the system founded on the British Crown and Dublin Castle would carry Ireland through two major wars and to the threshold of the Irish Free State and partition in 1920.

The architects of the Act of Union paid scant attention to the Irish executive. This institution was almost as ancient as the. Anglo-Irish connection itself. Immediately after the Normans invaded Ireland in 1172 they imported the office of Justiciar, or Lieutenant of the King.[1] This instrument had already served the Normans well in England, for this dynamic and bellicose race frequently dispatched its armies and its monarchs to make war on the continent. England was entrusted to a loyal surrogate on these occasions, and what proved convenient in England was soon seen to be indispensable in Ireland. The justiciar embodied every royal prerogative necessary to the government of restless Ireland: the incumbent was simultaneously military chief, head of the civil administration, and presiding judge.[2] During the thirteenth century the Justiciar's powers were circumscribed somewhat by the emergence of a council, a Parliament, and law courts based on Anglo-Norman precedents.[3] But as late as 1376 Edward I granted his viceroy wide powers to issue pardons, to revamp the Irish administration, to dispense justice, and to "perform all and sundry for the good rule, safety, and recovery of our land and people..."[4] These enormous delegated powers were gradually reduced, but the process was an uneven one.

The viceroys' autonomy (degree of autonomy accorded the viceroys depended upon several factors: the intensity of Irish unrest; the vitality of the monarchy in England and the extent of its control over Irish affairs; the resourcefulness of the viceroys themselves. During the Wars of the Roses which convulsed England for much of the fourteenth century, Ireland's chief executives almost established an independent monarchy, defying England on one hand and challenging Ireland's indigenous political system on the other. At length Henry VIII (1517-1547), the second vigorous Tudor monarch, broke the power of the Fitzgeralds, who had threatened to convert the office of viceroy into a hereditary dynasty.[5] For the first time Englishmen began to dominate the list of viceroys and under Elizabeth I (1558-1603) England's authority for the first time extended throughout Ireland.

After the Reformation viceregal privileges were allowed to erode. Incumbents became absentees, and a Lord Deputy chosen for experience and ability as a bureaucrat, rather than for rank, assumed the burden of defending the pretensions of the English Crown in Ireland. Oliver Cromwell temporarily disorientated the landed aristocracy descended from the old Norman families. Later, in the 1690s, persecution of Catholics focused on those ancient and powerful families who had remained true to the traditional faith. Their ruin advanced the pretensions of a new landed aristocracy, loyal to the Hanoverians but quick to resist London's intrusions into Irish affairs. This spirit of quasi-independence was embodied in the Irish Parliament, which after 1715 assumed the form which would persist until the Act of Union. Westminster laboured to reinforce the subordinate status of the Dublin parliament by refining its interpretation of Poynings' Law, a statute enacted in the Elizabethan period which seemed to confirm the Dublin parliament's subservience. A Declaratory Act in 1720 further strengthened Westminster's claims. Beyond this, West-

minster could depend upon the bench of bishops of the established church and officeholders beholden to viceregal patronage
generosity. They often used their parliamentary influence to
sustain successive viceroys' efforts to curb the Dublin legislature.

Despite these efforts and legal devices, Ireland's Protestant
landowners on occasion defied London's wishes. Sometimes they
balked at approving important fiscal measures. Occasionally
they used their influence in the House of Commons, where viceregal influence was weakest, to pass resolutions reflecting a
healthy defiance of London's wishes. To discourage this,
successive English ministries began entrusting Irish parliamentary
matters to "undertakers", Irish leaders who pledged to secure
parliament's cooperation at the price of controlling much of the
viceroys' patronage. When this system ran smoothly, there was
little need indeed for a resident viceroy, and by 1760 the trend
was towards a completely ceremonial Irish executive.

This trend was reversed after 1765. The patronage appetites of
the "undertakers" expanded steadily and in 1769 George
Townshend as viceroy determined to assume direct responsibility
for securing legislative approval of the necessary legislation.[6]
There were problems in the new arrangement. Irish policy had
traditionally been "conducted on well-understood principles about
which British statesmen, however deeply divided on other
subjects, were in agreement."[7] Central to these principles was the
conviction that Ireland should be isolated from political contact
with Britain's potential enemies, that the Protestant interest be
strengthened by assiduous application of penal laws against the
Catholic majority, and that the Irish economy must complement
rather than compete with that of Britain within the larger imperial
forum. In London these objectives transcended in importance the
means used to secure them. Townshend's decision to grapple
directly with the Irish parliament was therefore uncomfortable,
for it forced London to grapple with unpleasant patronage
decisions heretofore entrusted to the "undertakers". Townshend
and his successors were forced to construct coalitions of such Irish
politicians who could be relied upon, at a price, not to defy the
viceroy.[8] At Dublin Castle, that cluster of ancient buildings,
towers, and crenelated walls, a larger permanent bureaucracy
gradually succeeded to the responsibilities of the "undertakers".
Only a resourceful and vigilant viceroy could control this bureaucracy, and many did not succeed.[9]

Ireland's relationship to the British Crown had always involved certain implicit and fundamental contradictions; now they sharpened. Was the viceroy as Ireland's pre-eminent executive authority ultimately responsible to the Irish legislature, to the Crown, or to Westminster? If responsible to the Irish legislature, the imperial connection could not be guaranteed. If beholden to the Crown, the viceroy's prerogatives constituted an implicit affront to the emerging precepts of limited monarchy. If to Westminster, then the Dublin parliament must be subservient to the viceroy and through him to the government of the day in London. But increasing pressure from Irish public opinion, combined with the unnecessarily tactless behaviour of some viceroys, made Irish politicians' "allegiance to the castle... a political risk which called for the payment of rising premiums." [10] Viceroys found themselves dispensing patronage on a scale even more lavish than that which the "undertakers" had demanded earlier.

The constitutional crisis deepened during the last quarter of the eighteenth century. An enflamed Irish public opinion responded to British disasters in North America by demanding a fully autonomous Irish legislature, an end to corruption in the Irish administration, and reform of the overblown patronage apparatus. Legislative independence was conceded in 1782. Successive viceroys, nonetheless, were still expected to reconcile Dublin's legislative initiatives to policies articulated at Westminster. London despatched and recalled viceroys and at Westminster ministries rose and fell as the Americans moved towards independence. For a time coherent policy proved impossible. Had William Pitt's long ministry (1784-1801) not intervened at the height of the crisis, efforts to stem Ireland's bid for even wider autonomy might have failed completely. [11]

Under these conditions discussions in London almost inevitably turned towards a legislative union in which a restless Ireland would be reduced to the status of an English county. Such a project was first broached in 1779, but Ireland's passionate insistence on amending Poyning's Law subsequently made this impossible. In 1785 Pitt, after only one year in office, urged a programme of closer political and economic ties. [12]   These were debated vigorously until 1789, when King George III's first bout of insanity gave Irish "patriots" − that is, the element of the Protestant ruling classes which favoured a truly autonomous Dublin Parliament − an opportunity to offer the Prince of Wales, as regent, powers in Ireland which Westminster was determined to deny him in England. The viceroy proved powerless to prevent this attempt to excise the British Parliament from the Irish scene except by refusing to transmit the invitation to London. [13] The King recovered before Westminster's privileges were declared void, and the ancient Anglo-Irish connection was preserved. Pitt, nonetheless, strengthened his resolve to curb Ireland's separatist inclinations. [14]

Between 1790 and 1800 events supported the thesis that Irish viceroys could not simultaneously serve the Irish Parliament and the government in London. In 1790 Pitt forced Earl Fitzwilliam as viceroy to submit to the Irish Parliament a bill which the viceroy and his Irish administration both opposed. In the wake of this parody on responsible government one of Pitt's friends, the Earl of Mornington, proposed that the viceroy be transformed into a surrogate constitutional monarch, accepting as a ministry any group which could command a majority in the Irish Parliament. [15] Such a plan would have removed the constitutional debris which cluttered the Irish scene and raised the viceroy's prestige. But it might also have encouraged Ireland to pursue and implement economic and diplomatic policies diametrically opposed to those of Britain. This Pitt would not permit, and when Ireland was convulsed by rebellion in 1797 and 1798 he determined to extinguish the Irish Parliament. [16] Patronage promises and bribes were applied generously, and in 1800 the Irish Parliament voted itself out of existence. Irish legislative autonomy was a casualty of war and an unworkable constitutional system. It remained to be seen whether an independent Irish executive would be called for in the new unitary state.

THE IMPACT OF THE ACT OF UNION

In April 1801 Earl Hardwicke departed London for Dublin as the first Lord Lieutenant, or viceroy, to take office after enactment of the legislative union. He carried with him three large packets describing his powers and listing instructions. The first packet testified to the medieval origins of the office; in it could be found the extraordinary powers which had attached themselves to the Irish viceroyalty over the course of time, as well as the difficulties inherent in preserving British control in that turbulent land. For almost five hundred years every viceroy had been authorised to declare and wage war, administer justice, dispense patronage, requisition supplies, summon councils and parliaments and exercise authority in many other areas. He could require the King's vassals to meet their feudal obligations. He might commandeer materials, appoint deputies with full powers in his absence, grant offices, pensions and peerages, and pardon most crimes.[17] Over the course of centuries many of these powers had been weakened or had disappeared completely, but the viceroy's prerogatives were still considerable.[18] The Act of Union had extinguished his legislative powers and he would not have declared war without instructions. The Crown, on the advice of the government of the day, enjoyed right of nomination to most lucrative Irish offices. Other powers remained, however, as the basis for Dublin Castle's role in early nineteenth century Ireland.

A second packet of "official" as opposed to "formal" instructions more clearly defined the parameters of Irish executive powers. The viceroy was to audit and to inspect Ireland's military and civil establishments, and to demand an accounting from the Treasury and other offices. He was instructed to protect the established Church and to be careful and cautious in making appointments. Rather more recent was the injunction to "promote trade and manufactures", and in particular "to encourage Protestant citizens to establish manufactures in Irish cities." Other items reflected the Crown's concern about illicit coinage, the unauthorised export of woollens, the under-evaluation of lands for taxation purposes, and misappropriation of military funds, an endemic evil.[19] These instructions betrayed the King's disenchantment with the conduct of some eighteenth century viceroys who in the King's words on an earlier occasion had conducted themselves "like quacks" by engaging "in all matters from not knowing the magnitude of the undertaking." [20] Such conduct, the King observed, had permitted some people "in that uncivilised land" to manipulate viceroys and to profit from their ignorance of Irish affairs.[21]

The King was not alone in urging a stricter definition of viceregal powers. The Secretary for the Home Department in particular expected to see Ireland reduced to the status of an English county. Central to this was the question of patronage. The King touched on this sensitive topic in declaring that it should be "clearly understood that the union had closed the reign of Irish jobs." [22] Unfortunately the passage of this law had been facilitated by the most liberal dispensation of titles, places and pensions ever recorded in Ireland, so that these "union engagements" had to be settled before a higher line of conduct could be demanded of the Lord Lieutenant. For the moment, therefore, the viceroy was advised that his patronage decisions would be subject to a veto in London. Much confusion and acrimony was to attend patronage matters in the first three decades of the nineteenth century.

Almost as volatile an issue was control of the army.[23] Unlike his predecessor Earl Cornwallis, Hardwicke was not appointed Commander-in-Chief of the army when he became viceroy. Hardwicke was angered by this and he bitterly opposed the Duke of York and even the cabinet on this issue. Eventually the title was restored to the viceroy, and until the defeat of Napoleon in 1815 successive viceroys exercised important military functions. Thereafter the gradual development of a more efficient peace preservation force and a reduced danger of foreign invasion undermined these powers.

The extension of Westminster's immediate jurisdiction into Ireland posed enormous problems for the Lords Lieutenant. Logic dictated that Irish departments such as the Treasury be amalgamated with their English counterparts and that the Home Department also exercise a direct jurisdiction over Irish local government. Hardwicke's instructions pledged the ministry to work only through the viceroy, but this commitment was soon violated, especially by Henry Pelham, the ambitious Home Secretary of the day. Pelham first denied that Hardwicke retained the right to restrict trade between Ireland and Britain.[24] Hardwicke thereupon broadened the debate by accusing Pelham of trying to abolish the Irish Privy Council so as "to lessen the weight and authority of the Lord Lieutenant, and create infinite embarrassment in the execution of a variety of statutes..."[25] Hardwicke managed to parry Pelham's threat, but the Home Secretary's logic was incontrovertible: a single parliament demanded a single and uniform administration.

It took three decades to resolve jurisdictional disputes of this sort. Hardwicke's successors maintained substantial control over patronage. [26] London was also not unhappy to see the viceroy take the lead in enforcing unpopular laws in Ireland or in instituting repressive measures designed to keep the peace.[27] Viceroys won other victories, sometimes relatively minor ones, in their contests with London. [28] They also enhanced their prestige by taking the initiative in easing Ireland's distress during periods of disease and famine. [29] In doing so they obscured somewhat the tendency towards Ireland's integration into the British political and economic system. The office of viceroy became in one sense a hostage to Ireland's hope for a continued unique status within the United Kingdom, or, even better, to its dreams for home rule.

CHOOSING THE KING'S MEN

Who was chosen to be the King's surrogate in Ireland? In early centuries princes of the blood were sometimes despatched to what was for them often a miserable exile, isolated from family and deprived of adequate income. After 1300 the great Anglo-Norman families provided many viceroys. [30] Tudor monarchs were both wise enough and powerful enough to suspect the loyalty of such resident noblemen, so they appointed English aristocrats and soldiers instead; not until 1821 would another Irish-born aristocrat become viceroy. As long as "undertakers" were primarily responsible for the conduct of Irish affairs, even young noblemen "caught wild" at one of London's fashionable clubs and endowed with "second-rate abilities" might be chosen. [31] Late in the eighteenth century standards for selection rose, but men of wealth and pedigree remained the principal candidates. Ireland ceased to attract bold spirits such as those which secured Britain's domination in India.

The eight viceroys who ruled in Ireland between 1800 and 1830 were all aristocrats. [32] Only two, however, were wealthy by eighteenth century standards, when incumbents often enjoyed annual incomes in excess of £50,000, worth almost ten times that much by today's standards. The new viceroys brought a full range of experience in public service to their Irish posts — no more recruits from London social clubs. Hardwicke and Bedford commanded independent support in Parliament, Richmond and Anglesey could boast a distinguished military career, and Whitworth was a suave and experienced diplomat. Wellesley's Indian viceroyalty was already famous. None of the eight, however, played a prominent role in British politics after serving in Ireland. [33]

After 1800 the length of viceregal tenures became longer. tations to serve in Dublin. Even before 1800 the post was often described as a punishment of sorts. [34] Many considered the great expenses involved unwarranted in terms of the prestige derived. [35] From London's point of view the perfect candidate was one whom the Cabinet "wished to conciliate, but exclude from the cabinet..." [36] Under these conditions many leading aristocrats

27

were reluctant to accept the post.[37] On the other hand, Ireland demanded a leader skilful in dispensing patronage, firm in management of Irish notables, immune from corruption, and extraordinarily patient.[38] Each vacancy, therefore, prompted a number of refusals. Some were offended to have been approached.[39] Others throught themselves unequal to the task.[40] Still others insisted on certain conditions which London refused to concede.[41] A couple, such as Edward Clive, Earl of Powis, accepted the appointment, and then after closer scrutiny of the nature of the office asked to be excused.[42] Several refusals were leaked to the press before the Duke of Richmond accepted in 1807.[43] "Many," a Dublin newspaper observed wryly, "have declined the honour of being Viceroy."[44] Richmond himself accepted office in part to advertise his unhappiness that his military talents were being ignored.[45]

Between 1810 and 1820 the Perceval and Liverpool ministries seem to have found the task of finding suitable candidates for the office of viceroy particularly difficult. Richmond's tenure was extended from month to month after 1811 until a successor could be found. Whitworth, who was induced to accept, stood "very low on the list of Irish barons" and owed his pretentions to matrimonial considerations.[46] His selection shocked Richmond and generated universal amazement. The King tried to rectify the problems his low rank caused by granting him an earldom.[47] In 1817 Liverpool eagerly accepted Whitworth's suggestion that his friend Earl Talbot, a peer of modest rank and reputation, succeed him.[48] Talbot simply proved unequal to the demands of the office.

After 1820 competition for the post suddenly intensified. Wellesley was appointed over the protests of several disappointed peers.[49] Not only did Wellesley accept office with an almost pathetic alacrity but he also proved extremely difficult to dislodge.[50] Anglesey was recalled involuntarily after manifesting an alarming spirit of independence. The last viceroy of the period of this study, Hugh Percy, Duke of Northumberland, allegedly wanted the post to display his great wealth.

After 1800 the length of viceregal tenures became longer. During the last twenty years of the eighteenth century there were ten viceroys, and eighteen in the last forty years. Between 1800 and 1830 the average tenure was three years and eight months. In part this reflected the political stability represented by the Tory ascendancy; this certainly added to the years of service contributed by Hardwicke, Richmond and Wellesley. Only Bedford and

Northumberland were recalled because of a change in government.[51] A change in ministers without a change in party rarely prompted a viceroy's early recall and indeed often extended his stay.[52]

The context in which a viceroy resigned his office or was recalled to London was often unpleasant. Before 1815 the problem was usually to discourage incumbents from resigning prematurely. So weak was Spencer Perceval's ministry (1809-1812) that the prospect of finding a replacement for Richmond was unappealing in the extreme. Perceval preferred to appease Richmond if he would agree to remain a little longer.[53] Whitworth was also persuaded to remain; Liverpool refused to accept the viceroy's resignation until finally Whitworth became ill.[54] Pressure for removal increased sharply after this. Talbot's appointment resulted from Liverpool's failure to find a qualified successor to Whitworth. But after Talbot and Charles Grant his Chief Secretary proved incompatible, Liverpool was persuaded to appoint an entirely new team. Talbot was stunned at being "turned out of office in less time than I should deem it right to turn a servant away."[55] Whitworth took umbrage at the treatment meted out to his friend and it required the intervention of Robert Peel, friend to all parties, to smooth ruffled feathers.[56]

Wellesley was determined to remain in Ireland as long as possible. He complained of being "far gone in years, much broken in health, and much afflicted in spirit."[57] But he was determined to endure so as to revive his sagging reputation and repair his desperate financial situation.[58] Prime Minister George Canning tried to remove him in April 1827 because the King wanted a "Protestant" viceroy to balance the pro-Catholic sympathies held by Canning and other important members of the Cabinet. Wellesley threatened to make a scene. Canning died before he could devise a solution,[59] and Wellesley even refused to resign when news of his successor Anglesey's nomination began to circulate in Dublin.[60] Only the vain hope of being made Prime Minister induced him to rush to London in December, where he was studiously ignored and allowed to retire into obscurity.[61] When Anglesey fell foul of Wellington and Peel he defied the Prime Minister to dismiss him. Wellington accepted the challenge and Anglesey was recalled.[62] This opened the way for Northumberland, who went in early 1929. He resigned late in 1830 when the Whigs finally came to power after waiting nearly a quarter century.[63]

DRAMATIS PERSONAE

Eight viceroys comprise what may be called this study's cast of characters. Of the group, only Wellesley has been the subject of a detailed analysis elsewhere. Whitworth and Anglesey have been studied apart from their Irish years. Hardwicke and Richmond feature in the appropriate monographs and articles on Irish history. In all, the attention is scanty and yet they presided in Ireland during one of the most important periods in Irish history.

Philip Yorke, third Earl of Hardwicke, was born in 1757 and inherited his title in 1790. His viceroyalty extended from 1801 to 1806. Courteous, intelligent and conscientious, he was moderately popular in Ireland. [64] The Duchess and he tried to soften the disappointment felt in Ireland following the extinction of the nation's parliament.[65] He claimed to see a "spirit of improvement" in Ireland" [66] Hardwicke grew more sympathetic to Catholics' grievances while viceroy and after returning to England steadfastly supported Catholic relief. He died in 1834. [67] His reputation has suffered undeservedly because of "union engagements," the burden of which he was called upon to carry. He deprecated the entire exercise but felt compelled to honour these commitments. His struggles against Pelham preserved for Ireland more autonomy than the Act of Union admitted, and his "great good sense, moderation and propriety" should not be forgotten. [68]

Lord John Russell, sixth Duke of Bedford, was born in 1766. He succeeded his brother as Duke in 1802 and resided at Dublin Castle during the very short government of "all the talents" in 1806 and early 1807. The Russell family was deeply committed to Whig politics but the Duke's mark was a faint one in both houses of parliament. He was popular among Catholics in Ireland and he laboured to implement the Whigs' programme of accommodating Catholics' grievances.[69] After retiring from Ireland to his estate he enhanced his reputation as a scientific agriculturalist and he scoured Europe for painting and sculpture. His passion for collecting did not entirely divorce the Russell family from Irish affairs, for his third son, John, later featured prominently in the Whig party and played an important role in instituting administrative and ecclesiastical reforms in Ireland.[70]

Charles Lennox, fourth Duke of Richmond and Lennox, is remembered principally, according to one critic, "for the ball given by his wife on the eve of Waterloo".[71] This is unfair. Born in

1754, he spent most of his career in the army and duelled the Duke of York in 1789. Richmond succeeded Bedford in April 1807 and remained in Dublin until 1813. His wife and the Duchess of Bedford were sisters. After sixteen years' service in parliament as a loyal Pittite, Richmond's politics waxed emphatically conservative. Associates thought he was a difficult man to measure. Friends found Richmond "irresistably convivial" and enemies labelled him a drunkard. One by-product of his love of claret was a weakness for Dublin women, which divided the city's high society into hostile camps. According to Lady Bessborough, the aggrieved Duchess received a tender note which the Duke had intended for his mistress Lady Augusta Everitt.[72] This indiscretion was only one of many celebrated in the city. Despite the controversies thus engendered Richmond never tried to conceal his opinions.[73] He denounced Wellesley and the Whigs and publicly toasted his old duelling opponent when the Duke of York was charged with using extra-marital connections to help him dispense military patronage. [74]

These were Richmond's defects. Subordinates respected his candor and sense of fairness. Spencer Perceval, Prime Minister from 1809 until he was assassinated in 1812, described Richmond as "liberal, accommodating and friendly to the greatest degree" for being willing to remain in Ireland until such time as the government was strong enough to tackle the question of a successor. Two of the Marquess Wellesley's brothers served as Irish Chief Secretary under Richmond. One of them was Arthur, the future Duke of Wellington, who exerted a steadying influence on Richmond until he resigned office in order to join the British Forces in Spain. Thereafter many observers thought Richmond too strongly influenced by Patrick Duigenan, an ascerbic Orange Lodge enthusiast, and by the strong-willed Duchess.[76]

Richmond's tenure as viceroy has received mixed reviews. Lady Gregory lamented that he made little impact at a time when "in the new relations between England and Ireland a greater statesman might have done much to turn the bitter waters to sweet." [77] But Perceval's biographer Denis Gray considered Richmond "one of the best" viceroys of the era.[78] He succeeded in keeping Ireland "tranquil and unhappy," as one historian has put it.[79] His innovations in patronage distribution and his failure to move for tithe and ecclesiastical reform were, however, probably regrettable and he never established an empathetic relationship with the people.[80] Richmond died of hydrophobia in Canada only four years after leaving Ireland.[81] Richmond opposed Whitworth's appointment because Whitworth lacked rank.[82] Indeed, Whitworth's fame was of a different kind. He earned an enduring reputation when an enraged Napoleon allegedly drew his sword in response to Whitworth's announcement that Britain would retain Malta until France met certain provisions of the Treaty of Amien.[83] This confrontation between French emperor and British ambassador in effect signalled the resumption of the Great War. Whitworth brought to Ireland a glamorous reputation for other reasons as well. Falsely advertised as one of the many lovers of Catherine the Great, Whitworth did in fact marry his patron's widow, the wealthy Duchess of Dorset, in 1801. He possessed a "cool and sure intellect,... good sense, temper, firmness, and habits of business." He relied heavily on Peel as his Chief Secretary and on the imperious Duchess.[84] Whitworth therefore left few traces in Ireland; perhaps it was a sufficient accomplishment to depart Ireland moderately popular.

Charles Chetwynd, second Earl Talbot of Hensol, served under Whitworth in Russia from 1797 to 1800. Talbot shared Bedford's interest in agriculture and impressed acquaintances as a "jolly, good-natured farmer". His wife was Irish and while he was viceroy her relatives constantly pestered Talbot for favours.[85] Unfortunately, Talbot's ineptitude as an administrator was aggravated by the death of his son and then of his wife. In the wake of these disasters Talbot's principal legacy as viceroy to Ireland seems to have been a "large stock of Ayrshire cattle, store sheep and horses" which were auctioned off in Dublin after his departure.[86]

Wellesley's credentials and reputation were as impressive as those of Talbot were lackluster. Richard Colley Wellesley was born in Grafton Street in Dublin in 1760. He inherited his father's earldom in 1781. At Eton and Oxford he shared with William Grenville a love of the classics, and through Grenville became one of William Pitt's intimates. He sat in the Irish parliament for a brief period and then entered into the Pittite group at Westminster before sailing to India as Governor General in 1797. His Indian exploits earned him both fame and notoriety. By brilliant strategy he converted a detestation of Napoleonic France into a consolidation of Britain's Indian empire. The East India Company was horrified at his demonstrations of independence and his fiscal extravagance. In spite of this, he returned to England in 1806 anticipating a hero's welcome, only to find himself facing possible impeachment. In time these charges were quashed and in 1809

Wellesley undertook a special embassy to Spain. He returned late the same year to become Secretary of State for the Foreign Department. In 1812 he bid twice for the office of Prime Minister. He failed both times, refused the Irish viceroyalty, and retired into political obscurity and bankruptcy.

Wellesley was an old man — sixty one — when he was again invited to go to Dublin. His pro-Catholic views endeared him to many Irishmen and his Irish birth assuaged in some measure a systematic diminution of Ireland's national identity. But a perceptive ditty recognised the problem occasioned by Ireland's inflated expectations of what Wellesley could do:

Who that hath viewed him in his past career
Of hard-earned fame could recognise him here?
Changed as he is in lengthened life's descent
To a mere instrument's mere instrument... [87]

Wellesley himself entertained no such feelings of despair. He was determined in the first place to rise above religious factionalism.[88] Despite bouts of bad health he managed some heroic displays of energy.[89] Henry Goulburn, his Chief Secretary, was alternately distressed and amazed by all this.[90] So were Dublin and London when Wellesley proceeded to marry an American Catholic heiress.[91]

Wellesley's tenure was marked by an emerging Catholic militancy orchestrated by Daniel O'Connell. The Orange Movement responded with a vigour of its own. Tithe agitation spread and the potato crop failed in several areas. Extremist Protestants and militant Catholics harrassed Wellesley. Modern observers do not agree on Wellesley's effectiveness as viceroy; his was the first administration to grapple with some of Ireland's most pressing problems, but Wellesley's personal contribution to this is still disputed.

Wellesley's successor, Henry William Paget, Marquis of Anglesey, was born in 1764. He lived until 1858, only six years short of a century. He lost a leg and gained a reputation for bravery at Waterloo. Canning selected Anglesey in June 1827 but he did not reach Dublin until Wellington had succeeded Viscount Goderich as Prime Minister the following January.[92] Unlike many ultra-Tories Wellington feared that Anglesey would prove difficult on the Catholic issue.[93] And indeed it transpired that his "imprudence and unreserve" and his refusal to support "any measures contrary to his opinions" caused considerable pain.[94] Catholic leaders praised Anglesey's openness towards them, and with Protestants in panic Wellington ordered the viceroy home.[95] Anglesey departed Dublin enormously popular among Catholics and he insisted that he would conduct himself in similar fashion should he ever return.[96] At the time this seemed most unlikely, but when the Whigs came to power in 1830 they sent Anglesey back to Dublin. This encore was not successful; as one historian has noted, Anglesey's genius consisted in cultivating "two formidable oppositions," one conservative and ultra-Protestant, the other reformist and pro-Catholic.[97] The clashes resulting from this obscured Anglesey's real penchant for original and imaginative thinking on Ireland's economic and social problems. [98]

Hugh Percy, third Duke of Northumberland of the third creation (1785-1847), displayed a keen interest in slave emancipation upon entering parliament in 1806. In 1824 he financed Britain's embassy to the coronation of Charles X of France, a dazzling display of philanthropy of a sort. His garrulousness was legendary; Greville was not unfair in calling him "an eternal talker and a prodigious bore." [99] Peel commented that Northumberland learned quickly whenever he stopped talking long enough to listen. He favoured Catholic relief and he presided while the Catholic Emancipation Act was extracted from a reluctant parliament. His place in history may rest upon Peel's belief that in terms of temperament and ability he was the best viceroy of the era.[100] To most people, he was an "amiable and charitable Croessus." [101] His return to England ended the Tory ascendancy and marked the culmination of an important phase in British administration in Ireland.

1. One student of the emergence of Irish administrative institutions in the Middle Ages believes that the various titles had specific connotations and were not granted haphazardly. "Lieutenant of the King" was the highest designation. Those awarded this title entered into indentures with the King at the moment of their appointment, and the terms included agreement on a fee which the incumbents would receive for undertaking to govern Ireland. The office of "Justiciar" on the other hand was associated with a fixed salary. The incumbent's powers were set out in a patent and usually he was enjoined to act only with the advice of the council. His powers were also much more limited than those conceded to the "Lieutenant of the King". The office of "Deputy" was revived from time to time to supply a temporary executive officer when the Governors were absent. Sometimes the King appointed the Deputy; on occasion one Deputy appointed another. For a detailed treatment of this see H. Wood, "The Office of the Chief Governor of Ireland, 1172-1509", *Royal Irish Academy, Proceedings*, XXXVI, section C, pp. 206-12.

2. Jocelyn Otway-Ruthven, *A History of Medieval Ireland* (London: Ernest Benn, 1968), pp. 144-45.

3. M. V. Clarke, *Fourteenth Century Studies* (Oxford: Clarendon Press, 1937), p. 21.

4. Calendar of Ormond Deeds, II, 215, in Edmund Curtis and R. B. McDowell, eds., *Irish Historical Documents, 1172-1922* (New York: Barnes and Noble, 1943), pp. 61-62.

5. J. C. Beckett, *The Making of Modern Ireland, 1603-1923* (London: Faber and Faber, 1966), pp. 17-19.

6. Edith M. Johnston, *Great Britain and Ireland, 1760-1800: A Study in Political Administration* (Edinburgh: Oliver and Boyd, 1963), p. 5.

7. J. C. Beckett. "Anglo-Irish Constitutional Relations in the Later Eighteenth Century" *Irish Historical Studies*, XIV, 27.

8. V. T. Harlow, *The Founding of the Second British Empire* (2 vols.; London: Longmans, Green and Co., 1952, 1964), I, 546-50.

9. Johnston, *Great Britain*, pp. 72-73.

10. Beckett, "Anglo-Irish," p. 27.

11. *Ibid.*, pp. 37-38.

12. Herbert Butterfield, *George III, Lord North and the People, 1779-1780* (London. Beel, 1949), p. 105.

13. Johnston, *Great Britain*, p. 6.

14. 'Copy of a Memorandum Delivered by Mr. Cooke to Mr. Douglas", Clements Transcripts, V, 2474-79, cited in Donald ·G. Barnes, *George III and William Pitt* (Stanford: University Press, 1930), pp. 338-39.

15. Harlow, *Founding*, pp. 644-45; Great Britain, Historical Manuscripts Commission, *Report on the Manuscripts of J. B. Fortescue, Esq., Preserved at Dropmore* (Walter Fitzpatrick and Francis Binney, eds.; 10 vols.; London: His Majesty's Stationery Office, 1892-1927).

16. Robert B. McDowell, *Public Opinion and Government Policy in Ireland, 1801-1846* (London: Faber and Faber, 1952), p. 17.

17. "Powers of the Lord Lieutenant", British Museum, Hardwicke MSS, 35737/203, ff.; "Instructions", Henry Addington to Philip Yorke, Third Earl of Hardwicke, 29 April 1801, Hardwicke MSS 35705/16-23; "Private Instructions", William Cavendish Bentinck, Third Duke of Portland, to Hardwicke, n. d., Hardwicke MSS, 35707/32-35.

18. Otway-Ruthven, *Medieval Ireland*, p. 146; Johnston, *Great Britain*, p. 28.

19. 'Lord Lieutenant Appointed by Patent', draft of memorandum n. d., Hardwicke MSS, 35737/203; "Instructions to Hardwicke", Addington to Hardwicke, 29 April 1801. Hardwicke MSS, 35707/16-23.

20. George III to Lord North, 28 November 1775, quoted in Arthur Aspinall, ed., *The Correspondence of George III* (5 vols.; Cambridge: Cambridge University Press, 1962, ff.), MS No. 1774.

21. George III to Hardwicke, 9 May 1801, Hardwicke MSS, 35349/75.

22. George III to Addington, 11 February 1801, in George Pellew, *The Life and Correspondence of the Right Honourable Henry Addington, First Viscount Sidmouth* (3 vols.; London: John Murray, 1847), I, 303; also in Arthur Aspinall, ed., *The Later Correspondence of George III* (8 vols.;

Cambridge: Cambridge University Press, 1962 ff.), III, 504; Charles Abbot, Baron Colchester, *Diary and Correspondence* (3 vols.; London: Murray, 1861), I, 24.

23. "Instructions", Addington to Hardwicke, 29 April 1801, Hardwicke MSS, 35707/16-23.

24. Hardwicke to Addington, 2' December 1801, Hardwicke MSS, 35771/123.

25. Hardwicke to John Freeman Mitford, First Baron Redesdale, 27 May 1803, Hardwicke MSS, 35772/ 171; Colchester, *Diary*, printed in Richard Barry O'Brien, *Dublin Castle and the Irish People* (London: K. Paul, Trench, Tribner, 1909), pp. 89-90.

26. Charles Lennox, Fourth Duke of Richmond and Lennox, to Henry, Earl Bathurst, 22 February 1811, printed in Great Britain, *Historical Manuscripts Commission, Report on the Manuscripts of Earl Bathurst Preserved at Cirencester Park* (Francis Bickley, ed.; London: His Majesty's Stationery Office, 1923), p. 155.

27. Enclosure, Robert Peel to Richard Colley Wellesley, Marquess Wellesley, 19 January 1822; John Wilson Croker to Henry Goulburn, 31 May 1822; Goulburn to Wellesley, 3 July 1822; British Museum, Wellesley MSS 37298/ 54-55, 180; 37301/184-85.

28. *Annual Register*, XLV (1803), 356; John Russell, Sixth Duke of Bedford, to William Grenville, Baron Grenville, 7 July 1806; Grenville to Bedford, 11 July 1806, *Fortescue MSS*, VIII, 223-24, 231.

29. *Annual Register*, LXIV (1822), 38-39; *Dublin Evening Post*, 21 May 1822, p. 3, col. 1; Goulburn to Peel, 5 July 1824, British Museum, Peel MSS, 40330/74; also see Peel MSS, 40204/225, 40293/109-14, 40194/ 13-85, in Norman Gash, *Mr. Secretary Peel: The Life of Sir Robert Peel to 1830* (Cambridge: Harvard University Press, 1961), pp. 220-24; *Dublin Evening Post*, 12 June 1817, p.2, col. 4.

30. Otway-Ruthven, *Medieval Ireland*, p. 148.

31. G. C. Bolton, *The Passing of the Act of Union* (London: Oxford University Press, 1966), pp. 8-9.

32. The Marquess Cornwallis, who did not depart until after the Act of Union had come into operation- on 1 January 1801, is not included in this analysis.

33. R. B. McDowell, *The Irish Administration, 1801-1914* (London: Routledge and Kegan Paul, 1964), p. 53.

34. Great Britain, Public Record Office MSS, 30/8/326, in Johnston, *Great Britain*, p.26.

35. Aspinall, ed., *Correspondence of George III*, VI, no. 3857.

36. Charles Parker, *Sir Robert Peel* (3 vols.; London: John Murray, 1891), I, 333.

37. Cornwallis to Ross, 26 February 1801, in Charles Ross, ed., *The Correspondence of Charles, First Marquess Cornwallis* (3 vols.; London: J. Murray, 1859), III, 340-41.

38. James Harris, First Earl of Malmesbury, *Diaries and Correspondence* (4 vols.; London: R. Bentley, 1844), IV, 13; Colchester, *Diary*, I, 240-42; Pellew, *Sidmouth*, I, 346.

39. Aspinall, ed., *Later Correspondence*, III, 508.

40. Colchester, *Diary*, I, 242 (21 February 1801).

41. Aspinall, ed., *Later Correspondence of George III*, IV, 547; Lady Bessborough to Granville Leveson Gower, 10 November 1805, in Castalia Rosalind, Countess Granville, ed., *The Private Correspondence of Lord Granville Leveson Gower* (2 vols.; London: John Murray, 1916), II, 134; Earl Powis to Hardwicke, 19 January 1806, Hardwicke MSS, 35706/324; Francis Plowden, *History of Ireland, 1810-1811* (2 vols.; Dublin, 1811), II, 251.

42. *Dublin Correspondent*, 31 March 1807, p. 4, col. 4; 1 April 1807, p. 3, col. 3; Portland to the King, 31 March 1807, printed in Aspinall, ed., *Later Correspondence of George III*, IV, 549; Malmesbury, *Diaries*, IV, 380; *Evening Herald*, 3 April 1807, p.2.

43. *Dublin Evening Post*, 28 September 1813, p. 3, col. 1.

44. Aspinall, ed., *Later Correspondence of George III*, IV, 549; Lady Bessborough to Leveson Gower, March 1807, in Gower, *Correspondence*, II, 243; Portland to Richmond, 30 March 1807, National Library of Ireland, Richmond MSS, 60/243.

45. Dublin *Evening Herald*, 1 January 1813, p. 2, col. 2; Charles O'Mahoney,

The Viceroys of Ireland (London: John Long, 1912), p. 217.

46. Peel to Richmond, 15 May 1813, Richmond MSS, 69/1164; for the Whigs' reaction see Thomas Grenville to Lord Grenville, March 1813, 9 June 1813, printed in *Fortescue MSS*, X, 337; William Eden, Baron Auckland, to Grenville, June-July 1813, *Fortescue MSS*, X, 347; McMahon to Sir William Manners, 5 June 1813, in Arthur Aspinall, ed., *The Letters of King George IV, 1812-1830* (3 vols.; Cambridge: Cambridge University Press, 1938), I, 254.

47. O'Mahoney, *Viceroys*, pp. 218-19; O'Brien, *Dublin Castle*, p. 51; Gash, *Peel*, p. 229; Arthur Wellesley, First Duke of Wellington, to Robert Banks Jenkinson, Second Earl of Liverpool, n. d., printed in Arthur Wellesley, First Duke of Wellington, *Despatches, Correspondence and Memoranda* (8 vols.; London: J. Murray, 1867-80), I, 195; Francis Bamford and the Duke of Wellington, eds., *The Journal of Mrs. Arbuthnot* (2 vols.; London, Macmillan, 1950), I, 90.

48. Richard Ryder, Earl of Harrowby, to Bathurst, 24 November 1821, *Bathurst MSS*, p. 522.

49. *Evening Post*, 29 December 1821, p. 3, cols. 1-3; *Evening Mail*, 23 November 1825, p. 3, col. 2; Wellington to Bathurst, 2 and 7 January 1828, Bathurst MSS, 651-52; Peel to Anglesey, 26 January 1828, Peel MSS, 40325/1.

50. Hardwicke to Charles Yorke, 20 April 1804, Hardwicke MSS, 35705/248.

51. Bathurst to Richmond, 30 January 1811, 2 June 1812; Richmond to William Wellesley Pole, 13 June 1812, Richmond MSS, 61/345, 70/1318, 68/1064; Frederick Robinson, Viscount Goderich, to Wellesley, 29 November 1827, Wellesley MSS, 37305/198; Hardwicke to J. Sydney Yorke, 9 June 1803; Hardwicke to Charles Yorke, 3 May 1804; William Pitt to Hardwicke, May 1804, Hardwicke MSS, 35772/182, 35706/3, 38, 25; Richmond to Bathurst, 24 September 1809, 24 May 1812, Richmond MSS, 65/791, 72/1579.

52. Richmond to Bathurst, 20, 28 September 1812, *Bathurst MSS*, pp. 214, 215; Henry Addington, First Viscount Sidmouth, to Richmond, 25 September 1812, Richmond MSS, 65/829.

53. Peel to Charles Whitworth, First Earl Whitworth, 11, 30 March 1816, printed in Parker, *Peel*, I, 214, 219.

54. Charles Talbot, Earl Talbot, to Sidmouth, printed in O'Brien, *Castle*, p. 55.

55. Talbot to William Gregory, 10, 17 January, 1822, printed in Augusta Isabella Gregory, ed., *Mr. Gregory's Letter-Box, 1813-1830* (London: Smith, Elder and Co., 1898), pp. 169-70, 171-72; Whitworth to Talbot, 2 December 1821, Gregory, *Letter-Box*, p. 168.

56. Wellesley to William Conyngham Plunket, 19 March 1824, printed in David Plunket, ed., *The Life and Speeches of William Conyngham Plunket, First Baron Plunket* (2 vols.; London: Smith, Elder and Co., 1867), II, 145.

57. Col. Meyrick Shawe to William Knighton, 5 June 1827, printed in Aspinall, ed., *George IV*, III, 245.

58. Charles Arbuthnot to Peel, 6 July 1827, in Arthur Aspinall, *The Formation of Canning's Ministry, February to August 1827* (Camden Third Series, vol. LIX; London: Royal Historical Society, 1937), p. 254.

59. Wellesley to the King, 15 July 1828, Shawe to Knighton, 15 August 1827, printed in Aspinall, ed., *George IV*, III, 268, 287; Peel to Bathurst, 21 August 1827, *Bathurst MSS*, p. 644.

60. Wellington to Bathurst, 2 January 1828, *Bathurst MSS*, p. 651.

61. Henry William Paget, Marquess of Anglesey, to Wellington, 3 January 1829, British Museum, Huskisson MSS, 38757/177-78.

62. O'Mahoney, *Viceroys*, p. 233.

63. *Gentleman's Magazine*, n. s., III, 205; McDowell, *Irish Administration*, p. 53.

64. Mahoney, *Viceroys*, p. 233.

65. Hardwicke to Wickham, 18 May 1803, Hardwicke MSS, 35772/165; Margaret of Buckingham to Grenville, 17 May 1801, *Fortescue MSS*, VII, 19-20.

66. Sir Leslie Stephen and Sir Sidney Lee, eds., *The Dictionary of National*

37

Biography (Oxford: Oxford University Press, 1885-1900), XXI, 1269.

67. Cornwallis to Ross, 2 September 1802, in Ross, *Cornwallis*, III, 493; *Annual Register*, LIV (1812), 30.

68. *Fortescue MSS*, VIII, 97-98, 120-21, 128-32, 175-77, 224 486-88; see McDowell, *Public Opinion*, p. 69.

69. *Dictionary of National Biography*, XVII, 454-55.

70. Hereward Senior, *Orangeism in Ireland and Britain, 1795-1836* (London: Routledge and Kegan Paul, 1966), p.180; Gregory, *Letter-Box*, pp. 40-41; Parker, *Peel*, I, 101; Gregory to Peel, April 1813, Peel MSS, 40196/1, 40.

71. Lady Bessborough to Leveson Gower, 1 October 1808, Granville, *Correspondence*, pp. 333-34.

72. Richmond to Bathurst, 13 August 1807, *Bathurst MSS*, p. 62.

73. *Ibid.*, 12 September 1809, *Bathurst MSS*, p. 102; Robert Dundas to Richmond, 12 May 1809, Richmond MSS, 59/169.

74. Spencer Perceval to Bathurst, 25 January 1812, *Bathurst MSS*, p. 161.

75. Richard Grenville, Marquis of Buckingham, to Grenville, 3 January 1808, *Fortescue MSS*, IX, 164; Gregory, *Letter-Box*, pp. 40-41.

76. Gregory, *Letter-Box*, p. 41.

77. Denis Gray, *Spencer Perceval, 1762-1812: the Evangelical Prime Minister* (Manchester: Manchester University Press, 1963), p. 414.

78. Sidmouth to Richmond, 12 August 1813, Richmond MSS, 60/314.

79. "Memorandum Drawn as a Basis for Communication with A. Wellesley.

80. Croker to Yarmouth, 8 October 1819, Croker to Mrs. Croker, 8 October 1819, printed in Louis J. Jennings, ed., *The Correspondence and Diaries of John Wilson Croker* (3 vols.; London: John Murray, 1885), I, 136-37.

81. Richmond to Sidmouth, 19 May 1813, Richmond MSS, 62/467.

82. Gregory, *Letter-Box*, p. 41.

83. O'Mahoney, *Viceroys*, pp.216-18; Lord Sheffield to John Foster, 4 November 1813, printed in Gash, *Peel*, p. 131.

84. Peel to Liverpool, 31 October 1816, in Parker, *Peel*, I, 230; Gash, *Peel*, p. 229; Talbot to Gregory, 15 March 1821, printed in Gregory, *Letter-Box*, p. 140; Talbot to Peel, 6 May 1818, Peel MSS, 40194/248.

85. *Patriot*, 5 January 1822, p. 2, col. 4.

86. O'Mahoney, *Viceroys*, p. 226.

87. Goulburn to Bathurst, 22 December 1821, *Bathurst MSS*, p. 524; Shawe, "A Sketch of Some of the Measures of Lord Wellesley's Administration in Ireland", Aspinall, ed., *Letters of George IV*, III, 304.

88. Harrowby to Bathurst, 22 December 1821, *Bathurst MSS*, p. 526; Goulburn to Peel, 5 July 1824, Peel MSS, 40330/74; Goulburn to Peel, 10 July 1826, Peel MSS, 40332/52; Canning to Bathurst, 29 September 1824, *Bathurst MSS*, 574; Goulburn to Peel, 4 May 1822, 16 January 1823, Peel MSS, 40328/60, 40329/17.

89. *Ibid.*, 26 November 1824, Peel MSS 40330/235-36.

90. Goulburn to Peel, 16 October 1825, Peel MSS, 40331/176-78.

91. Galen Broeker, *Rural Disorder and Police Reform in Ireland, 1812-36* (London: Routledge and Kegan Paul, 1970), pp. 130-31; *Dictionary of National Biography*, XX, 1133-34.

92. Maj. Gen. Vivian to Knighton, 15 April 1827, printed in Aspinall, ed., *The Letters of George IV*, III, 253.

93. Anglesey to Peel, 27 January 1828, Peel MSS, 40325/3; Lyndhurst to Knighton, 20 December 1827, printed in Aspinall, ed., *Letters of George IV*, III, 253.

94. Charles C. F. Greville, *A Journal of the Reigns of King George IV and King William IV* (2 vols.; ed. Richard Henry Stoddard; New York: Scribners, Armstrong, 1875), I, 212.

95. Thomas Wyse, *Historical Sketch of the Late Catholic Association of Ireland* (2 vols.; London, 1829), I, 333.

96. Leveson Gower referring to Anglesey, printed in Gregory, *Letter-Box*, p. 244.

97. Daniel Owen Madden, *Ireland and Its Rulers since 1829* (London: T.C. Hewby, 1843-44), part I, p. 129.

98. Peel MSS, 40325, *passim;* also see

Anglesey to Henry Richard Vassal Fox, Third Baron Holland, 12 August 1831, Belfast, Northern Ireland Public Record Office, Anglesey MSS. T1068/7, p. 40; William M. Torrens, *Melbourne* (2 vols.; London: Macmillan, 1878), I 308.

99. Leveson Gower to Gregory, January 1829, *Letter-Box*, pp. 261-62.

100. *Dictionary of National Biography*, XV, 868.

101. Grenville, August 1829, quoted in Gregory, *Letter-Box*, p. 262; Madden, *Ireland*, part I, p. 55.

Duchess of Bedford, wife of John Russell, Duke.
Lord Lieutenant
March 1806–April 1807

Chapter 2
The Executive

A government of clerks – a government to be carried on by post and under the domination of spies, who were less than gentlemen, and more than ministers.

Henry Grattan on the Irish government, 21 April 1798

AS A RESULT of the Act of Union, Ireland's viceroys were expected to maintain lines of communication with the Crown, the Prime Minister, the Home Secretary, and the Cabinet. Direct correspondence with the King had already virtually ceased, but the intrusion of the Home Secretary more than supplied the deficiency. In many respects channels of communication and how they were employed document successive viceroys' struggles to maintain an independent jurisdiction while ambitious London officials and improved communications brought ever closer Pelham's dream of county status for Ireland.

THE ROLE OF THE CROWN AND THE PRIME MINISTER

Manuscript sources as early as the thirteenth century suggest that there was a vigorous correspondence between Dublin and London. During the succeeding one hundred years this contact was much less pronounced, and Poyning's Law was enacted in 1949 primarily to curb the Irish executive's increasing autonomy.[1] The slow intensification of Westminster's control subsequently. discouraged direct communications from the Crown, and by the mid-eighteenth century the Crown's role was slight. Thereafter George III took a much closer interest in Irish affairs and insisted on being a party to even relatively minor decisions. He complicated matters by claiming the right to read even the private correspondence which passed between Irish and English officials.[2] Indeed, it came to pass that "royal power was not so much

41

delegated to the viceroy as exercised through him."[3] In 1801 the King took time to warn Hardwicke of the dangers posed by certain Irish officials.[4] He also urged Hardwicke to follow Pelham's lead, and when Hardwicke stoutly refused to do so the King expressed his deep displeasure.[5]

The King's insanity in 1810 marked a dramatic and permanent reversal in the practice of direct intervention in Irish affairs. As Regent and King, George IV almost always communicated through his ministers. His principal concerns were related to patronage matters rather than to policy. In 1825 he decided against directly rebuking Wellesley for marrying a Catholic and permitting mass to be celebrated at the Royal lodge.[6] No other such initiative seems to have been given serious consideration.

The relationship of the viceroy to the Prime Minister was central to the smooth operation of the Irish government. At first Hardwicke found the relationship congenial, for Prime Minister Addington was quick to acquiesce in most of Hardwicke's suggestions. Upon returning to office in 1804 Pitt was astonished to see Hardwicke attempting, and often succeeding, to defy the ministry's wishes. Pitt sought to curb this by communicating directly with the viceroy's staff. He further angered Hardwicke by pledging patronage to unreconciled opponents of the Act of Union. Hardwicke demanded that "union engagements" be satisfied first; these were his instructions. The viceroy at length refused to sign a warrant prepared by Pitt to postpone meeting a commitment incurred in 1800, and Pitt died before the issue could be resolved.[7]

Bedford had no appetite for such independence. The Prime Minister, Baron Grenville, was acquainted with Ireland and might have reduced Bedford to little more than his agent had his ministry endured more than a year.[8] Portland was too old and feeble to struggle with Ireland; Perceval lectured Richmond on the need for certain reforms but left Richmond otherwise unfettered. From 1807 to 1812 the ministries of the day were often too weak to risk intervening in Irish affairs in such a way as to antagonise those vested interests on which the ministry relied for support. This afforded Richmond a good deal of autonomy, and within certain limits he was very much his own man.

Liverpoool was also inclined to limit severely his communications with Irish viceroys. On occasion Liverpool was moved to prepare a detailed letter advising viceroys on principles of patronage and administrative reform. At other times Liverpool failed to intervene. Even this would have been an entirely appropriate course of action. His reluctance to inform Talbot that he was soon to be removed from office was perhaps the most celebrated instance of such reluctance.[9] Canning was perhaps even worse. Although a longstanding friend of Wellesley, he neglected to inform the viceroy of his plans as Prime Minister and Wellesley's role in them.[10] Anglesey complained that Wellington never bothered to keep him informed of changing views on the Catholic question. The confrontation of two soldiers, "each expecting to be absolute in his own camp," should have suggested to Anglesey the declining status of the viceroy relative to that of Prime Minister.[11]

During the eighteenth century Cabinet members often communicated directly with the Irish viceroy. After Poyning's Law was amended in 1782 and after Westminster surrendered its veto over Irish legislation Henry Grattan and other Irish national leaders argued that all correspondence between London and Dublin should be addressed through the Prime Minister to the viceroy. Otherwise, they maintained, the Irish administration would be simply "a government of clerks" without any independent responsibilities. Grattan blamed many of Ireland's problems on the meddlesome tendencies of the Cabinet, but at length he condoned a limited traffic in informal communications.[12] After the Act of Union Pelham pressed to have all Cabinet correspondence pass through his ministry. Hardwicke protested. Richmond reopened the issue by directing letters to certain Cabinet members on important issues then under consideration[14] This was normally tolerated prior to 1820. Thereafter viceregal interference was not welcomed. In 1822 Wellesley failed to change Cabinet policy on several occasions. The Cabinet in turn neglected to consult the viceroy before reaching a decision, and Wellesley retaliated by ignoring the Cabinet.[14] After 1824 the Cabinet was so sharply divided on Irish questions that its members sometimes cultivated confidential contacts with Wellesley in an effort to buttress the pro-Catholic interest. Wellesley in return occasionally volunteered confidential information. This most irregular state of affairs was brought to a close in 1830 by putting the Chief Secretary in the Cabinet. Anglesey was infuriated by this experiment, and although it was not frequently repeated casual correspondence between viceroy and Cabinet virtually ceased.[15]

In 1800 a natural channel of communication was the Home Secretary's office. The acrimony which characterised relations between Hardwicke and Pelham prematurely focused attention on subjects which might have been resolved amicably over a longer period of time. Hardwicke conceded that the Act of Union called upon Ireland to adjust to English legal, fiscal, and administrative norms. But Ireland's condition could not admit of the traditional· county government; the viceroy needed a large discretionary power and direct access to the Cabinet and to the Prime Minister. Without this, sudden changes in Ireland's political temper could not be accommodated. As William Grenville noted on an earlier occasion, the fundamental differences between conditions in England and conditions in Ireland were imperfectly understood.[16·]

Pelham dissented. In Pelham's mind the Act of Union had limited the viceroy to maintaining the peace, and even policies in this area should be fashioned in London.[17] He accused Hardwicke of promoting federalism and even separatism. For three years Hardwicke and Pelham waged a private struggle, and it touched upon points personal and constitutional. Hardwicke defended his right, for example, to restrict agricultural imports when they tended to depress Irish agricultural prices.[18] Pelham complained bitterly to the King when a new Chief Secretary was appointed without his approval. Philip Yorke, Hardwicke's brother and a member of the Cabinet, denounced "this dirty shabby trick" and tried to have Pelham removed from office.[19] Later Pelham supported the Duke of York's efforts to deprive Hardwicke of his military patronage and he resisted proposals to raise the viceroy's salary. Yorke also charged that Pelham delayed communications intended for Dublin; this "astonishing perseverance in the disgusting and offensive negligence and inattention" threatened to undermine completely the Irish government.[20] Tempers flared in February 1803 when Pelham inadvertently received a packet of Hardwicke's letters critical of his conduct and intended for the Prime Minister. Pelham threatened to resign and hoped that the King would order Addington to dismiss Hardwicke instead.[21] The ploy failed; Addington accepted Pelham's resignation and Yorke succeeded him as Home Secretary.[22]

Between 1803 and 1812 a rapid succession of Home Secretaries in effect surrendered the initiative to the incumbent viceroy. In 1812 Addington (by this time styled Earl Sidmouth) began a term of office which spanned a full decade of endemic unrest and much hardship among the lower classes of both Britain and Ireland. Sidmouth urged Whitworth and Talbot to emulate his own stern and occasionally repressive policies. Until he resigned in 1818 as Chief Secretary, Peel shielded the two viceroys from Sidmouth's ambitious and at times alarmist policies. Thereafter Talbot tended to rely heavily on Sidmouth and inadvertently opened up to him a new world of spies, potential undercover agents, and real or imagined dangers to the state. Sidmouth convinced himself that Irish conditions were so serious that he recommended Talbot's recall.

Peel became Home Secretary shortly after Wellesley arrived in Dublin. Peel succeeded in establishing his own authority in Ireland much as Pelham had tried and failed to do two decades earlier. Peel's experience in Irish affairs, his balanced conservatism, and his patience inevitably placed Wellesley at a disadvantage. Wellesley's outlook on Catholic relief and other contentious issues differed sharply from Peel's. But Peel resolved to establish a "cordial relationship" with Wellesley; Wellesley in turn testified (perhaps insincerely) to Peel's "wisdom and honour" and a "judgement so correct, acute, and honest."[23] Over the years their correspondence remained polite enough, even if Peel privately complained that Wellesley was often unwilling to grapple with unpopular or complex issues.[24] Soon enough the Home Secretary's skill and industry were reflected in bills prepared for Parliament. This marked the first time that the Home Secretary participated so actively on Ireland's behalf in this most crucial of functions.

Peel was briefly out of office in 1827. He resumed his position in January 1828 more powerful than ever. Anglesey complained of this, to no avail.[25] Under the Whigs the Home Secretary's role in Irish affairs was further strengthened, and strengthened at the expense of the Irish Lord Lieutenant.

PROPOSALS FOR REFORM

After 1800 improvements in communications gradually undermined Dublin Castle's autonomy. As late as the 1780s Lords Lieutenant compensated for deficiencies in official correspondence by turning to family members, members of parliament, agents and secretaries.[26] Most viceroys chided London about slow responses to their requests. Letters went unanswered for months and when instructions finally arrived they might be outmoded.[27] Deficiencies were due in part to carelessness, in part to disinterest, and in part to a calculated impoliteness. London often changed its procedures for communicating with Dublin in an effort to define more accurately the role of the Treasury, the Secretaries of State, the Undersecretaries, the viceroy's London agents, and the small bureau for Irish affairs.[28] A major innovation in 1782 designated the Home Department as the principal clearing house for Irish correspondence, but by 1800 there was general dissatisfaction with Anglo-Irish communications.[29]

The Act of Union presented an admirable chance to reform the system. Pelham and Hardwicke feuded over this and everything else. Finally, in 1803, Pelham accused Hardwicke of gross negligence in failing to discern and submit evidence of an impending insurrection. It transpired, however, that Hardwicke had forwarded the relevant reports directly to Addington.[30] Pelham had also undertaken to communicate privately and directly with Hardwicke's subordinates.[31] That most problems reflected a clash of personalities as well as principle was reinforced when Yorke succeeded Pelham. He proposed that Hardwicke and he (as Home Secretary) correspond officially, confidentially and frequently. The Irish Chief Secretary would correspond directly with the Home Secretary only in unusual cases, but he could contact the Undersecretaries of State whenever necessary.[32] All other correspondence would pass through the viceroy's hands. Hardwicke acquiesced in this, even though some points were similar to those which he had resisted when Pelham suggested them earlier.

After 1804 viceroys complained frequently that no one in London took time to keep them informed. The post between London and Dublin was reduced to only forty hours, but viceroys found themselves at the mercy of their better-informed Irish Chief Secretaries.[33] In 1817 no one in London bothered to appraise Talbot of a change in electoral tactics regarding a vacancy at Trinity College. In the confusion the government's candidate was defeated. Peel lamely explained that he assumed letters sent to Talbot's subordinates were always shown to the viceroy.[34]

In 1822 Wellesley offered a simple solution: all Dublin-bound correspondence would come to the viceroy and all items for London would be addressed to the Home Secretary.[35] Wellesley wanted to interdict the Goulburn-Peel correspondence, which he failed to do.[36] Peel insisted that the Home Secretary must be permitted direct access to the Irish Chief Secretary, and he promised that Goulburn would relay all relevant news to

Wellesley. This was hardly likely to allay Wellesley's suspicions, and Wellesley embarked upon a series of elaborate reports designed to elicit a clear response from members of the Cabinet other than Peel. Their length only served to see them end up after all in Peel's hands.[37] Peel faced unavoidable delays in preparing suitable responses, and of course Wellesley complained bitterly.[38] Anglesey did the same and Peel chastised him for depending too heavily on private and casual correspondence.[39] Northumberland suffered no illusions as to the superintending role of the Home Secretary; he directed everything to Peel and cared little who in Dublin was honoured by receipt of London's correspondence.[40]

By 1830 viceroys were forced to depend heavily on their Chief Secretaries. London made most decisions and correspondence took on a peremptory rather than an interrogatory tone. Parliament resorted more frequently to its own commissions, some of which also included Ireland. Irish affairs qualified as domestic rather than imperial problems. Almost imperceptively but inexorably events conspired to elevate the powers of the Irish Chief Secretary.

THE RISE OF THE CHIEF SECRETARY

The growth of the Chief Secretary's importance preceded the Act of Union. Insufficient attention has been paid to finding why the Chief Secretary's functions and growing powers were directly related to the Lord Lieutenancy. Until the last third of the eighteenth century the Chief Secretary to the Lord Lieutenant was simply that: selected by the viceroy and placed under his immediate control. Destruction of the "undertakers" system after 1767 marked a new chapter in the history of Irish administration. The "undertakers" had secured an amenable parliament in return for control of a large portion of the viceroy's patronage. But Irish politicians' demands became excessive and after that time viceroys determined to reside permanently in Dublin and to negotiate directly with parliament. Soon enough the Chief Secretary became the focus of transactions involving military matters and the treasury and revenue boards.[41] In 1781-82 William Eden observed that his office was "rapidly becoming a testing ground for aspiring British politicians." [42] Fifteen years later the rise of the Chief Secretary's prestige and power was confirmed in the performance of the young Lord Castlereagh, who could "redeem a mediocre viceroy if competent, and overshadow him if brilliant." [43] He tended to overshadow.

What factors enhanced the importance of the Chief Secretary? As early as the 1770s one viceroy observed that by "placing his secretary between himself and the people" the Irish constitution shielded the viceroy from the vexations of trying to manage an Irish legislature whose deliberations he could not shape directly.[44] Pitt agreed after the appointment of a new Chief Secretary in 1784 temporarily disoriented the entire administrative apparatus in Dublin.[45] Because they sat in parliament, and because they often negotiated directly with the Irish political proprietors, Chief Secretaries were capable of "great power and mischief."[46]

Nonetheless, as Professor R. B. McDowell had observed, until 1800 the Secretaryship was "decidedly" inferior to the Lord Lieutenant. The Chief Secretaries served for too brief a period. Their understanding of Irish affairs was often faulty. Many were young and inexperienced; only gradually was the potential value of the office to a politician's career recognised. Quick-witted Irish politicians often exploited the Secretaries' ignorance and credulity. In emergencies viceroys negotiated directly with leaders of the Irish parliament. Robert Peel noted at a much later date that as long as the Chief Secretary functioned in the forum of the Irish Parliament he remained subordinate to a resident viceroy.[47]

Castlereagh and the Act of Union together demonstrated that the Chief Secretary's office could challenge the viceroy for primacy in Ireland.[48] Castlereagh's powerful family connections, unsurpassed parliamentary skills and great experience in Irish affairs set powerful precedents.[49] Removal of Irish legislators to Westminster forced the viceroy to depend on his Secretary for information and advice. Liverpool later advised Richmond that since the Chief Secretaries "have the labouring oar of Irish business in the House of Commons" viceroys must support them in their parliamentary business and use of patronage.[50]

Not until 1812 was the full potential of the office of Chief Secretary realised. A succession of seven secretaries between 1801 and 1809 gave every advantage to a viceroy with several years' experience in office. Upon his appointment in 1812 Peel "considered [his] office quite identified with that of the Lord Lieutenant, as I can do no act whatever independent of his authority...."[51] But when Whitworth succeeded Richmond as viceroy Peel possessed the greater experience, and his biographer Professor Norman Gash dates the emergence of the Chief Secretaryship as the principal office in the Irish administration from that time.[52] Another observer has held that the Chief Secretary's power was reinforced by a tendency among viceroys themselves to sacrifice their autonomy by confining themselves too rigidly "to social functions and the dispensing of patronage."[53] Personalities — Castlereagh and Peel vs. Whitworth and Talbot — and the new parliamentary forum provided by Westminster shifted power degree by degree to the Chief Secretary.

The advantages of the longer view were not available to the Chief Secretaries themselves, and the institutional development of the office followed an irregular course. After 1767 the Chief Secretary's increased responsibilities were reflected in a reorganisation at Dublin Castle. Most important was the emergence of two Undersecretaries, one for civil and another for military affairs, to replace antiquated bureaus and offices over which the Chief Secretary often had only indirect control.[54] More difficult was the task of defining just what were the viceroy's responsibilities. Castlereagh's tenure as Chief Secretary terminated with the Act of Union, and Hardwicke arrived in Dublin to find the office in a state of great confusion.[55] Was the Chief Secretary henceforth to be the "efficient" minister for Ireland or merely an assistant to the Home Secretary in matters related to Ireland? Was he responsible to the Home Secretary or to the viceroy? Should he reside in London or in Dublin?[56] Hardwicke proposed that these questions be addressed immediately. But little was done and a succession of Chief Secretaries treated the office as one of little importance: Nicholas Vansittart never came to Ireland; William Wickham was too ill to work; Sir Evan Nepean took a seat on the Admiralty Board while still holding his Irish office.[57] Hardwicke complained that the cabinet made no attempt to recruit a qualified individual.[58]   In 1804 he urged Pitt to nominate as Chief Secretary someone able to defend the Irish administration in Parliament and able to confront rather than surrender to well-entrenched Irish bureaucrats.[59] When this appeal fell on deaf ears Hardwicke urged his brother Yorke as Home Secretary to view the Irish Chief Secretary's office as "equal to a Secretary of State" and deserving of a seat in the Cabinet when the incumbent came to England.[60]   In his distress at the state of affairs Hardwicke apparently failed to see that implementing his proposals would permit the Chief Secretary to challenge the viceroy.

Even Hardwicke's brother proved unresponsive. Hardwicke's correspondence contains dozens of acrimonious exchanges with Chief Secretaries whose work he deprecated. In each case Hardwicke issued detailed instructions about what he expected them to do, warned them about Irish politicians and bureaucrats, betrayed his disillusionment when they failed to meet expectations, and complained bitterly to London of their incompetence and unfitness.[61] Hardwicke alleged that they soon fell under the evil influence of Irish vested interests or simply refused to apply themselves.[62] Worst of all, Hardwicke's criteria were systematically ignored; announcement of one appointment was gazetted even before the viceroy was appraised of the list of candidates.[63] Repeated promises that henceforth "regularity and organisation" would characterise the conduct of the Chief Secretaryship came to nothing.[64]

All of these problems seemed to culminate in the Chief Secretaryship of Sir Evan Nepean. Nepean was appointed in February 1804. Hardwicke issued all the familiar warnings about attempts by the Chancellor of the Irish Exchequer to become "the efficient minister of Ireland," about the entrenched position of the Undersecretaries, and about numerous other problems.[65] Nepean listened impatiently. He had served in numerous administrative posts and had been Chief Secretary once before. At this juncture he looked forward to higher office in England. He refused to fight Hardwicke's battles against Dublin Castle but did circumscribe the Undersecretaries' power by personally handling every detail of administration. Unfortunately, in Hardwicke's view, this also encouraged the Secretary to listen sympathetically to the viceroy's critics, to the neglect of his duties in Parliament. At length Nepean resigned. Hardwicke took advantage of the moment to write that Nepean was consistently ill-informed and frequently exposed his ignorance in "the most lamentable blunders". He was "positively the most unfit man that ever was appointed." [66]

This exchange is all the more remarkable because Nepean's career had heretofore been a distinguished one. Perhaps, some whispered, the fault lay instead with Hardwicke. Nepean complained bitterly of Hardwicke's deficiencies. But Pitt in his final months of life was too weak physically and politically to contemplate removing the viceroy. [67] Hardwicke endured two more Chief Secretaries before the Tories fell from power in 1806. One of them, Charles Long, wrestled successfully with the various boards and Undersecretaries and battled with Hardwicke as well.[68] In his widely advertised efforts to shape the Chief Secretary's office into a more effective instrument Hardwicke came rather close to undermining it completely.

Hardwicke's departure failed to arrest the rapid turnover in Chief Secretaries, but relations with the viceroy certainly became more amicable. Bedford's secretary William Elliott had served as military Undersecretary for five years, which was invaluable, and his personal charm, excellent political connections and somewhat mysterious reputation as a "soldier of fortune" were also useful. That the office was not held in high esteem is suggested in Arthur Wellesley's stipulation that he be allowed to surrender the office at any time if an opportunity for continental service with the army appeared on the horizon. This was no idle reservation, for soon enough Arthur was invited to join British and German forces on the Rhine. It was an offer he could not refuse, and he promptly turned over his duties to Richmond. Richmond soon enough complained that in Wellesley's absence a "vast number of people" refused to deal with anyone but the viceroy himself, and that as a result he was forced to attend personally to the bulky correspondence. [69] Wellesley returned from the Continent, finally resigned and sailed for Spain. Richmond thereupon declared that he preferred no secretary to a weak one. [70] Whitehall listened; none was appointed for most of a year.

Robert Dundas, later Lord Melville, managed to clear a year's backlog of work during his six month appointment. His successor was William Wellesley-Pole, Arthur's brother. He brought to the task good connections, limited talents, and an overriding determination to strengthen his position in the Queen's County. He was unpopular with Catholics, and his inability to humour disappointed office-seekers angered many Protestants as well. [71] But Richmond supported Wellesley-Pole's initiatives unstintingly until the Chief Secretary suddenly announced his conversion to the pro-Catholic cause in May 1812. [72] Wellesley-Pole volunteered that he had long harboured pro-Catholic sympathies. Richmond immediately and violently denounced his Chief Secretary and the pro-Catholic press lost not a moment celebrating the spectacle of an Irish administration motivated by diametrically opposed policies. [73] Wellesley-Pole thereupon resigned his office. Richmond vented his frustration by launching a libel suit against one of the opposition newspapers. [74]

Whatever the inconsistencies of his policies, Wellesley-Pole demonstrated how important a familiarity with Irish conditions and length of tenure could be in reviving the prestige of the Chief Secretary's office. And the Catholic issue would eventually induce Whitehall to strive for the very objective which Richmond detested: either the Viceroy or the Chief Secretary would be appointed on the basis of some sympathy towards Catholics' aspirations.

Peel's impact has already been alluded to. An early biographer declared that "successive Lords Lieutenant resigned, Mr. Peel governed." [75] Peel soon established an ascendancy in the Liverpool ministry's Irish policies.[76] He worked exceedingly well with the initially sceptical Richmond.[77] Soon enough Richmond was content to leave most business in Peel's hands, and the bureaucracy's resistance melted before Peel's dextrous strategy.[78] Richmond's confidence in Peel was strikingly demonstrated when the Chief Secretary confronted the contentious Maynooth issue in Parliament in March 1813. The viceroy's letter of advice contained two opinions, one "personal" and the other "public". "Take whatever course you please," he told Peel. "You may decidedly quote me as perfectly agreeing with you. You will be a better judge on the spot than I am." [79]

"Armed with seniority and experience," Peel was clearly ascendant over Whitworth.[80] Whitworth accepted this state of affairs gracefully, and the government of Ireland was described as "a model of unity and efficiency." [81] Peel defended the viceroy in Parliament; Whitworth sustained the Chief Secretary in Ireland. Peel determined patronage policies and Whitworth rebuffed supplicants who tried to circumvent the Chief Secretary. [82] The Irish press took note of the shift of work to Peel, and Whitworth confirmed it in 1816 by agreeing to stay in Dublin an extra year only if Peel continued as Chief Secretary.

By 1817 Peel was acutely conscious of his ascendancy over Whitworth. He reacted sharply when the Corporation of the City of Dublin commissioned Peel's portrait but neglected to invite Whitworth to sit as well.[83] Peel felt the embarrassment; it reinforced his determination to leave Ireland with Whitworth so as not to stifle Whitworth's successor. [84] But Talbot refused to face a general election without Peel, so Peel remained. Talbot proved so dependent on his Chief Secretary — he cleared even his household appointments with Peel — that he was little prepared to cope with the reforming zeal of Charles Grant.[85] As a result, the Talbot-Grant administration was perhaps the least efficient of the era. Grant possessed little executive or political experience and strongly opposed Talbot's conservative politics. Grant was also "vacilating and procrastinating". He appeased Catholics by making promises which London refused to implement. The Castle staff laboured to undermine Grant's pro-Catholic position.[86] O'Connell on the other hand praised Grant ("the mildest, kindest and best mannered man Ireland has ever seen"). Such compliments only aggravated Protestants' suspicions. Under the stress of rural agitation, which spread and intensified rapidly after the summer of 1821, Talbot and Grant proved completely unable to agree on the essentials of their response. Talbot favoured a more forceful policy and eventually implemented it over Grant's protests.[87] The Liverpool Cabinet looked on in undisguised horror and at length Talbot hinted that Grant should be dismissed.[88] But times had changed; no longer was a Chief Secretary to be dismissed at the viceroy's command. London concluded that both men, because they failed to "draw together", should be replaced.[89]

This sad affair established the concept of a "team"; the team would feature prominently in most subsequent appointments.[90] Wellesley's nomination depended upon finding him a stable and efficient secretary. Henry Goulburn was this; he was also Peel's intimate friend and disciple. Goulburn knew better than to confront Wellesley; with Peel as Home Secretary he need only circumvent the viceroy. The Goulburn-Peel correspondence testifies to the success of this strategy.[91] Fortunately, Goulburn and Wellesley were busy enough in separate jurisdictions to reduce the number of inevitable clashes. Goulburn's parliamentary burden was unusually heavy: tithes, insurrection acts, suppression of the Catholic Association, and vestry, municipal and judicial reforms were some of these responsibilities. He travelled to Dublin once a year, where Wellesley often pleaded ill-health to avoid meeting him.[92] On occasion Wellesley proved demanding, usually, however, Goulburn was forced to press Wellesley to expedite his paperwork. At Westminster liberals complained that Goulburn and Peel were too strong for the viceroy.[93] In Dublin, however, Wellesley channeled his invective harmlessly into letters to his friend William Plunket.

Wellesley outlasted Goulburn, who resigned with Peel in April 1827.[94] William Lamb understood Wellesley's "very susceptible temperament" far better than had Goulburn.[95] At first they rather liked each other; later their relationship would turn bitter.[96] Lamb found Anglesey much less amenable, saw his recommendations politely ignored, and left Ireland before Anglesey was replaced.[97] Francis Leveson Gower thus became the third Chief Secretary in eighteen months. Nonetheless, the importance of the office was secure; Leveson Gower's successor would enter the

Cabinet.

During this thirty year period the criteria and procedures touching upon selection of the Chief Secretary changed profoundly. Before 1783 most secretaries were chosen directly by the viceroy; even Cabinet approval was sometimes missing. In that year, however, the viceroy Northington was not consulted when Pelham was selected.[98] By 1789 William Pitt as Prime Minister enjoyed a decisive say.[99] The last Irish Parliament reaffirmed the ancient right of the viceroy to choose his own Chief Secretary.[100] This mattered little, as Hardwicke's complaints indicated.[101] It appears that three of his five Chief Secretaries — Abbot, Nepean, and Vansittart — were chosen entirely independently of Hardwicke.[102] In the last instance George Canning received and rejected an officer, and Vansittart consulted several sources — but not Hardwicke.[103] Richmond vainly opposed Wellesley-Pole ("he would incline to do jobs for the Queen's county" — his political influence was centred in modern County Laoise)[104] and resented not being consulted on Peel. "Nobody cares less about form than I do," Richmond observed, "but it might have been awkward" if he had refused his consent.[105] Talbot opposed Grant, again to no avail.[106] Wellesley was never consulted about Goulburn, nor Anglesey about Leveson Gower.[107] Anglesey was candid enough to tell his new Chief Secretary of his opposition but pledged to act "as if the appointment had originated in me."[108] In 1831 Stanley's voice was decisive in selecting the viceroy; the reversal was complete.

Who became Irish Chief Secretary? Most striking was the paucity of Irishmen. Castlereagh in 1797 was the first Irish-born Secretary in thirty years; only the two Wellesley brothers were Irish-born appointees during the next third of a century.[109] The pattern was intentional. Richmond complained of Wellesley-Pole's Irish connections, and Peel later urged that Irishmen not be appointed.[110] Parliamentary experience was also useful, although prior to 1812 this was not given priority.[111] Peel, however, demonstrated that Irish matters demanded first rate parliamentary credentials, and Grant was appointed largely on the basis of his potential in debate.

Administrative expertise was always valued. Nepean's reputation here more than countered objections that he was "entirely unconnected with the..... country and business" of Ireland.[112] Wellesley-Pole was advertised as "quick, steady, intelligent, zealous and indefatigable."[113] Dundas too was "an excellent man of business – fit for any situation."[114]   Peel, although young, was considered steady and reliable.[115]   But administrative expertise took second place to parliamentary talents and ideological factors.[116] This concern about political bias reflects the altered role of the Chief Secretary. Grant balanced Talbot and Goulburn balanced Wellesley. But in 1827 Lansdowne urged on Canning the need to choose the Chief Secretary first. He cited the importance of having a pro-Catholic who could work with the Cabinet.[117] Wellesley was thus pressed to resign; the King would not permit both viceroy and Chief Secretary to be "catholic".[118]

Certainly the prestige attached to the office of Chief Secretary rose rapidly between 1800 and 1830. Hardwicke reflected the majority view in 1804 in holding that the office held no promise for a young politician.[119] Yorke complained that most incumbents were too easily influenced by parties opposed to the government.[120] Until 1812 the Cabinet's first choice often rejected the post or expected a better position to follow.[121] In 1807 the Earl of Rosse wrote Arthur Wellesley that he could take Wellesley's place in his absence; he spent considerable time in Dublin in any event and could without convenience reside even longer.[122] When Peel accepted office in 1812 he was only twenty-four and conceded that he wanted to bring himself to the Ministry's attention.[123]   Liverpool later explained Grant's appointment by complaining that no one else was willing to go to Ireland.[124] Goulburn demonstrated, as did Peel, that the office was so onerous that rewards were in order. In 1830 Stanley accepted the challenge of the office when Grey persuaded him that the fate of the ministry depended upon it.

By 1830 the rising prestige of the office was prompting proposals for changing the formal relationship between viceroy and Chief Secretary. Pelham early on proposed to subordinate both the viceroy and Chief Secretary to the Home ministry. Hardwicke was prepared to sacrifice the Chief Secretaryship to save his own office.[126] Indifference saved them both. But in 1812 Richmond was alarmed by a proposal that the Chief Secretary be raised to Cabinet rank. This would undermine his own position, he concluded.[126]   Nearly twenty years passed before Edward Stanley gained entrance; this was done over the opposition of the incumbent Lord Lieutenant.[127]   The precedent subsequently caused problems; some nominees refused office unless placed in the Cabinet.[128]   For the next forty years the Chief Secretary

55

was frequently, and the viceroy rarely, admitted to the Cabinet. This situation clearly made the viceroy supreme only when he was in the Cabinet. In 1905 this "practical paradox" led to problems which perhaps later would have destroyed the arrangement even had war not intervened.[129]

In retrospect it is surprising that the Chief Secretary's pre-eminence was not established earlier. Improved transportation, Parliament's triumph over the Crown, collective responsibility in the Cabinet all supported the pretensions of the Chief Secretary against the viceroy. But until 1830 the viceroy remained the single most important factor in Irish government.

FOOTNOTES   CHAPTER 2

1. Beckett, *Modern Ireland*, p. 51.

2. Johnston, *Great Britain*, pp. 12-13.

3. *Ibid.*, p. 16.

4. George to Hardwicke, 8 May 1801, Hardwicke MSS, 35349/73.

5. John Holland Rose, *Pitt and Napoleon: Essays and Letters* (London: C. Bell and Sons, 1912), pp. 243-44; Hardwicke MSS 35744/49, cited in Aspinall, ed., *Later Correspondence of George III*, IV, 156; Hardwicke to Charles Abbot, 29 November 1803, Hardwicke MSS, 35772/269.

6. Peel to Goulburn, 12 November 1825, Peel MSS, 40331/192-94.

7. Plowden, *Ireland*, II, 224-34.

8. Grenville to Bedford, 11 March 1807; Bedford to Grenville, 1 April 1807, *Fortescue MSS*, IX, 68-72, 129-30.

9. Wellesley to Liverpool, 22 November 1824, printed in C. D. Yonge, *The Life and Administration of Lord Liverpool* (3 vols.; London, 1868), pp. 312-13.

10. Goulburn to Wellesley, 21 April 1827, Wellesley MSS, 37305/95; Lamb to Lansdowne, 3 August 1827, in Aspinall, *Formation*, p. 276.

11. Wellington to Peel, 5 November 1828, cited in Parker, *Peel*, II, 73, and in Wellington, *Despatches*, V, 366; Gregory, *Letter-Box*, pp. 240-41; Anthony E. M. Ashley, *The Life and Correspondence of Henry John Temple, Viscount Palmerston (2 vols.; London, 1879), I, 183.*

12. Henry Grattan on the position of Irish ministers, Irish House of Commons, 21 April 1798, *Parliamentary Register* (Dublin 1795 ff.), XV, 189-90, cited in Curtis and McDowell, eds., *Irish Historical Documents*, p. 226.

13. Grattan, 21 April 1795, *Parliamentary Register*, XV, 189-90, in Curtis *et al.*, *Irish Historical Documents*, p. 226.

14. Wellesley to Richmond, 1 February 1809, Richmond MSS, 58/47; Richmond to Bathurst, 1 June 1812, *Bathurst MSS*, 176; Dundas to Richmond, 25 September 1809, Richmond MSS, 59/174.

15. Peel to Wellesley, 31 January 1822, Wellesley MSS, 37298/116; George Canning to Plunket, 27 December 1823; William Wynn to Plunket, 24 June 1823, printed in Plunket, ed., *Plunket*, II, 144, 132-38.

16. A. D. Kriegal, "The Irish Policy of Lord Grey's Government", *English Historical Review*, LXXXVI (January 1971), 28-29.

17. Hardwicke to Pelham, 8 February 1803, Hardwicke MSS, 35772/87.

18. Grenville to Buckingham, September 1798, printed in Richard Plantagenet Temple-Nugent-Brydges-Chandos-Grenville, Duke of Buckingham and Chandos, *Memoirs of the Courts and Cabinets of George III* (2 vols.; London, 1853-55), II, 404-407.

19. Colchester, *Diary*, quoted in O'Brien, *Castle*, pp. 91-92; also see "Introductory Paper from Lord Pelham to Lieutenant Colonel Littlehales for His Excellency the Lord Lieutenant", n. d., Hardwicke MSS, 35771/97-99.

20. Hardwicke to Redesdale, 27 May 1803, Hardwicke MSS, 35772/171.

21. Yorke to Hardwicke, 12 February 1802, Hardwicke MSS, 35701/237.

22. *Ibid.*, 30 May 1803, Hardwicke MSS, 35702/195.

23. Peel to Wellesley, 17 January 1822, Wellesley MSS, 37298/40-41; Wellesley to Goulburn, 1822, Peel MSS, 40328/197.

24. Broeker, *Rural Disorder*, p. 132.

25. Peel to Anglesey, 10 January 1829, Peel MSS, 40326/181.

26. Great Britain, Historical Manuscripts Commission, *Thirteenth Report*, Appendix III, p. 400; Public Record Office MSS, 30/8/326; Buckingham, *Courts and Cabinets*, I, *passim;* Johnston, *Great Britain*, p. 25.

27. British Museum Add. MSS 33101, cited in Johnston, *Great Britain*, p. 25; Robert Henley, Second Earl of Northington, to Portland, 1783, British Museum Add. MSS, 38716/145.

28. Dublin Public Record Office, State Papers 63/452, f. 172; Aspinall, ed., *Correspondence of George III*, V, no. 3190; *Calendar of Home Office Papers, 1773-75*, no. 14; Johnston, *Great Britain*, p. 28.

29. Johnston, *Great Britain*, pp. 77-78, 87-88.

30. Thomas Pelham to George III,

13 September 1803, printed in Aspinall, ed., *Later Correspondence of George III*, IV, 132-33.

31. Charles Lindsay to Abbot, 26 October 1801, Dublin, State Paper Office, Official Papers, Second Series, Vol. I (1791-1810), Carton 518, Nos. 113-16; Hardwicke to Charles Yorke, 20 August 1803, Hardwicke MSS, 35772/234.

32. Charles Yorke to Hardwicke, 18 August 1803, Hardwicke MSS, 35702/339.

33. Hardwicke to Charles Yorke, 7 March 1804, Hardwicke MSS, 35705/152.

34. Peel MSS, 40194/255-63, noted in Gash, *Peel*, p. 230.

35. Peel to Goulburn, 12 September 1822, Peel MSS, 40328/133.

36. Peel to Wellesley, 16 February 1822, Wellesley MSS, 37298/227; Peel to Goulburn, 10 September 1822, Peel MSS, 40328/130.

37. Goulburn to Peel, 26 November 1824, Peel MSS, 40330/236; for examples of Wellesley's reports see *The Patriot*, 22 June 1822, p. 2, col. 5, and 9 February 1822, p. 3.

38. Wellesley to Plunket, 19 March 1824, printed in Plunket, ed., *Plunket*, II, 145.

39. Anglesey to Peel, 31 March 1828; Peel to Anglesey, 7 April 1828; Anglesey to Peel, 16 July 1828; Peel to Anglesey, 19 July 1828, Peel MSS, 40325/6-7, 21, 119, 125; Croker, memorandum, 9 January 1829, printed in Croker, *Diaries*, I, 403-406.

40. Peel to Hugh Percy, Duke of Northumberland, n. d., Peel MSS 40327/12.

41. William Eden to North, 1781, printed in William Beresford, ed., *Correspondence of the Right Honourable John Beresford* (2 vols.; London: Woodfall and Kinder, 1854), I, 168-69; Johnston, *Great Britain*, pp. 34, 44.

42. Beresford, *Correspondence*, I, 145-46; Johnston, *Great Britain*, p.37.

43. R. Ross to Arthur Hill, Second Marquess of Downshire, 29 August 1798, Belfast, Northern Ireland Public Record Office, DOD 607, cited in Johnston, *Great Britain*, p. 38.

44. *Harcourt Papers*, IX, 254.

45. Charles Manners, Seventh Duke of Rutland, ed., *Correspondence between the Rt. Hon. William Pitt and Charles, Duke of Rutland, Lord Lieutenant of Ireland, 1781-1787* (London: A. Spottiswoode, 1842), p. 128.

46. John Hely-Hutchison to Alexander Wedderburn, First Baron Loughborough, 1793, Historical Manuscripts Commission, *Thirteenth Report, Appendix IX*, p. 328; Johnston, *Great Britain*, p. 40.

47. O'Brien, *Dublin Castle*, p. 83.

48. McDowell, *Irish Administration*, p.57.

49. *Ibid., Public Opinion*, pp. 66-67.

50. Liverpool to Richmond, September 1812, Liverpool MSS, 38238/43.

51. Peel to Liverpool, 20 October 1813, printed in Parker, *Peel*, I, 110-111.

52. Gash, *Peel*, pp. 110-11, 129.

53. D. A. Chart, *Ireland from the Union to Catholic Emancipation* (London: J. M. Dent and Sons, 1910), pp. 180-81.

54. John Hobart, Second Earl of Buckinghamshire, memorandum, Public Record Office, SP 63/457, ff. 119-21; Johnston, *Great Britain*, pp. 48, 50, 59.

55. Abbot to Addington, 27 October 1801; Hardwicke to Charles Yorke, 16 December 1801, Hardwicke MSS, 35771/117-20, 131-32.

56. "Considerations upon the Situation of the Lord Lieutenant and his Chief Secretary", 20 September 1801, Hardwicke MSS, 35771/101-104.

57. Redesdale to Abbot, 30 October 1823, printed in Colchester, *Diary*, III, 269; Hardwicke to Charles Yorke, 8 February 1802, Hardwicke MSS, 35701, cited in McDowell, *Public Opinion*, p. 67.

58. Wickham to Grenville, 9 February 1802, *Fortescue MSS*, VII, 71; Hardwicke to Pitt, 9 July 1804, Hardwicke MSS, 35709/89-90.

59. Hardwicke to Pitt, May 1804, Hardwicke MSS, 35709/29.

60. Hardwicke to Charles Yorke, 15 November 1804, Hardwicke MSS, 35706/108-11.

61. *Ibid.,* 31 July 1801, Hardwicke MSS, 35771/67.

62. Robert Hobart to William Eden, First Baron Auckland, n. d. (c. October 1801), printed in George Hogge, ed., *The Journal and Correspondence of William Eden, Lord Auckland* (4 vols.; London, 1861-62), IV, 145; Hardwicke to Charles Yorke, 13 April 1804, Hardwicke MSS, 35705/238.

63. Wickham to Grenville, 9 February 1802, 4 March 1802, *Fortescue MSS,* VII, 77, 86.

64. Redesdale to Addington, 11 August 1803, in Pellew, *Sidmouth,* II, 213.

65. McDowell, *Public Opinion,* p. 67; Hardwicke to Evan Nepean, 17 January 1804, Hardwicke MSS, 35708/224-26.

66. Hardwicke to Charles Yorke, 15 November 1804, 23 January 1805, Hardwicke MSS, 35706/108, 111, 156; also see Hardwicke to Charles Yorke, 8 February 1805, Hardwicke MSS, 35701.

67. Thomas Grenville to Grenville, 20 September 1805, *Fortescue MSS,* VIII, 304.

68. Redesdale to Abbot, 30 October 1823, Colchester, *Diary,* III, 269.

69. Richmond to Bathurst, *Bathurst MSS,* cited in Aspinall, ed., *Later Correspondence of George III,* IV, 633.

70. Richmond to Arthur Wellesley, 8 June 1808, printed in Arthur Wellesley, Duke of Wellington, ed., *Supplementary Despatches and Memoranda of Arthur Wellesley, the First Duke of Wellington* (15 vols.; London: John Murray. 1858-72), Vol. V *(Ireland),* pp. 444-45. Herein referred to as *Ireland.*

71. Richard Ryder to William Wellesley Pole, 25-26 July 1811; Ryder to Richmond, 26 July 1811; Wellesley Pole to Ryder, 30 July 1811, cited in Gray, *Perceval,* p. 419; Richmond to Bathurst, 21 February 1811, *Bathurst MSS,* p. 155; copy in Richmond MSS, 61/337.

72. Richmond to Perceval, 3 April 1812, Richmond MSS, 74/1770.

73. Richmond to Peel, 5 March 1813, Parker, *Peel,* I, 78.

74. See the review article on Richmond in the Dublin *Evening Post,* 5 January, 7 January 1813, as well as subsequent remarks on 6 March and 11 March 1813.

75. Parker, *Peel,* I, 35.

76. Peel to Liverpool, 31 October 1816, in Parker, *Peel,* I, 230.

77. Richmond to Peel, 4 August 1812, Richmond MSS, 61/415; Peel to Richmond, 4 September 1813, Richmond MSS, 71/1413.

78. Parker, *Peel,* I, 35.

79. Richmond to Peel, March 1813, Peel MSS, 40185/190; Gash, *Peel,* p. 129.

80. Gash, *Peel,* p. 130.

81. *Ibid.,* p. 227; Peel to Whitworth, 10 April 1816, Parker, *Peel,* I, 223.

82. Peel MSS, 40193 (Whitworth-Peel Correspondence), *passim.*

83. *Ibid.,* 24 July 1817, p. 3, col. 1.

84. Gash, *Peel,* pp. 227-28; O'Brien, *Dublin Castle,* pp. 96-97.

85. Talbot to Peel, 31 July 1817, 11 May 1818, Peel MSS, 40194/167, 251.

86. *Dictionary of National Biography,* VIII, 381.

87. Gregory, *Letter-Box,* p. 116.

88. *Ibid.,* p. 128.

89. Harrowby to Bathurst, 24 November 1821, *Bathurst MSS,* p.522.

90. Liverpool to Bathurst, 22 December 1821, *Bathurst MSS,* p.525.

91. Goulburn to Peel, 15 November 1825, Peel MSS, 40331/211-14; Goulburn to Peel, 22 October 1825, Peel MSS, 40331/180; Goulburn to Peel, 24 March 1823, Peel MSS, 40329/49.

92. Goulburn to Peel, 20 April 1824, Peel MSS, 40330/61.

93. Buckingham to Plunket, 21 December 1823, Plunket, ed. *Plunket,* II, 141.

94. Goulburn to Wellesley, 14 April 1827, Wellesley MSS, 37305/89.

95. Torrens, *Melbourne,* I, 259; Lamb to Wellesley, 28 April 1827, Wellesley MSS, 37305/97; Lamb to Lansdowne, 3 August 1827, printed in Aspinall, *Formation,* pp. 276-77.

96. Shawe to Knighton, 15 August 1827, in Aspinall, ed., *The Letters of George IV,* III, 287.

97. O'Brien, *Dublin Castle,* pp. 57-58.

98. Northington to North, 1783, BM Add. MSS, 37873/76, cited in Johnston, *Great Britain*, p. 36.

99. Great Britain, Historical Manuscripts Commission, *Thirteenth Report*, Appendix III, p.512.

100. Ireland, *House of Commons Journal*, XVII, 684.

101. *Ibid.*

102. Michael MacDonagh, *The Viceroy's Post Bag: Correspondence Hitherto Unpublished of the Earl of Hardwicke, First Lord Lieutenant of Ireland after the Union* (London: John Murray, 1904), p.4; Addington to Yorke, 5 February 1804, in Pellew, *Sidmouth*, II, 242.

103. Canning to Granville Leveson Gower, 11 January 1805, Granville MSS, cited in Aspinall, ed., *Later Correspondence of George III*, IV, 270; Nicholas Vansittart to Hardwicke, 5 April 1805, Hardwicke MSS, 35716/15.

104. Richmond to Bathurst, 4 October 1809, *Bathurst MSS*, p. 126.

105. Wellesley Pole to Richmond, 4 August, 10 August 1812, Richmond MSS, 60/292, 296; Richmond to Peel, 4 August 1812, Peel, I, 34; Richmond to Bathurst, 5 August 1812, *Bathurst MSS*, p. 193.

106. Peel to Liverpool, July 1818, Peel MSS, 40181/135; also see Peel MSS 40295/78, 93, 132; 40194/121, noted in Gash, *Peel*, p. 233.

107. Anglesey to Peel, 13 June 1828, Peel MSS, 40325/56.

108. Wellington to Anglesey, 15 June, 18 June 1828, Wellington, *Despatches*, IV, 489, 491; Anglesey to Peel, 21 June 1828, 23 September 1828, Peel MSS. 40325/59, 40326/63; Anglesey to Leveson Gower, 21 June 1828, Plas Newydd Papers, cited in George Charles Paget, Marquess of Anglesey, *One-Leg: The Life and Letters of Henry William Paget, First Marquess of Anglesey* (London: Reprint Society, 1963), p.198.

109. Johnston, *Great Britain*, p.44; J.L.J. Hughes, "The Chief Secretaries of Ireland", *Irish Historical Studies*, VIII, 69.

110. Peel to Liverpool, 31 October 1816, cited in Parker, *Peel*, p.229.

111. Leveson Vernon Harcourt, ed., *The Diaries and Correspondence of the Rt.*

Honourable George Rose (2 vols.; London: R. Bentley, 1860), II, 172.

120. Charles Yorke to Hardwicke, 21 June 1804, Hardwicke MSS, 35716/121.

121. Vansittart to Hardwicke, 11 July 1805, Hardwicke MSS; Huskisson to Richmond, 5 April 1808, Richmond MSS 59/142.

122. The Earl of Rosse to Arthur Wellesley, 20 February 1809, Arthur Wellesley to Rosse, 25 February 1809, Wellington, *Ireland*, p.585.

123. Parker, *Peel*, I, 35.

124. Liverpool to Peel, 17 June 1818, Peel MSS, 40181/145; Broeker, *Rural Disorder*, p.105.

125. Hardwicke to Charles Yorke, 8 February 1802, Hardwicke MSS, 35701, in McDowell, *Public Opinion*, p. 68.

126. Richmond to Wellesley Pole, 15 March 1812, Richmond MSS, 62/1452.

112. Thomas Grenville to Grenville, n.d., *Fortescue MSS, VII*, 206. For Addington's comment on Nepean see Addington to George III, 10 January 1804, in Aspinall, ed., *Later Correspondence of George III*, IV, 149.

113. First Earl of Mulgrave to Richmond, 4 October 1809, Richmond MSS, 59/186; Robert Banks Jenkinson, Baron Hawkesbury, to Richmond, 18 November 1808, Richmond MSS, 73/1643.

114. Liverpool to Richmond, September 1809, cited in Aspinall, ed., *Later Correspondence of George III*, V, 405.

115. *Ibid.*, 1 August 1812, Richmond MSS, 74/1914.

116. Gregory, *Letter-Box*, pp. 247-48.

117. Lansdowne, memorandum, 22 April 1827, in Aspinall, *Formation*, pp. 156-57.

118. Canning to Wellesley, 22 May 1827, Wellesley MSS, 37297/272-80.

119. Hardwicke to Hawkesbury, 24 July 1804, Hardwicke MSS, 35709/97-99.

127. Charles Grey, Second Earl Grey, to Anglesey, Plas Newydd MSS, 9 March 1831, in Arthur Aspinall, "The Cabinet Council, 1783-1835" *Proceedings of the British Academy*, XXXVIII (1952), 160-61.

128. Henry Brougham, *Life and Times* (3 vols.; New York; Harper and Row,

1871), III, 231; Parker, *Peel,* II, 264.

129. Arthur Balfour to the Earl of Dudley, in Charles Petrie, *Walter Long* *and His Times* (London, 1936), pp. 95-97; see McDowell, *Irish Administration,* pp.161-62.

Charles Lennox, Duke of Richmond
Lord Lieutenant
April 1807–June 1813

Chapter 3
The Irish Administration

A small knot of men, powerful with the arts of counter-action and conversant with official details of business, active and energetic in mischief but from want of sympathy and common interest with the mass of people incapable of doing good. *Thomas Spring Rice, 1826.*

THE PRINCIPAL FIRST OFFICERS

EXTINCTION OF THE Irish Parliament permitted the viceroy to focus his attention on administrative matters. The Chief Secretary was drawn even deeper into politics at Westminster, where Ireland's many serious problems often prompted legislators to propose reforms more extensive than any which might have been tolerated in Britain itself. Eventually many departments of the Irish government were to be integrated into their British counterparts, but until 1830 the pace of amalgamation was slow and uneven. The Irish Exchequer was abolished, but viceroys continued to superintend an administrative apparatus not substantially different from what it had been in the eighteenth century. In some respects, the viceroy's responsibilities increased. After 1800 the public was quicker to complain of administrative irregularities tolerated in earlier periods. Executive powers remained defective, but Westminster expected viceroys to grapple more successfully with bureaucratic vested interests which the Act of Union had done little to diminish.

In 1801 Hardwicke inherited an administrative system in which inefficiency was reinforced by precedents and procedures sanctified over the course of several centuries. The Privy Council was one such institution. For three hundred years the Council had consisted of officials responsible for the day-to-day conduct of Irish affairs. The chief executive officer solicited advice from those inclined to support his point of view. Despite the emergence of a clerk of the Council, therefore, the Council itself never achieved a corporate unity comparable to the Privy Council in

England.[1] After 1782 the problem of dealing with an autonomous parliament enhanced the Council's role, for its members often possessed the experience and skills which the viceroy needed.[2]

The Act of Union dealt the Council's powers a serious blow, and a lack of corporate identity helped to frustrate Hardwicke's efforts to employ it against Pelham. In 1803, for example, Hardwicke informed Pelham that the Privy Council must approve all reforms in the Irish administration, even those enacted by parliament. In addition many ancient and modern laws could not be carried into execution unless the Council certified them. And finally, asserted Hardwicke, the Council continued to enjoy immediate jurisdiction over tariffs, coinage and trade.[3] Pelham was astonished by all this, which was based on Hardwicke's thesis that in the absence of contrary provisions in the Act of Union, the Privy Council's powers remained intact. Hardwicke's position was technically correct, nonetheless, and for the moment Pelham was barred from undermining Ireland's fiscal and commercial autonomy. In 1804 Hardwicke mobilised the Privy Council to debate a controversy dealing with coinage matters.[4] Thereafter the Council's pretensions were gradually undermined.

The remainder of Ireland's administrative system was also exposed to the reform impulse. As early as 1770 Dublin Castle's inefficiency and corruption had promoted a reform movement. Not a great deal was accomplished during the next thirty years, according to Sir John Mitford, who under the title of Lord Redesdale became Lord Chancellor in 1802. He complained that until 1800 the methods which the government had been compelled to employ had "given a corrupt character to the whole people of Ireland, and behaviour which in England would have excited surprise and indignation was not considered lamentable. It was considered a fair advantage."[5] Redesdale's arrival signalled a renewal of reform efforts. He was assisted by Chief Secretary Charles Abbot, who reorganised the Revenue Boards and the Board of Stamps. Pressure from Parliament and from a commission on Irish officials' emoluments was also a factor.[6]

Eradicating malfeasance was not enough; even when honest the Irish administration was grossly inefficient.[7] Irish officers were sensitive to this and yet resented London's intrusions. John Fitzgibbon, Lord Clare, echoed the sentiments of many Irishmen in condemning Abbot and his reforms: "I will never consent to be gibbeted in this country," he wrote to a former Irish Chief Secretary, "by the insolence and impotence of any little coxcomb... sen[t] over here to goad and degrade every gentleman of Ireland."[8] Clare pressed his point that efficiency purchased at the price of alienating the loyal part of the Irish population would gain Britain very little. Administrative reforms should proceed only as fast as Ireland could digest them.

After 1800 reforms were slowly implemented. Meanwhile the Irish administration continued to depend on four traditional instruments of support. The civil and legal departments included the offices of Lord Chancellor, Chancellor of the Exchequer, Solicitor General and Attorney General. The Military Department was responsible for the large army normally barracked in Ireland, as well as the garrison and fort facilities. The viceroy's personal secretary and the Irish Office in London comprised a third instrument, and the viceregal household staff a fourth.

Of all these, the Civil departments most accurately reflected the worst features of Ireland's unreformed and antiquated administration. Several powerful politicos competed for influence over the minor departments and over their offices and sinecures. The Revenue Board (divided by Abbot into customs and excise), the Board of Accounts, the Post Office, the Stamp Office, the Board of Works and the Bank of Ireland bristled with sinecures. Their work was routine and the burden was light enough. They offered the viceroy certain patronage opportunities, and over the years their staffs had remained solidly Protestant and politically conservative. They tended to treat proposals for reform as Catholic-inspired plots which must be detected and stamped out. Such attitudes were not limited to mere functionaries. The Earl of Clare as Lord Chancellor was one of this school.[9] Clare was a hardworking, mordantly forthright "unscrupulous political intriguer," bitterly anti-Catholic "as only the grandson of a Catholic peasant could be."[10] His relatives were powerful and entrenched, and he characterised his opponents, including anyone sympathetic to Catholics, as sentimental fools.[11] He derided Hardwicke's efforts to salvage for Ireland some shreds of autonomy even as he condemned Whitehall's reformist intrusions. He supported the Act of Union and aspired to be virtually the nation's ruler.[12] When it appeared that Hardwicke might fill vacancies in the legal departments without consulting Clare, he demanded a "full explanation". Hardwicke proceeded to make the appointments in defiance of Clare's wishes. Clare died in 1802 before he could attend to the insult.[13]

Redesdale was cut from the same cloth. Hardwicke wanted an

Irish-born Lord Chancellor — the country abounded with un-employed lawyers — but Redesdale was favoured by London's reformers and even the King. Redesdale was both brilliant and ambitious. He had succeeded Addington as speaker of the House of Commons and surrendered it only upon receiving a handsome annuity of £10,000, a peerage, and other rewards. Hardwicke soon concluded that like Clare, Redesdale hoped to rule Ireland, and feared that his reactionary bent would soon incite re-bellion.[14] Redesdale's aggressiveness taxed Hardwicke's patience and terrified the Civil Departments. His tenure ended when the Whigs took office in 1806.

The Whig Chancellor George Ponsonby held office only briefly. His Tory successor, Manners, shied away from Clare's and Redes-dale's ambitious behaviour. He held the office twenty years. His anti-Catholic opinions were congenial to Richmond and Talbot and Whitworth found them endurable. Under Wellesley, however, Manners openly sided with the Protestant interest against the viceroy's pro-Catholic advisers. Wellesley tried to dismiss Manners by goading him into some indiscretion; Manners waxed angry but not angry enough. At any rate, the office of Lord Chancellor had declined considerably in prestige by the time he resigned in 1827.[15]

In 1800 the Chancellor of the Exchequer was an ageing Irish politician, Isaac Corry. Corry had strenuously opposed the Act of Union but he held on to this office and to its handsome emolu-ment. Most Irish revenue had long since been granted in perpetuity to the Crown. The United Kingdom Exchequer anticipated an early absorption of Corry's office, and many assumed that Corry would bring to a close the line of incumbents. He did not. Hardwicke needed every available office to meet patronage requirements and the post of Chancellor of the Exchequer was too valuable to extinguish. Corry's successor was John Foster, a proud, intelligent and experienced Irish political leader. Foster's service in a series of important Irish offices, culminating in the speakership of the Irish Parliament from 1785 to 1800, made him a truly formidable figure.[16] Foster was determined to revive the importance of his new office, and to do so tried to revive its ancient prerogatives. He proceeded to exploit patronage resources boldly and negotiated independently with Parliament. Hardwicke and Richmond both failed in efforts to dampen his enthusiasm. Redesdale criticised his "overbearing conduct... assumed con-fidence and affected obsequiousness." Redesdale also contrived to have Foster's finance bills blocked in the House of Lords and at length Foster resigned.[17]   Thereafter this office declined in importance. Wellesley-Pole attached it to his Chief Secretaryship in 1811. Thereafter it was briefly restored to an Irish politician, Vesey Fitzgerald, who soon enough alarmed Liverpool by his attempts to emulate Foster.[18] Liverpool pressed it on Peel, who refused to follow Wellesley-Pole's example.[19]   The office was thereupon extinguished and a potential challenge to viceregal administrative authority was put to rest.[20]   Subsequently other fiscal responsibilities were transferred to England.[21]

A diminished Lord Chancellorship and an extinguished Chancellorship   of the Exchequer enhanced the role of the Attorney General, William Saurin. Saurin was the son of a Presbyterian minister and early on imbibed an Orange separatism which led him into violent opposition to the Act of Union. He argued that Parliament could not abrogate either a nation's right to a separate identity or its right to recover it by rebellion if necessary. His talents and influence were enormous in their time, and in 1803 Whitehall proferred the office of Solicitor General to him despite his dangerous views. He refused but in 1807 he accepted office as Attorney General. For the next fifteen years he fashioned a diehard anti-Catholic interest. In 1813 he confronted O'Connell in a famous defamation and treason trial, forged a bitter hatred of the eloquent Catholic advocate, and even supported plans to influence jury opinion against O'Connell in a famous trial. He befriended Peel and viewed Wellesley's appointment with misplaced equanimity stemming from a confidence that Wellesley could be brought to heel. Wellesley was not cowed, however, and indeed fortified himself by securing permission to remove Saurin even before he left London. Although Saurin was only Attorney General by title, Wellesley observed acidly, he had in fact "been viceroy for fifteen years". Saurin refused to accept a peerage and a handsome pension. "In truth," Wellesley later recorded, "I had nothing left to offer except the Lord Lieutenancy of Ireland". To this there were two objections: "First, he had already held the office for fifteen years, next, I − I was viceroy." [22]   Saurin was thereupon dismissed. Never before had so entrenched a part of the Dublin Castle interest been so abruptly and spectacularly dislodged.[23]

With Saurin gone most of the powers of this office soon decayed. Peel and Goulburn opposed Wellesley's friend and champion of Catholic claims, William Plunket, lest Plunket distribute legal appointments to pro-Catholics as Saurin had favoured the extreme Protestant interest.[24] Plunket's appointment had been extracted from Liverpool, however, who was impressed by Wellesley's argument that the nomination of Plunket would demonstrate the new administration's impartiality on the religious question.[25] Protestants lost no time in charging that Plunket and not Wellesley ran the country, and that Plunket would soon surrender the Castle bureaucracy to O'Connell himself.[26] This was of course a wild exaggeration, but it resulted in informal restrictions on the powers he enjoyed in office. This impotence, ironically, was demonstrated most clearly on the question of the Catholic Association.[27] While Wellesley laboured to sustain the government in the face of O'Connell's para-political Catholic Association, Plunket found himself caught in the middle. Catholics complained that he was too ready to obstruct legitimate forms of agitation. Peel marvelled at Plunket's string of failures in securing convictions against O'Connell and his friends. These painful circumstances desponded Wellesley's affection for his Attorney General, in that both men were caught in the same predicament. Plunket's friendship, if we may believe the viceroy, became a source of great consolation "in this troublesome and thankless station," and on occasion Wellesley exhorted Plunket not to stay out of his company an unnecessary moment.[28] Plunket resigned office when Wellesley's departure became known. His pro-Catholic bias prejudiced his bid to become Lord Chancellor but there was room for his services in the the judiciary. Under the Whigs Plunket long remained an important factor in Irish politics.

From 1800 to 1830 the office of Solicitor General produced no challengers to viceregal pretentions. In accordance with British practice it was inferior to the Attorney General's office in prestige and power, giving legal advice as appropriate and at the request of the government that was appropriate to its position. In Ireland considerable prestige was derived from incumbents' claims to leadership of the legal profession, a profession which in Ireland was second to none in potential political clout. From 1805 to 1822 Charles Kendall Bushe held the office. A brilliant lawyer and eloquent orator, he strenuously opposed the Union and supported Catholic claims. Saurin and the Orange faction isolated him for more than a decade.[29] In 1822 he was shifted to the King's Bench as Lord Chief Justice, a "promotion" which reflected fears that Wellesley, Plunket and Bushe together would comprise too potent a pro-Catholic interest. When discouraged, Wellesley sought solace in Bushe's pithy, invigorating conversation, and the Bench profited from his abundant good sense.[30] His successor as Solicitor General, Henry Joy, has been described as a brilliant practical lawyer and "one of the bitterest bigots that Irish Toryism ever nurtured."[31] But Joy was also cautious, and his copious and conflicting recommendations to Wellesley on how best to handle the Catholic Association distressed Goulburn and Peel, who wanted Joy to serve as ballast to Plunket.[32] But Joy preferred holidays in England to his Irish duties, which delighted Wellesley.[33] For his labours he was rewarded with the Attorney Generalship in 1827. His successor as Solicitor General, John Dogherty, was a sociable, amiable politician miscast as a barrister. He employed charm to supply some want of professional talent. Canning was his relative and he ignored protestations that Dogherty's appointment would distress the entire legal profession.[34] Canning died before Dogherty's deficiencies were confirmed in his confrontations with O'Connell.[35]

Between 1800 and 1830 incumbents in the great offices of Ireland reflected more Whitehall's determination to sustain a particular balance in politics than to secure talented individuals for government service. It is true that Redesdale, Foster and Saurin were men of weight and talent beyond what was warranted by these appointment practices. Others were adequate to their limited responsibilities. None laboured as assiduously or developed as essential a role as did the Civil Undersecretary. Here lay potential for enormous influence. As intermediary between Ireland's politically active classes and the Castle bureaucracy sometime surrogate Chief Secretary and as supervisor of the day-to-day official mechanism, the Civil Undersecretary touched upon all facets of Irish government. To the incumbent of this office came confidential information of all types. The duties of the office were multifarious, and as a result the inexperienced viceroy was virtually at his mercy.[36] When Sir Charles Saxton surrendered the office in 1812, Liverpool advertised the importance of the Civil Undersecretary by apprising Richmond of potential difficulties inherent in training a successor.[37] Hardwicke had earlier relied heavily on Samuel Marsden to supply the defects he attached to successive Chief Secretaries.[38] Sexton in turn was diligent in educating Richmond on the state of the country. But in William Gregory, who replaced

Sexton in 1812, the office became a truly formidable instrument; between 1812 and 1830 Irish political developments were intimately connected with Gregory.

The key to power here was confidence. Gregory soon established an intimacy with Peel which extended in time to Saurin and Whitworth and later to Talbot. Gregory acquired considerable influence in the determination of patronage, administrative decisions, and even larger questions of policy. At one point in 1815 Gregory found himself in charge when Napoleon attempted his return to power. He undertook to place Ireland's military establishment on the appropriate footing and directed the incarceration of likely subversives. Both Whitworth and Peel were in England at the time and Whitworth made no immediate arrangements to return to Dublin. Instead, he forwarded the necessary instructions to Gregory.[39] The Under-secretary enhanced his mandate by sifting carefully all reports of rural unrest and by appointing agents to keep suspicious persons under close surveillance. Exhausted but elated, Gregory directed Irish affairs from the Castle until Whitworth reached Dublin a month later.[40]

In 1818 Charles Grant claimed that Gregory was "the master of the whole machine of government" in Ireland. Liberals resented his influence, and many assumed that Wellesley would dismiss him forthwith. He did not. When Gregory disputed Wellesley on a point of policy in one of their early meetings Wellesley reminded him that he must either execute the orders given or resign; his resistance had "gone to the very verge of duty". Gregory desisted; his friends urged him not to resign, and Wellesley thereafter proved less demanding.[41] Wellesley must have realised Gregory's expertise was essential, and within a year the Viceroy and Under-secretary had established a mutually satisfactory *modus operandi.* Wellesley abhorred administrative details; Gregory retained his influence by insuring that the Castle bureaucracy functioned smoothly. Thomas Wyse, the Catholic barrister, confirmed this:

> The petitioner at the Castle did not ask what the Lord Lieutenant thought but what the Lord Lieutenant's secretary thought, or rather what his secretary's secretary thought. It was not Lord Wellesley, nor even Mr. Goulburn, but it was Mr. Gregory who held in his hand the destinies of Ireland.[42]

Gregory was relieved when Wellesley departed. But Anglesey arrived determined to remove him. Gregory was an...

70

arch jobber. A man who has the press at his command – a determined intriguer. False as hell. A violent anti-Catholic – a furious Tory – and quite ready to betray the secrets of anyone whose confidence he obtains. It is a misery to feel that you have a spy in your camp and I intended to make a point of having him removed.[43]

Anglesey's resolutions failed him. Lamb advertised Gregory's importance at the Castle and he was retained. Finally in 1830 Anglesey insisted on Gregory's removal as a condition for his own return to Dublin.[44] Gregory's resignation symbolised better than any other development the decaying influence of the ultra-Protestant interest at Dublin Castle.

Gregory's durability suggests the control which the permanent Irish administration enjoyed in relation to successive viceroys. A bureaucracy recruited through patronage methods often identified with powerful Irish families and dedicated to preserving a tradition of Protestant hegemony would have been difficult to challenge. When it was fortified by years and decades of administrative experience it could defy all but the most determined viceroys. Bedford, for one, "found himself at the head of a hierarchy of government servants who could be counted on to disregard the spirit of the policy he had been sent to implement."[45] He wisely refrained from trying to revamp the entire bureaucracy. In his melodramatic fashion Wellesley alleged that he was "degraded, villified, an object of scorn and detestation, without protection or even care; anxious to save the country; able to save it as far as relates to my powers; frustrated, baffled and betrayed by my own agents, encompassed by traitors even at my own table; the whole machinery of my own government working to my destruction...."[46] This was certainly overdrawn. But a more temperate man, Thomas Spring Rice, wrote in 1826 that the Irish bureaucracy formed "a small knot of men, powerful with the arts of counteraction and conversant with official details of business, active and energetic in mischief but from want of sympathy and common interest with the mass of people, incapable of doing good."[47] There was much truth in this, although motives were not always as objectionable and selfish as pictured. The bureaucratic apparatus was indeed immune in large measure from public opinion and public scrutiny. After 1830, in part because of the impact of Catholic Emancipation, in part because of direct control from London, the permanent bureaucracy of Dublin Castle became more responsive to Irish requirements.

Separate from the durable permanent Castle administration was the small and disjointed staff immediately dependent upon the viceroy. It consisted of a personal secretary, a small secretarial staff, an office in London, and the Lord Lieutenant's household.[48] Well before 1800 the personal secretary had ceased to play a meaningful role in Irish affairs.[49] The nominee, often a relative, looked after such personal matters as viceroys saw fit to entrust to him. On occasion matters of extraordinary sensitivity were involved. The most effective member of this group seems to have been the first, Charles Lindsay. As Hardwicke's personal secretary he served as special emissary between London and Dublin and eventually obtained a bishopric. Wellesley's natural son Edward Johnstone was certainly the most inept and most meddlesome.[50] The Irish Office in London, established to facilitate the flow of correspondence between London and Dublin after passage of the Act of Union, was technically responsible to the Chief Secretary and forbidden to communicate with any other agency in London. In practice it served largely as a listening post and secretarial service.[51]

The personal household carried forward a full panoply of ancient offices, most of which were entirely sinecurial. The retinue's size reflected successive viceroys' wealth and love of show and London's toleration of the idea that viceregal influence was enhanced by a careful attention to ceremony and display. In 1792 Earl Harcourt's comparatively modest staff consisted of six aides-de-camp, two chaplains, a steward, two gentlemen of the bed-chamber, other gentlemen at large, two pages, a rider, and footmen and porters. Some were paid from £200 per annum secured from fees for "transmisses of bills." [52] The Marquis of Buckingham (1787-1790) surrounded himself with seven chaplains. [53] Other offices included a chamberlain, master of the revels, the Ulster king of arms with his heralds and pursuivants, master and composer of the music, an orchestra of kettle drums, trumpets, violins and other instruments, and a company of footguards armed with battle axes.[54] After 1800 the list was gradually reduced.[55] Anglesey seems to have made the most drastic cuts to avoid that "absurd affection of state" which his friends assured him separated Dublin Castle from the people.[56]

Economies in the viceregal household endangered the "warm berths in the Castle" enjoyed by friends and relatives of influential people.[57] Many offices were considered to be virtually personal property, as Talbot found out in 1817 when he tried to install his own relations and "personal friends".[58] Anglesey was advised to dismiss Wellesley's servants, with their "corrupt" and "ruinous" system of plunder.[59] Most celebrated was Wellesley's decision to fire Sir Charles Vernon in 1823 for allegedly toasting Wellesley's hoped-for departure. Vernon was growing senile and had been in office fifty years. Wellesley was severely censured for his alleged cruelty.[60]

The usefulness of the household offices could not be proven easily, even one hundred and seventy-five years ago. They not only provided places for friends and relatives, but they excited the jealousy of others. Many incumbents looked upon household offices as simply a base from which to bid for more lucrative positions. Charles Chester, chaplain to Hardwicke, confidently expected a bishopric. Richmond's military companions, Whitworth's old school acquaintances, remnants of Wellesley's Indian staff, and Anglesey's sons and relatives all looked forward to greater boons[61] While waiting they competed among themselves for the Castle apartments, a place of honour at the viceroy's table, and other small marks of distinction.[62] Although frivolous, the household retinue was expensive. In 1823 Joseph Hume, the radical M.P., estimated that £85,000 was spent each year to maintain the Castle, the viceroy's lodge in Phoenix Park, and the gardens. The figure excluded public expenses.[63] The household staff could also complicate administrative functions. Allegedly the household influenced the wives of Richmond and Whitworth. Anglesey complained that the household, even after a purge of Wellesley's friends, was a vexatious burden.[64]

THE LORDS JUSTICES

An institution of transitory importance was the Lords Justices. Before 1770 the inconvenience of viceroys' extended absences was relieved by transferring supreme authority to the Primate, the Lord Chief Justice and less regularly the Lord Chancellor. More ancient yet was the practice of entrusting viceregal powers to the Privy Council if the viceroy died in office or left the country without appointing a viceroy. After 1800 only the committee system of the Lords Justices was used at all, and this rarely. Hardwicke entrusted his powers to them when he toured Ireland. The Primate, William Stuart, performed so impressively that

Hardwicke's opponents urged the viceroy to continue travelling. Stuart and Gregory directed affairs for two months in 1815.[65] Wellesley resigned his commission into the hands of the Lords Justices in 1827 rather than await Anglesey's arrival.

Thus the administrative system centred on Dublin Castle complemented and at times contested the authority of the Lord Lieutenant. The various subsidiary departments sought independence by establishing direct links to London, by advertising to certain precedents to expand their prerogatives, and by relying on an entrenched bureaucracy. London sometimes encouraged these irregularities. "In a country situated and governed as this is," Peel observed on one occasion, "there ought to be a paramount authority somewhere, an authority not merely superior to all others, but one upon which all others are dependent."[66] He feared that Dublin Castle at times undermined rather than underpinned the incumbent viceroy to the extent that it circumscribed the viceroy's decisive response to crises which threatened the Irish policy. Viceroys for their part sought to increase their leverage by directing attention to patronage and to the cultivation of a sympathetic public opinion.

1. Otway-Ruthven, *Medieval Ireland,* p.151.

2. Bolton, *Passing,* pp. 8-9.

3. Hardwicke to Pelham, 8 February 1803, Hardwicke MSS, 35772/88.

4. Hardwicke to Charles Yorke, 12 April 1804, Hardwicke MSS, 35705/220.

5. Redesdale to Liverpool, 18 October 1821, Liverpool MSS, 38290, in McDowell, *Public Opinion,* p.48.

6. McDowell, *Public Opinion,* p.78.

7. Redesdale to Abbot, 30 October 1823, printed in Colchester, *Diary,* III, 269.

8. John Fitzgibbon, First Earl Clare, to Eden, 22 October 1801, cited in Robert B. McDowell, "Some Fitzgibbon Letters from the Sneyd Muniments in the John Rylands Library," *John Rylands Library Bulletin,* XXXIV (1952), 551.

9. In 1823 Hume noted that in Ireland only 25 magistrates of 466 were Catholic, in the Royal Dublin Society none of 7, in the Bank of Ireland only 6 of 127. No Catholics sat on the Paving Board, the Wide Streets Commission and several other municipal boards in Dublin. In the Excise 6 of 265, in the Customs 11 of 296, and on the Linen Board 3 of 71 were Catholic. Hume computed that in Ireland only 106 Catholics held one of the 2459 offices paid by public funds. Great Britain, *Parliamentary Debates,* 2 Hansard, IX (1823), 1214-15.

10. Bolton, *Passing,* p.9.

11. Harlow, *Founding,* p.629.

12. Hardwicke to Addington, August 1801, printed in MacDonagh, *Post-Bag,* pp.62-63.

13. McDowell, "Fitzgibbon Letters," p.500.

14. Buckingham to Grenville, 17 September 1803, *Fortescue MSS,* VII, 188.

15. Coulburn to Peel, 17 January 1825, 24 March 1825, Peel MSS, 40329/22, 50.

16. Bolton, *Passing,* pp.9-10.

17. Redesdale to Addington, 15 January 1805, in Aspinall, ed., *Later Correspondence of George III, IV,* 220; *Redesdale to Vansittart,* 24 May, 17 June, 20 June 1805, BM Add. MSS 31330; Redesdale to Charles Long,

7 November 1804, London, Public Record Office, PBO, Chatham MSS, 330, cited in McDowell, Public Opinion, p.67.

18. Liverpool to Vesey Fitzgerald, 4 October 1813, Peel MSS, 40181/39-41.

19. Gash, *Peel,* p.112.

20. Liverpool to Peel, 21 October 1813, Parker, *Peel,* I, 113.

21. *56 George III,* c. 98; *3 George IV,* c. 56. (The Boards of Customs of Ireland and Great Britain were fused and put under Treasury supervision. In 1827 the Boards of Stamps of the two countries were united. In 1831 the Post Offices were amalgamated, and in 1832 the duties of the commissioners of public accounts for Ireland were transferred to London. For this see McDowell, *Irish Administration,* pp.78-79.

22. Dennis Gwynn, *The Struggle for Catholic Emancipation, 1750-1829* (London: Longmans and Co., 1928), p.189.

23. Goulburn described Saurin's inflexibility on the eve of Wellesley's move to dismiss him in a letter sent to Peel 24 March 1823, Peel MSS, 40329/51.

24. Goulburn to Peel, 8 November 1823, Peel MSS, 40329/205.

25. Liverpool to C.W.W. Wynn, 15 [?] November 1821, printed in Plunket, ed., *Plunket,* II, 93.

26. Goulburn to Wellesley, 2 January 1826, Peel MSS, 40332/2.

27. Plunket to Wellesley, 23 December 1822, Wellesley MSS, 37300/98-105.

28. Wellesley to Plunket, 21 March 1823, Plunket, ed., *Plunket,* II, 134-36.

29. Whitworth to Peel, 10 May 1814, Parker, *Peel,* I, 138-39; Gash, *Peel,* p.99.

30. "Historical Sketches," Vols. IV and V of Henry Brougham. *Works* (London: R. Griffin and Company, 1855-61), IV, 195-206.

31. Madden, *Ireland,* pt. I, pp. 58-59.

32. Joy to Wellesley, 12 May 1823, Peel MSS, 40324/152.

33. Wellesley to Canning, 12 June 1827, Wellesley MSS, 37297/353-55.

34. Canning to Wellesley, 1 June 1827, Wellesley MSS, 37297/335-36.

35. Madden, *Ireland*, pt. 1, pp. 61-63.

36. Gash, *Peel*, I, 37.

37. Liverpool to Peel, 10 September 1812; Peel to Liverpool, 14 September 1812, Parker, *Peel*, I, 37.

38. Hardwicke to Pitt, 24 July 1804, Hardwicke MSS, 35709/106-7.

39. Whitworth to Gregory, 15 March 1815, Gregory, *Letter-Box*, p.70.

40. Whitworth to Gregory, 17 April 1815; Gregory to Whitworth, 15 April 1815, Gregory, *Letter-Box*, p.83.

41. Gregory to Peel, 2 February 1822, Peel MSS, 40334; McDowell, *Public Opinion*, p.69; Gregory to Talbot, 19 January 1822, Gregory, *Letter-Box*, p.173.

42. O'Brien, *Dublin Castle*, p.56.

43. Anglesey to William Lamb, 17 September 1827, Plas Newydd MSS.

44. Anglesey, *One Leg*, p.188.

45. Senior, *Orangeism*, p.179.

46. Wellesley to Plunket, 19 March 1824, Plunket, ed., *Plunket*, II, 146.

47. David Spring Rice to Merrick Shawe, 29 November 1826, Wellesley MSS, 37304; McDowell, *Public Opinion*, p.68.

48. There was also, of course, a military responsibility exercised through the military departments: see Chapter V.

49. Johnston, *Great Britain*, p.70.

50. Goulburn to Peel, 2 November 1822, Peel MSS, 40328/173-74; *Dublin Evening Mail*, 10 October 1825, p.3, col.3.

51. Johnston, *Great Britain*, pp.79-80; Hardwicke to Pelham, 24 May 1803, Hardwicke MSS, 35770/26-30.

52. Blaquiere to Harcourt, 1792, *Harcourt Papers*, IX, 18.

53. Historical Documents Commission, *Thirteenth Report*, Appendix III, p.296.

54. McDowell, *Irish Administration*, p.53.

55. *Ibid.*, p.53; The *Patriot*, 6 April 1822, p.3, col.4.

56. Forbes to Anglesey, printed in Anglesey, *One Leg*, p.185.

57. Historical Manuscripts Commission, *Thirteenth Report*, Appendix III, p.204.

58. Talbot to Peel, 10 August, 1817, Peel MSS, 40194/169; The *Patriot*, 6 April 1822, p.3, col. 4.

59. Forbes to Anglesey, printed in Anglesey, *One-Leg*, p.185.

60. Dublin *Evening Post*, 13 February 1823, p.3, col.3; *Ibid.*, 20 February 1823, p.3, col.4.

61. Whitworth to Peel, 21 June 1813, Peel MSS, 40187/9; Dublin *Evening Post*, 18 December 1821, p.2, col.4; Anglesey, *One-Leg*, p.184.

62. Arthur Wellesley to an unnamed person, February 1809, printed in Wellington, *Ireland*, p.571.

63. Hansard IX (1823), 1218-20.

64. Forbes to Anglesey, printed in Anglesey, *One-Leg*, p.185; Lamb to Spring Rice, 15 December 1827; Torrens, *Melbourne*, I, 291.

65. Whitworth to Gregory, 18 March 1815, Gregory, *Letter-Box*, pp.63-64; Peel MSS, 40190/76, 86, 104; 40288/84-87; 40200/20-273, cited in Gash, *Peel*, pp.133, 135.

66. Peel to Liverpool, 20 October 1813, Parker, *Peel*, I, 110-11.

Charles Whitworth, Viscount and Earl Whitworth
Lord Lieutenant
June 1813–August 1818

Chapter 4
Patronage and Political Management

"You will become very familiar before you leave Ireland with the expression: 'My father over and over again refused a peerage'."

Peel to De Grey, 23 November, 1841

THE PATRONAGE FACTOR IN IRISH POLITICS

IN THE EARLY nineteenth century, as in the eighteenth, patronage issues constituted an important ingredient in Irish political life. Granting preferment on the basis of political or personal favouritism intensified as the Irish parliament waxed independent. It reached a climax of sorts in "union engagements", when a number of Irish legislators were offered pensions, places and peerages in return for their willingness to support abolition of the Dublin parliament. Thereafter these commitments had to be met. The "reign of jobs" continued, and a lavish and assiduous distribution of political favours dominated the correspondence of successive viceroys.[1]

Ireland's patronage system was sustained by more than the unhappy events attendant on the Act of Union. In England greater wealth had "emancipated society from undue dependence on the court and the administrative system. In Ireland the Protestant caste had been permanently conditioned to look almost solely to the state for support and nourishment."[2] Charles Fox noted that one would sooner find an Irishman without a brogue as without a job. Peel observed that he had "never yet met a man in Ireland who has not either himself refused honours from the Crown, or was not the son of a man who had, or who had not married the daughter of a man who had been hardhearted enough to refuse the solicitations of the government..."[3] Viceroys found vexatious the petitions for patronage coming from all directions. They came from the famous and the obscure, from political opponents and political supporters.[4] They took every conceivable form, from demands for a salute on the streets to appointment to high office.[5] The "whole accumulated host" bothered Whitworth so much that he surrendered control over patronage to Peel.[6] Even in 1830 Anglesey was forced to "devote many hours politely refusing requests".[7]

Because patronage transactions pervaded Irish politics every viceroy demanded the right to control them; otherwise it would be "utterly impossible to conduct the King's business".[8] Even before 1800, however, the Crown and the government of the day had laid claim to a vital share of appointments to Irish offices.[9] In 1786 Rutland pleaded with Pitt for a chance to make his wishes known, at least "from time to time".[10] Hardwicke demanded a veto over London's choices.[11] Bedford's earliest complaints were directed against attempts to deprive his office of control over patronage.[12] Richmond set out for Dublin with a pledge from Perceval that no offices or pensions would be awarded until Richmond had submitted his recommendations.[13] Six years later Liverpool reaffirmed the principle that the viceroy's prerogatives would be preserved intact.[14] In thanking Liverpool Peel testified candidly to the intrinsic importance of viceregal control over patronage: until "the time arrives that the government of this country can be conducted on different principles," he observed, "you must either try to carry on the government without such support, or you must (and I fear there is no misapplication of the term) purchase it." [15] Peel repeated these sentiments even after he had retired from office, and Wellesley agreed heartily.[16]

Despite these protestations London was quite unwilling to forego a decisive voice. At the time of the Act of Union the King urged that civil patronage be entirely decided in England.[17] Hardwicke conceded that the Crown had traditionally reserved "to its own immediate disposal" the major Irish civil and ecclesiastical offices. He was also willing to concede all honours except knighthoods, a half dozen Castle positions (all of the second rank), the office of Provost of Trinity College, and military patronage. In return, however, Hardwicke wanted London's support against Irish families when they bid for the right to fill the lesser (but often lucrative) secular and ecclesiastical positions.[18] Hardwicke's initiative settled nothing and his successors may have thought that he had conceded too much. The jurisdictional debate continued.

A series of unwritten rules governed distribution of patronage at the government's disposal. Unless a new political party took office, unredeemed pledges made by one viceroy became the responsibility of the next.[19]   When Hardwicke pleaded to be relieved of some "union engagements" contracted prior to 1801 Pelham advised him curtly that the established English practice must also apply to Ireland, "for if a contrary principle had been adopted the favours conferred by one Lord Lieutenant would not be considered by those who received them as influencing their support of his successor." [20] Hardwicke continued to remonstrate, but in vain.[21]   In 1807 Arthur Wellesley reminded Richmond that before he made new commitments there remained a large number of earlier ones to be satisfied. Promises to Irish loyalists who had suffered during the rebellion of 1797-8 had been neglected Hardwicke had been preoccupied with "union engagements" and "had no inclination to reward loyalists... The Duke of Bedford would have preferred to reward a rebel. Thus," Wellesley concluded, "the burden falls on you..." [22] In 1813 even Peel toyed briefly with the idea of urging Whitworth to ignore the enormous backlog of requests.[23]   Ultimately he decided against it, and he asked Richmond to supply a full list.[24]   Talbot was dismayed by the length of Whitworth's unfulfilled list and sadly admitted his obligation to satisfy the applicants.[25]

Offices once rewarded became virtually the property of the incumbent. Only gross malfeasance or notorious political disloyalty were deemed sufficient reasons to revoke an appointment (titles, of course, could not be extinguished under normal circumstances). A few bold spirits who opposed the Act of Union too vehemently were punished. John Beresford on behalf of "the whole body of official men" in Ireland complained of "so much rough and ill-timed harshness dealt out" to these few unfortunates.[26]   Bedford refused to remove Tories whose politics were moderate.[27] This principle extended in an attenuated form even to the highest efficient offices of the Irish Administration, which explains in part Saurin's shock when Wellesley dismissed him. Even non-hereditary honours were normally handed down. Wellesley struck a blow against this when Castlereagh's titles as a Derry regimental commander and governor were denied to the third Marquess.[28]

The Irish Pensions Act of 1793 established a third restriction. Thereafter the Government was limited to annual increases of £1,200 in the Irish pension list until the total pension list fell below £80,000. This occurred in 1813. Prior to 1813 Richmond complained incessantly of his inability to do anything substantial, even for indigent aristocrats.[29]   In 1813, therefore, Richmond planned more lavish awards, only to be told that the limit of £1,200 per annum had been in force so long that it could not now be ignored.[30] Thus the size of the pension list continued its steady decline.

Improvements in standards of conduct came into play after 1800. They were perhaps more noticeable in terms of ecclesiastical than civil patronage; at least some churchmen laboured to effect the needed reforms.[31] New standards gradually elevated the tone of civil patronage. Hardwicke opposed nominating absentees for the representative peerage and later Liverpool informed Wellesley that "residence, respectability and local consequence" were "indispensable conditions" for those chosen to represent Ireland in the House of Lords.[32]   Anomalies in post office patronage attracted Hardwicke's notice in 1802 and in 1816 Whitworth resolved to press for further reforms in this area.[33] Nominations to the Irish Privy Council were scrutinised more carefully.[34]   In 1822 King George IV urged the candidacy of a friend for an Irish peerage. Liverpool replied that it had been "strongly impressed upon the mind of Marquess Wellesley, that Irish honours should be confined to services and *personal consequence* in Ireland."[35]

Public opinion played its part. In 1806 Bedford's Chief Secretary resisted some demands put forward by Sir John Newport, an influential Irish M.P., by explaining that honouring them would "create a good deal of invidious observation."[36] In 1807 Richmond was admonished to do nothing which would not withstand close parliamentary scrutiny.[37]   Under Bedford and Wellesley a few posts of the second rank were opened to Catholics for the first time.[38] Reforms came too slowly to attract universal attention, but progress was substantial. In 1829 Leveson Gower observed that the "patronage of the Lord Lieutenant ha[d] been put on a footing which left no prospect of being able to serve anyone" in whom there was a merely personal interest.[39]   This was close enough to the truth to suggest that changes in patronage distribution had been substantial.

Even in its relatively purified form the patronage arena witnessed a contest between the viceroy and other groups. The military, the Crown, Whitehall, M.P.s and the Church all resented reductions in patronage at the disposal of their own leadership. The King and the incumbent prime minister often contested the other's right to nominate candidates for the major civil and ecclesiastical offices. Church reformers resented the Crown's intrusions. Everyone lamented the rapacity of Irish families. Viceroys for their part claimed the right to regulate, or at least to appear to regulate, all Irish patronage. Therefore even when patronage distribution assumed a higher tone, passions ran high and correspondence continued to reflect the enormous importance of patronage in the governance of Ireland.

For successive viceroys the Crown's prerogatives posed the most serious challenges to their authority in Ireland. Precedent offered no defence against the King's legal claim to virtually all substantial ecclesiastical and legal patronage and much civil and military patronage as well. The viceroy could remonstrate, delay, threaten to resign, and suggest alternate candidates. But royal involvement in Irish affairs fluctuated sharply, and a viceroy could never be sure whether he would prevail. Sometimes the intrusions came on short notice, and ramifications were often painful. On one occasion Hardwicke committed a vacancy in the representative peerage to one of his "union engagements" creditors, only to hear that the King had awarded the same office to a friend. Hardwicke wrote directly to the King threatening to resign and hinting that royal initiatives of this type would soon destroy the union.[40] Hardwicke's brother intercepted the letter and broke the news in a more delicate fashion. The King acquiesced, and Hardwicke's subsequent decisions were usually upheld.[41]

Bedford had to contend with George, the Prince of Wales, many of whose proposals for Irish places and peerages were so patently inappropriate that Grenville had little difficulty inducing the King not to approve them.[42] Richmond was less fortunate. Portland as Prime Minister was slow to support viceregal pretensions against those of the Crown. Perceval was made of sterner stuff, but after 1810 the government was forced to contend with the Prince of Wales as Regent.[43] A series of scuffles followed before the Regent ceased to seek favours for friends. During his Dublin visit in 1821 he exercised the Crown's rights with "great discretion".[44] And by his death in 1830 the monarch's role in Irish affairs had declined to an almost purely formal one.[45]

The ministry of the day provided a more potent and more durable threat to the viceroy. In the aftermath of the Act of Union Whitehall assumed an immediate jurisdiction over Irish patronage. Pelham informed Hardwicke that he would shoulder this responsibility.[46] Hardwicke retorted that this was both "discourteous and dangerous".[47] Later he claimed he would never defy Whitehall on the matter of patronage, but demanded the right to submit recommendations.[48]

Hardwicke was determined, however, to do more than play a ceremonial role. Under normal circumstances a nominee was chosen after informal consultations between London and Dublin. The final decision was thereupon made in London and forwarded to the viceroy. He in turn prepared a "private and confidential" letter requesting the nomination, which the Crown then approved. Hardwicke refused to subscribe to this formula. On at least one occasion Hardwicke refused to send the formal request because he disapproved of the nominee.[49] In another instance he forwarded the name of a friend after refusing to certify London's choice.[50] On two separate occasions Pelham used strong language in upbraiding Hardwicke for his obstreperousness in refusing to certify patronage awards to two individuals on the "union engagements" list.[51] Hardwicke defended his conduct on the grounds that his choices were better qualified. When Pitt returned to office in 1804 Hardwicke refused to approve the allocation of £1,200 from Irish funds to a pension for Isaac Corry and baldly claimed priority for "union engagements". Pitt in turn opposed Hardwicke's nominees. Tempers flared. Pitt finally inclined towards compromise, but "Hardwicke rose in tone and consequence as Mr. Pitt declined in health and influence".[52] Pitt died before he could give Corry his pension.[53]

Bedford and Grenville encountered no such difficulties. Bedford was uncertain as to his prerogatives and Grenville assumed almost complete control.[54] Fox complained that Bedford was too much neglected, but his own death, Bedford's malleability, and the ministry's early demise rendered Fox's observations obsolete.[55] Richmond no doubt envied Bedford in that the Whigs were free of "union engagements". At first the Portland ministry planned to settle these vexatious claims directly; this would allow Richmond to focus on other matters.[56] But Richmond's indulgent character soon embarrassed London, as he silenced Irish petitioners with promises of office and honours.[57] Richmond was admonished and he in turn rebuked his staff.[58] Unfortunately, Perceval needed the support of Irish M.P.s and therefore felt obligated to honour Richmond's ill-advised promises.[59] Finally in 1812 Peel showed Richmond a list of London's complaints on this score. Richmond in turn charged that the Cabinet had employed Irish patronage to undermine the viceroy's authority.[60]

Difficulties eased considerably after 1812. Liverpool curbed the appetites of his ministers while in Ireland Peel assumed direct control over patronage matters. Whitworth supported Peel and was glad enough to let Peel wrestle with the burdensome correspondence. The pension list was revamped and reduced.[61] Peel celebrated the unprecedented "honest" use of patronage, and as his powers grew he ceased to refer to Whitworth any appointments except the most important.[62] Talbot was equally acquiescent.[63]

Wellesley arrived in Ireland to find viceregal prerogatives in patronage distribution far decayed. His temperament dictated that he attempt to reverse this condition. Even before going to Dublin Wellesley sought to clarify his patronage powers.[64] Liverpool was prepared to concede to Wellesley the right to make the initial choice, but he as Prime Minister would exercise a veto. Wellesley's jurisdiction was not to extend to Irish offices in departments already integrated into their British counterparts. Wellesley bridled at this but acquiesced.[65] In practice, Wellesley's interest in patronage matters proved to be erratic. He showed little interest in the legal offices until he saw that they could be used to honour certain Catholics. But he laboured strenuously to oust Orange Lodge sympathisers from their strongholds. He also focused attention on local patronage in his efforts to upgrade the calibre of the magistracy.[66]

In all, Wellesley's efforts did little to reverse earlier trends. Liverpool held scrupulously to his pact with Wellesley, but he exercised his veto whenever he saw fit. This was demonstrated in dramatic fashion in 1826 when Liverpool resisted pressure from the Duke of Wellington and Wellesley together to place their brother Gerald on the Irish bench of bishops. Wellington argued that the Irish viceroy's powers allowed him to appoint, whatever Liverpool's objections might be. Liverpool would not hear it. When Canning assumed office he declared flatly that he would make the nominations directly.[67] In a final and perhaps symbolic gesture, when Anglesey opposed a pension for Lady Westmeath in 1828, Wellington was alleged to have obtained the King's sign manual (the seal used to show that viceroys acted in the King's place) and to have validated the grant himself.[68] The age in which Irish petitioners looked to Dublin Castle to meet their patronage requirements was slowly drawing to a close.[69]

PATRONAGE AND LOCAL INTERESTS

The competition between Dublin Castle and the county politicians for control of local patronage remained a lively topic throughout the period covered by this study. The unique character of each county interest, the entrenched position of county and borough officials, and their crucial role in keeping Ireland quiet discouraged the Lord Lieutenant from promoting major patronage reforms. Irish M.P.s provided incumbent ministries with a substantial reservoir of support and no government could neglect the Irish legislators without undermining their attachment. The great families of the land also demanded a sympathetic hearing. They supplied M.P.s. for the unreformed parliament, and their weight in the Irish administration helped to shape the legislation.

At the basis of the patronage issue was the paucity of offices in relation to claims upon the government's generosity. The viceroy was forced to defend his rights against the principal Irish office-holders. When Hardwicke invited Clare to submit three names for an impending vacancy on the legal bench Clare refused. He would "not submit to an appeal" from his recommendations, "or to a scrutiny of it by any man"; the office was his alone to fill.[70] The keenness of this competition was demonstrated vividly when Bedford came to Dublin.[71] The leading Whig families, long denied preferment, fought for the vacant collectorship at Derry.[72] Grenville tried to settle the dispute after Bedford failed.[73] In the process, Grenville and Bedford learned firsthand that families regarded certain offices as virtually personal property.[74] Even prominent Tories could not be dislodged except at the viceroy's peril.[75] The ministry's Irish supporters grumbled loudly and accused Grenville and Bedford of an insensitivity to patronage customs even as Bedford resigned office in the spring of 1807.[76]

Perhaps aware of Bedford's problems, Arthur Wellesley undertook an unusually detailed assessment of county patronage when Richmond and he took office. The Act of Union had brought about important changes in political attachments; implementing "union engagements" had strengthened the influence of certain families at the expense of others. Many Irish borough franchises had been extinguished. Opponents of the Act of Union now moved to reconcile themselves to Dublin Castle. One new index of prominence was the Irish representative peerage. Arthur Wellesley's report, with subsequent amendments, reflected many of these changes in its analysis of sixty-three parliamentary constituencies. The role of family interests was assessed and offices at the Government's disposal were described in some detail. Many

85

boroughs, some with more than one M.P., were absolutely proprietary, and their patrons either sold their influence outright to the Government or negotiated for local patronage. About twenty-five of the sixty-three constituencies were controlled by landlords other than the great patrons, and in seventeen of them a coalition of smaller interests prevailed. These "independent" M.P.s also demanded favours.[77] The great families exerted a preponderant influence in most of the remaining thirty-eight constituencies. In the counties, each represented by two seats, two families often shared control and divided the patronage.

Several factors influenced Dublin Castle's efforts to line up support in the Irish constituencies on the basis of an allocation of patronage. When the government was weak the constituencies available for purchase rose in price. Richmond complained that the Irish government could not meet the price, and in 1814 Peel observed that expectations were so inflated that even baronetcies and peerages were sometimes refused unless accompanied by an emolument.[78] An M.P. who failed to attend parliament was threatened with loss of a voice in local patronage matters, but the threat was rarely carried out lest the M.P. join the opposition. M.P.s who bore a handsome share of their own election expenses were entitled to share local patronage; occasionally even an unsuccessful candidate would be so rewarded. Opposing interests were sometimes admitted to a share of the patronage if such tenderness might promote a change of allegiance in the future.[79]

Inevitably a viceroy's correspondence box was burdened by petitions for preferment, reminders of commitments long outstanding, accusations of bad faith, threats to join the opposition, and even threats to disclose the sordid details of unsuccessful negotiations to the public. Viceroys responded with all the discretion and good humour they could muster, and they scrutinised their adversaries as carefully as circumstances would permit. The right party suitably rewarded was enormously useful. A diligent and loyal M.P. observed in 1815 that if properly compensated he could "do your business there, get you soldiers, ... support your revenue by influence," suppress smuggling, "quiet disturbances, everywhere supporting the laws and keeping up the standard of loyalty." [80] This was not an idle boast.

The M.P.s pitch was often repeated; perhaps he was more articulate than most. Many applicants were bound to be disappointed. Irish county patronage was indeed plentiful, but much was tightly controlled by local interests and more was pledged to government supporters at election time. In 1807 Hawkesbury shocked Richmond in reporting that the recent election had so seriously limited Dublin Castle's cornucopia that henceforth government supporters aspiring to be M.P.s must purchase their own seats.[81]   Richmond experimented in an effort to ease the pressure, but he failed.[82]   In 1814 Peel lamented that "nothing is more mistaken than the extent of the Lord Lieutenant's patronage," at least that not commandeered by local interests.[83]   Not until Wellesley was installed did the power of local interests subside. He successfully challenged some choices, only to discover that the patronage which he coveted often melted away in the face of Benthamite demands for economy and reform.[84]

Viceroys sometimes compromised their potential influence by ignoring local conditions.[85]   Viceroys often proved insensitive to local customs or placed their trust in thoroughly disreputable characters.[86]   Prior to Peel, chief secretaries held office for too brief a period to master patronage intricacies.[87] Peel was different. Not only did he use his familiarity with every aspect of Irish affairs to establish an ascendancy over Whitworth and Talbot, but he continued to display his superior abilities as Home Secretary. Peel's ascendancy, based on hard work and probity, was really not challenged until the Whigs undertook full scale patronage reform after 1830.

At the basis of patronage management was the need to create and sustain a large and pliable Irish parliamentary majority. This work was well known before the Act of Union, when ministries bargained with the great Irish families who controlled two-thirds of the boroughs and predominated in the county seats. But elections were infrequent (the Irish parliament elected in 1727 sat for thirty-three years) and Viceroys negotiated instead with individual members.[88]   Eventually enactment of a limit on the duration of parliaments and finally the Act of Union changed substantially the role of Dublin Castle. Landlords' influence remained weighty, as late as 1830 thirty-four of the county seats (seventy-two in all) still belonged to families who had represented the county in the Irish Parliament before 1800. Another seven sat for boroughs. But for penal laws seven of the eight Catholics in parliament in 1830 might also have sat prior to the Act of Union.[89] After the Act of Union only five constituencies, returning seven members, were "decidedly open," and of these only Dublin was keenly contested. Prior to the Great Reform Act of 1832 only two additional boroughs deviated sharply from the pattern of traditional control.[90]

Despite continued influence of traditional interests, general elections became more frequent after 1800 and modest efforts at electoral reform forced Dublin Castle to be more sensitive to public opinion. Irish interests saw new opportunities to exploit differences between Tories and Whigs. Whitehall in turn became more directly involved.[91] The timing of elections was a closely-guarded secret and a Lord Lieutenant might be surprised by news of an early poll.[92] In the rush viceroys were sometimes unsure which candidates to support, and on occasion elections were poorly managed indeed.[93]

Within all these constraints each Viceroy laboured to encourage the government's candidates, purchase available seats, and offer financial assistance to certain worthy but financially distressed aspirants. Prior to poll viceroys penned letters of encouragement and conducted personal interviews with as little publicity as possible. [94] They listened to the problems of Irish M.P.s sympathetic to the Government and paid careful attention to rumors of shifting allegiances.[95] They reported to London every constituency development, every initiative for a new local alliance.[96] On the basis of intelligence thus collected Dublin Castle then proceeded to advise London where to place bids for the purchase of a controlling interest in certain constituencies during the next election. Each bid reflected London's estimation of its polling prospects, the cost of purchase, and financial resources available. Usually only four or five seats were purchased outright; in the elections of 1806 and 1807 eight boroughs were made available, but most of them proved too expensive.[97] Peel observed later that the number of seats thus purchased was patently insufficient to secure a safer electoral majority, but they did afford the Ministry an opportunity to return some specific individuals valuable to the Government. [98] Occasionally this system was abused, as seen in Richmond's effort to return one of his friends.[99] Thus, Liverpool's aversion to the whole concept of purchasing support, and Peel's success in producing large Irish majorities by more orthodox means, led to a sharp reduction in the use of secret service funds to purchase seats. Peel warned one Irish nobleman not to mention the subject to Liverpool; the Irish government was prepared "to faint with horror at the mention of money transactions." [100] Wellesley and Anglesey denied these funds to Protestant stalwarts searching for a constituency, and on one occasion Anglesey even threatened to employ them against the government of which he was a member. No wonder that by 1830 purchasing seats was a thing of the past.[101]

The other side of parliamentary management was to impress on Irish M.P.s the need to support the ministry which sustained their pretensions. "One great and important object of the Lord Lieutenant," Redesdale observed in 1805, should be to demonstrate "that it was for the interest of Ireland that they [M.P.s] should, in a body, generally support the King's ministers in Parliament, and by making themselves of importance to government, obtain for Ireland what they might think necessary for the advantage of the country." The Irish, then, were expected to follow the example of the Scottish representation by supporting the ministry of the day whatever its ideological character. Although hostile to heavy-handed pressure, Irish M.P.s were amenable to whatever influence a discreet and resourceful viceroy could exert on behalf of his government.[102] Several devices were particularly effective: support for measures popular among Irish legislators; pressure for constant attendance; admonishing those M.P.s indebted to the Government but stingy in support of its policies.

Several viceroys incurred London's displeasure by lobbying for proposals popular in Ireland. Hardwicke and Wellesley were reminded that their function was limited to representing the Crown in Ireland. Hardwicke in particular vocalised the complaints of Irish legislators who believed that their advice had been ignored and hoped that London would pay "more attention to Irish concerns." [103] Wellesley repeated these sentiments, but the Cabinet in turn complained that Irish legislators should first pay more attention to the need for regular attendance. These exhortations were particularly forceful when a new session approached, and on such occasions viceroys wrote many letters on the Ministry's behalf.[104] Criticism of Irish M.P.s' absenteeism surfaced every year. In 1809 Dundas complained to Richmond that the Irish had been "very lukewarm in their attendance and support" and had returned to Ireland shortly after the session began. He urged Richmond to beat the bushes.[105] On the eve of crucial votes in the Houses of Commons letters were sent out. In June 1804 for example, letters were posted "to all the absentees in Ireland" likely to support the Government.[106] In January 1811, as the Regency crisis deepened, Wellesley-Pole forwarded to Richmond a lengthy list of Irish absentees who should be contacted directly. [107] And in 1822 Goulburn begged Wellesley to despatch Irish M.P.s to London; English country gentlemen were "very unmanageable" and Irish support was urgently required.[108]

When these exhortations failed – and often they did – viceroys adopted other expedients. Innocent bribes, such as invitations to Castle functions, a viceregal visit to the M.P.s in their constituencies, a friendly and flattering word, all were calculated to prevent Irish legislators from "becoming like sheep without a shepherd." [109] Hardwicke and Bedford were the most successful in this art of cultivating Irish M.P.s; Bedford issued a standing invitation to legislators whenever they passed through Dublin.[110] Wellesley was least successful; he despised most of them and scarcely concealed his contempt. They complained of his autocratic behaviour and of his insatiable need for praise.[111]

How effective was the viceroy's role in Irish political management and patronage distribution? Some practices, including the use of secret service funds, strike modern observers as unseemly, even if the scope of such operations steadily diminished between 1800 and 1830. Cultivating legislators' friendship seems to have taxed the patience of many viceroys, and they complained that such work was petty and demeaning. A lord lieutenant often lacked the necessary political ken; aristocrats shied away from the art of gladhanding. They had come to Ireland to rule, to dazzle, to persuade and impress; here, as the Crown's surrogate they aspired to make a decisive contribution to the government of Ireland.

1. George III to Addington, 11 February 1801, printed in Aspinall, ed., *Later Correspondence of George III*, III, 504; also see Colchester, *Diary*, I, 224, and Pellew, *Addington*, I, 303; Hardwicke to Pelham, 26 August 1801, Hardwicke MSS, 35771/53; see Bolton, *Act*, passim, and Edward Brynn, "Some Repercussions of the Act of Union on the Church of Ireland, 1801-1820," *Church History* (September 1971).

2. Charles James Fox to Bedford, June 1806, printed in John Russell, First Earl Russell, ed., *Memoirs and Correspondence of Charles James Fox* (4 vols.; London: Richard Bentley, 1853-57), IV, 143.

3. Peel to Earl de Grey, 23 November 1841, Peel MSS, 40477, cited in McDowell, *Irish Administration*, pp.47-48.

4. Richmond to the Earl of Cossillis, 30 June 1812, Richmond MSS, 74/1828.

5. MacDonagh, *Viceroy's Post-Bag*, p.12.

6. Parker, *Peel*, I, 160.

7. Anglesey, *One-Leg*, p.184.

8. Historical Manuscripts Commission, *Fourteenth Report*, Appendix I, p.344; Dublin, Public Record Office, . SP 63/475/100; Johnston, *Great Britain*, p.29.

9. *Harcourt Papers*, IX, 32; Historical Manuscripts Commission, *Fourteenth Report*, Appendix X, pp. 303-304; British Museum Add. MSS 34418/19; Public Record Office, Home Office MSS, 101/14/191.

10. Rutland to Pitt, 13 September 1786, Rutland, *Pitt-Rutland*, pp.151-52.

11. Hardwicke to Addington, 26 August 1801, Hardwicke MSS, 35771/51-52.

12. Elliot to Grenville, 25 March 1806, *Fortescue MSS*, VIII, 69-70.

13. Instructions to Richmond, 1807, Richmond MSS, 60/258, paragraph 19.

14. Liverpool to Peel, 4 October 1813, Parker, *Peel*, I, 109-110.

15. Peel to Liverpool, 20 October 1813, Parker, *Peel*, I, 110-12.

16. "Copy of Memorandum by the Duke of Richmond to Mr. Peel," 10 November 1813, Richmond MSS, 60/304; Richmond to Peel, 5 April 1816, Richmond MSS, quoted in McDowell, *Irish Administration*, p.48.

17. George III to Addington, 11 February 1801, printed in Aspinall, ed., *Later Correspondence of George III*, III, 504.

18. Colchester, *Diary*, quoted in O'Brien, *Dublin Castle*, pp.87-88.

19. Dublin, Public Record Office, MSS State Papers OPP 162/756, 30/8/331, f.307.

20. Pelham to Hardwicke, August 1801, in MacDonagh, *Post-Bag*, p.66.

21. Hardwicke to Pelham, 21 July 1802, in MacDonagh, *Post-Bag*, pp. 120-21.

22. Wellesley to Richmond, 14 July 1807, Richmond MSS, 58/26.

23. Peel to French, 5 June 1813, Richmond MSS, 71/1461d.

24. Peel to Richmond, 4 September 1813, Richmond MSS, 71/1413.

25. Talbot to Viscount Forbes, 16 February 1818, Peel MSS, 40194/213.

26. John Beresford to Auckland, 20 November 1804, Beresford, *Beresford*, I, 305.

27. Elliot to Grenville, 20 May 1806, *Fortescue MSS*, VIII, 145.

28. Robert Stewart, Third Marquis of Londonderry, to Wellington, 12 July 1823; Wellington to Londonderry, 18 August 1823; Aspinall, ed., *George IV*, III, 7, 8, 9.

29. Richmond to Henry Boyle, Third Earl of Shannon, 27 November 1808, Richmond MSS, 74/1928.

30. Peel to Richmond, 31 March 1813, Richmond MSS, 71/1426.

31. See Chapter VII.

32. Hardwicke to Yorke, 20 August 1801; Liverpool to Wellesley, 16 November 1822, Wellesley MSS, 37300/12.

33. Wickham to Addington, 15 August 1802, Hardwicke MSS, 37552/30-35; Dublin *Evening Post*, 5 March 1814, p.3, col.2.

34. Hardwicke to Pelham, 1 December 1802, Hardwicke MSS, 37552/59.

35. Liverpool to George IV, 22 January 1822, printed in Aspinall ed., *George IV*, II, 498.

36. Elliot to Grenville, 14 June 1806, *Fortescue MSS*, VIII, 197.

37. Hawkesbury to Richmond, 28 May 1807, Richmond MSS, 70/1323.

38. Shawe, "Sketch," printed in Aspinall ed., *George IV*, III, 297-98; Grenville to Spencer, 18 December 1806, *Fortescue MSS*, VIII, 479.

39. Leveson Gower to Murray, 6 April 1829, printed in Leveson Gower, *Letter Books*, cited in McDowell, *Irish Administration*, p.48.

40. Hardwicke to Charles Yorke, 1802, Hardwicke MSS, 35702; McDowell, *Irish Administration*, p.48.

41. Hardwicke to Charles Yorke, 20 August 1801, Hardwicke MSS, 35771/45; Hardwicke to George III, 25 August 1801, printed in Aspinall, ed., *Later Correspondence of George III*, III, 597; Hardwicke to Addington, 26 August 1801, Hardwicke MSS, 35771/51-52; Hardwicke to Charles Yorke, 7 September 1801, Hardwicke MSS, 35771/61; the correspondence is conveniently printed in MacDonagh, *Viceroy's Post-Bag*, pp.54-65.

42. Grenville to Windham, 16 April 1806, Grenville to Bedford, 22 September 1806, Bedford to Grenville, 18 November 1806, *Fortescue MSS*, VIII, 99-100, 350, 437.

43. Denis Gray, *Spencer Perceval, 1782-1812: the Evangelical Prime Minister* (Manchester: Manchester University Press, 1963), p.414; Bathurst to Richmond, 9 October 1811, Richmond MSS, 61/344.

44. Richard A. Brashares, "The Political Career of the Marquess Wellesley in England and Ireland," (Ph.D Dissertation, Duke University, 1968), p.521.

45. Wellesley to Canning, 1 June 1827, BM Add. MSS, 38103/115ff.

46. McDowell, *Public Opinion*, p.68.

47. Hardwicke to Abbot, 27 June 1801, Hardwicke MSS, 35771/22.

48. Hardwicke to Charles Yorke, 30 March 1804, Hardwicke MSS, 35705/218.

49. Hardwicke to Pelham, 21 July 1802, MacDonagh, *Post-Bag*, pp.120-121.

50. Hardwicke to Charles Yorke, 13 August 1803, MacDonagh, *Post-Bag*, pp.123-24.

51. MacDonagh, *Post-Bag*, pp.89-91.

52. Plowden, *Ireland*, II, 250-51.

53. Aspinall, ed., *Later Correspondence of George III*, IV, 235.

54. Bedford to Grenville, 18 August 1806, *Fortescue MSS*, p.287.

55. *Ibid.*, p.368; Fox to Grenville, March 1806, *Fortescue MSS*, VIII, 495; Grenville to Elliot, 8 July 1806, *Fortescue MSS*, VIII, 227.

56. Hawkesbury to Richmond, 22 April 1807, Richmond MSS, 58/2.

57. Arthur Wellesley to Richmond, 22, June 1807, Richmond MSS, 58/22.

58. Richmond to Dundas, 10 May 1809, Aspinall, ed., *Later Correspondence of George III*, V, 177.

59. Arthur Wellesley to Richmond, 6 July 1807, Richmond MSS, 58/28.

60. "Copy of Memorandum Given by the Duke of Richmond to Mr. Peel," 10 November 1813, Richmond MSS, 60/304.

61. Parker, *Peel*, I, 275.

62. Peel to Whitworth, Peel MSS, 40191/215, in Gash, *Peel*, p.124.

63. Peel to Gregory, n. d., Parker, *Peel*, I, 161.

64. Goulburn to Wellesley, 20 March 1822, Wellesley MSS, 37298/325.

65. Goulburn to Peel, 16 April 1824, Peel MSS, 40330/43-44.

66. Wellesley to Liverpool, January 1824, Liverpool MSS, 38103/93-99.

67. Canning to Wellesley, 24 May 1827, Wellesley MSS, 37297/283-84.

68. Anglesey to Peel, 26 July 1828; Peel to Anglesey, 30 August 1828; Anglesey to Wellington, 11 August 1828; Leveson Gower to Anglesey, 21 August 1828; Plas Newydd MSS, printed in Anglesey, *One-Leg*, p.206; Charles Greville, *A Journal of the Reigns of King George IV and King William IV* (Edited by R. H. Stoddart; 3 vols.; New York; Scribners, Armstrong, 1875), I, 136.

69. Leveson Gower to Murray, 6 April 1829, printed in Leveson Gower, *Letter Books*, cited in McDowell, *Irish Administration*, p.48.

70. Fitzgibbon to Eden, 17 November 1801, in McDowell, "Fitzgibbon Letters," p.501.

71. Bolton, *Act*, p.216.

72. Grenville to Bedford, 23 August 1806; Bedford to Grenville, 26 August 1806, *Fortescue MSS*, VIII, 293-95.

73. Bedford to Grenville, 9 September 1806, 22 September 1806, *Fortescue MSS*, VIII, 313, 350.

74. *Ibid.*, 26 August 1806, *Fortescue MSS*, VIII, 294-95.

75. *Ibid.*, 6 February 1807, 18 February 1807, *Fortescue MSS*, IX, 29, 44.

76. Elliot to Grenville, 4 March 1807, *Fortescue MSS*, IX, 65. There were in fact thirty-two counties with two members each; two cities with two members each; thirty-one boroughs and the college constituency.

77. Edward Wakefield, *An Account of Ireland: Statistical and Political* (2 vols.; London, 1812), II, 305, 310, 385.

78. Peel to Gregory, 21 July 1814, Parker, *Peel*, I, 161.

79. Arthur Wellesley, "House of Commons' Representation of Ireland in the Parliament of 1807-1812," BM Add. MSS, 40221/15-62, printed in Arthur Aspinall and E. Anthony Smith, ed., *English Historical Documents, 1783-1832* (London: Eyre and Spottiswoode, 1959), pp.265 ff.

80. Browne to Peel, 6 March 1815, Peel MSS, 40217, cited in McDowell, *Irish Administration*, p.47.

81. Hawkesbury to Richmond, 28 May, 4 June 1807, Richmond MSS, 70/323.

82. Richmond to Sidmouth, 24 September 1812, Richmond MSS, 74/1811; Clare to Bathurst, 1 January 1813, *Bathurst MSS*, p.22.

83. Peel to Fitzgerald, 26 September 1814, Parker, *Peel*, I, 161.

84. Joy to Peel, 4 May 1829, Peel MSS, 40327/20-27; Goulburn to Peel, 5 May 1823, Peel MSS, 40329/74.

85. Hardwicke to Addington, 6 August 1801, Hardwicke MSS, 35771/35; Redesdale to Hawkesbury, 1 October 1805, BM Add. MSS, 38241/241; Grenville to Bedford, 14 August 1806; Bedford to Grenville, 6 February 1807, *Fortescue MSS*, VIII, 273; IX, 29, 44.

86. Arthur Wellesley to Richmond, 18 March 1808, in Wellington, *Ireland*, p.368; Richmond to Liverpool, 21 October 1809, Richmond MSS, 1364.

87. Dublin *Evening Post*, 18 February 1813, p.2, col. 3.

88. Sullivan, "Irish Parliament," p.1; Harlow *Founding*, I, 508.

89. McDowell, *Irish Administration*, p.43.

90. *Ibid.*: pp: 44-45.

91. Grenville to Addington, 6 December 1801, *Fortescue MSS*, VII, 69; Elliot to Grenville, 20 April 1806, *Fortescue MSS*, VIII, 109-19.

92. Hawkesbury to Richmond, 22 April 1807, Richmond MSS, 70/1346.

93. Talbot to Peel, 15 May 1818, 19 May 1818, Peel MSS, 40194/257.

94. Hawkesbury to Richmond, 22 April 1807, Richmond MSS, 70/1346.

95. Talbot to Peel, 11 June 1818, Peel MSS, 40194/263.

96. McDowell, *Irish Administration*, p.46.

97. Sullivan, "Irish Parliament," p.26.

98. Peel to Liverpool, 29 September 1813, BM Add. MSS, 38195.

99. Hawkesbury to Richmond, 28 May 1807, Richmond MSS, 70/1323.

100. Peel to the Earl of Desart, 19 October 1812; Peel to Croker, 1 October 1812, Parker, *Peel*, I, 46-47.

101. Stanley to Anglesey, 2 February 1831; Anglesey to Grey, 7 February 1831; Grey to Anglesey, 8 February 1831; Anglesey to Grey, 10 February 1831, Plas Newydd MSS, printed in Aspinall and Smith, eds., *English Historical Documents*, IX, 278-79.

102. Redesdale to Hawkesbury, 1 October 1805, Liverpool MSS 38241/241, printed in Aspinall and Smith, eds., *English Historical Documents*, IX, 270-79.

103. Hardwicke to Nepean, 22 June 1804, Hardwicke MSS, 35750/157.

104. Richmond to the Duke of Abercorn, 8 January 1810, Richmond MSS, 73/1757; Hawkesbury to Richmond, 15 June 1807, Richmond MSS, 70/1357.

105. Dundas to Richmond, 4 May 1809,

Melville MSS, printed in Aspinall, *Later Correspondence of George III*, V, 272.

106. Nepean to Hardwicke, 8 June 1804, Hardwicke MSS, 35750/76.

107. Wellesley Pole to Richmond, 7 January 1811, Richmond MSS, 64/727.

108. Goulburn to Wellesley, 13 February 1822, Wellesley MSS, 37298/202.

109. Redesdale to Hawkesbury, 1 October 1805, Liverpool MSS, 38241/241.

110. *Annual Register*, XLVI (1804), 6-7, 45.

111. Peel to Wellesley, 8 February 1822, Wellesley MSS, 37298/157; Austin Mitchell, *The Whigs in Opposition, 1815-1830* (Oxford: Clarendon Press, 1967), p.177; Richard Wellesley to Wellesley, 25 April 1822; Goulburn to Wellesley, 23 April 1822, Wellesley MSS, 37315/268-69, 37297/94-95.

Richard Colley Wellesley, Marquess Wellesley
Lord Lieutenant
December 1821–December 1827

Chapter 5
Public Opinion and the Viceregal Image

Private Chaplain's Office, Phoenix Park: February 17, 1826. There will be a Rosary at the Lodge on the Evening of Monday the 20th inst. The Ladies and Gentlemen who attend are requested to bring their own beads.

Entry in Dublin Evening Mail, 17 Feb. 1826

AT LEAST SIX forces helped to shape Irish public opinion in the early nineteenth century: the press; the courts; the Orange Movement; Catholic agitation; parliamentary politics; and social functions centred on Dublin Castle. Of all these, most attention was focused on the role of the press.[1] Peel declared on one occasion that the press was in large measure responsible for periodic disturbances in Ireland; it never enlightened the public mind or contributed to the improvement of morals or the happiness of the people.[2] Traditionally Ireland's press was highly partisan, easily corrupted by government favour, and volatile. The "Castle press" sustained government policies and in turn received certain government funds. Many newspapers and journals were too small to survive without subsidies, and these publications rarely hesitated to change editorial policies to meet the prejudices of the government of the day.[3] A financially precarious "opposition" or "independent" press criticised officials lustily and slandered indiscriminately.

THE PRESS

Dublin Castle was never quite sure how to deal with the press. It rarely paid any attention to provincial newspapers, and thus Irish political journalism took on a decidedly Dublin orientation.[4] In Dublin itself successive viceroys pursued contradictory and often self-defeating policies towards the press. Pro-government and anti-government newspapers clashed most violently under

Richmond, when the opposition *Evening Post* almost single-handedly took on the "sophistries," "rubbish," and "roaring, waving rhodomontade" of several Government-supported newspapers.[5] Finally, under Wellesley, government-subsidised newspapers and journals clashed with each other on the Catholic issue, and the absurdity of sustaining such a system with public funds gradually became apparent to all.[6] Until 1830, nonetheless, the dynamics of the Castle press were fundamental to the process of shaping Irish public opinion.

The Castle press was sustained by several ingenious devices. Some newspapers received payments ostensibly intended to defray the cost of publishing legal notices. Funds from the King's secret service accounts found their way discreetly into the hands of obliging editors. Journalists obtained sinecurial positions and favoured newspapers were sometimes permitted to use government pouches, or "expresses," to obtain London news before it reached their competitors. Of all these devices perhaps the role of secret service funds was vital. In 1793 the Irish parliament placed a limit of £5,000 each year on secret service funds to be used in "detecting or defeating treasonable conspiracies, insurrection or rebellion".[7] Because most of this money was applied to pensions, Peel declared in 1813 that only £1,000 remained unpledged.[8] Two modern observers of the Irish press during that period estimate that before 1820 some £2,000 or £3,000 per year was devoted to the press.[9] No records were maintained, however, and when M.P.s were bold enough to demand an audit their bids were turned back: publicity "would defeat the very purpose of the grant". [10]

The career of one John Giffard highlights viceroys' problems with the press. Giffard and some journalist friends held pensions when in 1805 Hardwicke attempted to establish an amicable relationship with moderate elements of the "catholic press". Giffard misconstrued Hardwicke's intentions and delivered a highly intemperate speech in the Common Council of Dublin against petitions for Catholic relief then in circulation. Hardwicke appropriated Giffard's sinecure and threatened to cut off secret service funds to his newspaper, the *Dublin Journal.* The *Journal* thereupon condemned Hardwicke, while Giffard himself pleaded privately with Hardwicke to restore his sinecure because of his age. Hardwicke refused, but London supplied a pension.[11] In 1808, under pressure from the Dukes of York and Cumberland, Richmond restored Giffard to his sinecure. Hardwicke raised the issue in parliament. Arthur Wellesley criticised Hardwicke for having penalised Giffard and questioned "the propriety of avoiding to appoint any man to office in Ireland whose opinions were inimical to the Roman Catholics".[12] Giffard quickly resumed his pattern of indiscretions. In 1813 he angered Peel by publishing in his government-supported newspaper "a gross forgery professing to be a protest of the Catholics of Ireland against a bill for their relief". Peel failed in an attempt to terminate Giffard's secret service stipend.[13] In 1816 and 1817 he again angered Peel with antics which "always injured the cause he espoused".[14] His services were finally terminated in the 1820s.

Giffard's case demonstrated the inadequacy of the subsidised press. In 1810 Richmond and Wellesley Pole selected the recently launched *Patriot* to supply appropriate assistance "on every emergency". The editor, William Corbett, developed an insatiable appetite to match his obstinacy, and the *Patriot* soon proved to be "as discreditable as it was expensive to maintain".[15] Nonetheless, it continued to enjoy government funds until 1825.[16] Other newspapers such as the *Correspondent* and the *Hibernian Journal* received about £400 per annum between 1810 and 1820.[17] Peel tried to remove them from the list of the government's beneficiaries but William Gregory proved to be a resourceful custodian of these unworthy publications.[18]

Parliament also supplied Dublin Castle with some £10,500 per year under the appelation of "Proclamation Fund". Of this only some £3,500 was in fact spent on proclamations; much of the remainder served as subsidies to cooperative newspapers. Proclamations were occasionally printed in the opposition press, but most went to friendly papers.[19] Because these subsidies were by law tied to the publication of official notices, a Government paper sometimes printed the same notice several times or inserted old proclamations. In 1808 one paper warned of a fever which had raged in Gibraltar in 1805, issued outdated advice against the exportation of certain goods and repeated obsolete criteria for recruiting naval personnel. Proclamations for one county appeared in newspapers remote from the affected area, or were repeated year after year.[20]

The idea of favouring certain newspapers with access to government pouches apparently began under Bedford. He afforded to the *Correspondent*, his own creation, the chance to print continental news a full day earlier than competitors.[21] Dublin journalists stormed at this practice, but Richmond continued it and even launched a faster pouch service. At times this disoriented Dublin's financial markets, and after 1815 the practice declined as better communications undermined the government's advantage.

Was the subsidised press useful to the Irish administration? To the extent that some viceroys wished to depart from an ultra-Protestant stance subsidies could be useful. Hardwicke and Bedford both used subsidies to offer Catholics a chance to publicise their position.[22] There was less reason to rely on it under Richmond, Whitworth and Talbot. On one occasion, when pressed in parliament to justify the expenses involved, Peel asked Gregory what he should say. Gregory in turn asked Peel, "what can you say in defence of the system, except that your adversaries expended large sums in the same way". [23] Parliament's interest waned, and then waxed again, so that Peel "trembled for the proclamations".[24] Whitworth sided with the reformers after tangling with Giffard.[25] Grant expressed his resentment at the bigoted tone of the subsidised press, but did little more than this.

Wellesley lost no time after his arrival in demanding that subsidies to the Orange press be stopped, and he set in motion a successful assault on the whole system. At first Gregory and Goulburn deflected Wellesley's effort and Goulburn even feigned ignorance of the whole problem.[26] The one newspaper which switched its allegiance to the viceroy was almost immediately crippled because Gregory saw to it that its subsidy was withdrawn. To combat Wellesley's pro-Catholic sympathies, the Orange interest also launched a new paper, the *Dublin Evening Mail.* Indeed, Wellesley claimed, the paper existed "for the express purpose of writing down" his government. Wellesley's nominees for chief constable, he added, "upon applying for the commissions [were] required to subscribe to the *Evening Mail* in order that they might be edified by daily libels upon their benefactors." [27] Wellesley neglected to mention that the principal "Castle-Catholic" organ, the *Patriot,* used a large subsidy to roast Goulburn in its pages from time to time, and he refused to curb the *Patriot* when Goulburn complained.[28]

In 1827 Lamb observed that the practice of subsidies had "nursed up about three times as many newspapers as would naturally exist" in Ireland.[29] He joined Wellesley in urging that the whole system be terminated. There was considerable resistance to this within the Castle bureaucracy.[30] In 1828 Anglesey asked Peel to end the system, noting that he was a principal object of attack. Peel agreed and without supplying any explanation simply advised

Anglesey to cease all subsidies.[31] Anglesey did so, and in 1830 Leveson Gower was able to declare that the Government no longer exercised any influence over the Irish press.[32]

The impact of the subsidies system on the Irish press was quite as pernicious as on Dublin Castle itself. Peel noted that the violence of the press made impossible the "formation of wholesome public opinion in Ireland".[33] The Government "planted" material, much of it partially fraudulent and unprincipled.[34] Irish newspapers demonstrated their own credulity by printing "every idle tale invented and blazoned forth by the London newspapers".[35] Libel suits were common and often themselves became newsworthy events. Cobbett, editor of the influential *Political Register,* was charged in 1804 with having libelled Hardwicke.[36] Richmond was restrained from launching numerous suits but did terminate his career as viceroy with two controversial legal initiatives.[37] One, brought against John Magee of the *Dublin Evening Post,* inadvertently advertised the talents of Daniel O'Connell.[38] Magee was convicted of libel for characterising Richmond's anti-Catholic policies as a "monument of legal vengeance" but his newspaper's circulation multiplied.[39]

Subsidies, law suits and bigotry did encourage the revival of the Irish press after a period of somnulence brought on by the rebellion of 1797-98. In the wake of the insurrection the press was hesitant to criticise the government of the day. In addition, Hardwicke and Bedford were popular enough among influential Catholic elements to reduce criticism.[40] Richmond, on the other hand, excited many patriots' passions, and a vigorous press debate followed. The opposition press painted Richmond as a "military viceroy" who must be harbinger of "military measures".[41] He was subjected to unwarranted personal attacks, with charges of alcoholism and sexual improprieties predominantly featured: the "liberty of the still" was more sacred to him than the liberty of the press.[42] Unfortunate and unfair as much of this certainly was, opposition to Richmond guaranteed the revival of a viable opposition press. Whitworth garnered "golden opinions from all sorts of men" and Talbot was treated gently.[43] But Castle policies were attacked with unparalleled pointedness and audacity, and no administration could face the future immune from the criticism of a hostile press.

Under Wellesley press freedom became a permanent feature of the Irish scene. Certainly no viceroy received a more enthusiastic editorial welcome. "The great talents and decided character of the

100

noble Marquess," cried out the *Dublin Journal,* "will crush the factions which have so long distracted Ireland."[44] "The tone of official men," added the *Dublin Evening Post,* "is no longer exasperating and insulting."[45] Even five months later the *Post* could declare "that government has the universal support of the press."[46] Such euphoria could not last. Wellesley's Catholic sympathies emboldened the nationalist newspapers and circulation increased sharply. They exploited Wellesley's highly developed theatrical inclinations by sharpening their own rhetoric. The *Correspondent* might deprecate the impact of such impassioned language on the "prejudices of brutal or ignorant wretches," but it could not soften the tone of the press.

After 1825 Wellesley's influence over the press declined sharply; Catholics and Protestant journalists alike criticised his marriage. "At sixty-six," warned the *Dublin Evening Mail,* "love will make an old man that has more toes than teeth, attempt even a more foolish thing than dancing."[47] Their children would become the first disciples of "a new sect... [of] Conciliators," something "betwixt and between Catholic and Anglican."[48] Orange newspapers invited the faithful to bring their rosaries to the lodge.[49] As O'Connell's influence increased and as the Protestant reaction intensified, Dublin Castle became the focus of some devastating and tasteless ridicule. After journalists wearied of this, the press settled down into a partisan, ideological and even apocalyptic frame of mind, quite independent of the influence once exerted by the Castle.

THE PUBLIC IMAGE

Viceroys supported philanthropies, encouraged Ireland's commerce, and set the tone of society. They were expected to salve the nation's wounded pride after the loss of its own legislature. A calculated and ostentatious support for legitimate popular charities was central to every viceroy's work. Hardwicke and Whitworth taxed their private fortunes to meet these requirements. Whitworth in particular excelled in the unexpected and spontaneous act of generosity.[50] Richmond's failure to do so reinforced his unpopularity. Wellesley had declared bankruptcy in 1816 and he could not exceed his salary of £20,000 without inflaming his creditors; this dampened any tendency towards magnificent gestures.

Whatever their financial situation, all viceroys could encourage

Irish trade. Viceroys vowed to wear clothes of Irish manufacture. Indeed, Richmond pledged that every item in his viceregal equippage would be obtained in Ireland. The press celebrated the determination of the Duchess to use Irish cloth for her dresses.[51] Wellesley insisted that a shamrock be impressed upon livery buttons. "This may appear trifling to some," observed the *Post*, with suitable hauteur, "but little things are great to little men."[52] Anglesey preferred a simpler mode after his friends warned him against these calculated extravagances.[53] He pleased the crowds by having the band play Irish airs. Perhaps this was sufficient; he was a popular viceroy.

Viceroys were encouraged to promote the economic welfare of Ireland's large and largely indigent population. Talbot emphasised agricultural improvements, awarded handsome prizes, and contributed a fine collection of livestock for stud.[54] Whitworth and Wellesley earned credit for reacting quickly to rural distress resulting from a failure of the potato crop. These contributions were of marginal effectiveness; the age tolerated little interference in the economy and Westminster was quick to oppose any initiatives by Dublin Castle prejudicial to low taxes or British commerce.[55]

On numerous occasions a well-timed initiative focused public attention on the incumbent viceroy. Catholics applauded Hardwicke's opposition to a policy of severe reprisals in the aftermath of Emmet's insurrection, and their enthusiasm proved so embarrassing that he felt obliged to entertain the leaders of the Orange lodges at the Castle.[56] Wellesley tried to turn an alleged assassination plot into support for his campaign against the Orange extremists. The "flagitous faction" prompted addresses of thanksgiving for his escape, but try as he might he could not sustain popular enthusiasm.[57] At length his "escape" struck many as more ludicrous than miraculous.[58] He then turned, as had his predecessors, to the safer device of public addresses. Many of these oratorical exercises can be found in contemporary newspapers. Irish societies and public corporations competed with each other and with the viceroy in devising baroque and ponderous speeches full of flattery, hyperbole, and fatuous misinterpretations of contemporary developments. Certainly Wellesley's Etonian classical style defeated all rivals.[59] When in Dublin Goulburn laboured to edit Wellesley's florid language, but many examples reached the prints relatively unscathed.[60]

The Irish Lord Lieutenant stood at the apex of the nation's

social structure. In the early nineteenth century Ireland was extraordinarily conscious of rank and was also sensitive to any inference of inferiority to the British. The landed aristocracy often measured its importance in terms of visible wealth and the entrepreneurial element was as yet too small to offer a chastening alternative. Many Irish noblemen justified their habitual extravagance by claiming that such lifestyles more than martial demonstrations helped to preserve law and order in the provinces. Dublin played a central role even after the Act of Union. The viceroy's responsibilities probably increased as absenteeism diminished and as Dublin laboured to hide the loss of status as a capital by a calculated increase in the trappings of power.

Until 1830 every viceroy was selected with an eye to supporting the pageantry and pressing social burdens traditionally attached to the office. Nineteenth century viceroys failed to match the financial resources of their recent predecessors. But no viceroy was a commoner, nor would Ireland have tolerated such. Dublin seldom criticised a viceroy's extravagance; often he was pressed to open his pocketbook wider. More than one incumbent found demands on his purse more than he could bear. Wellesley once temporarily suspended all entertainment; he satisfied his many creditors but not Dublin society, and he was forced to soften his economies in order "to put the people of Dublin in good humour".[61] The newspapers pretended to be astounded and alarmed that he had gone a whole month without giving a dinner.[62]

Viceroys were expected to provide in Dublin what the royal household offered London: audiences, interviews and levees; benefit performances and charities; civic celebrations and military exercises; touring and travelling; Castle entertainments; and special ceremonies to mark royal birthdays, the arrival of a new viceroy and public holidays. Of the "routine" responsibilities perhaps most important was the annual shift from the Castle to the summer home in Phoenix Park. This expedition each May, trifling in geographic terms, marked the end of Dublin's social season, as the return to the Castle marked its resumption.[63] Both residences were frequently renovated, but apparently they remained endemically uncomfortable. At the end of the period Anglesey still complained that they were both "filthy beyond description" and very expensive to maintain.[64] Nonetheless during the winter, men of rank sat down to long and arduous dinners at the Castle, and in warmer periods ladies competed for

103

invitations to card parties at the lodge. Dublin's newspapers described the ladies' gatherings in detail complete with menu, table decorations, guest list and wearing apparel.[65] Men entrusted a precis of conversations to their diaries and on occasion took note of the wine list. In all cases the emphasis was on monitoring the list of candidates for Castle largesse; a society so dedicated to rank could not relax and enjoy these festivities.

Audiences, interviews and levees combined serious business and social functions. Viceroys' schedules betrayed their constant confrontations with petitioners, social climbers, lobbyists and curiosity-seekers. Hardwicke granted two audiences each week except when the Chief Secretary resided in Ireland; then he gave one and the secretary gave two. Whitworth seems to have granted audiences more frequently, whereas Wellesley quite often pleaded illness as justification for going weeks without granting any interviews or audiences.

Levees called for the attendance of the entire resident nobility; absence was interpreted as disaffection with the government unless the illness was obvious and obviously serious. The principal gentry and great officers of state also attended, sometimes in military uniform.[66] But the receptions held by the first lady set the city's social tone. In a newspaper notice dated 7 January 1807 the chamberlain informed "the nobility and the ladies and gentlemen, who have been presented to her Grace the Dutchess [sic] of Bedford," that she would be at home every second Thursday until further notice.[67] These entertainments were often expensive and elaborate. Every viceroy from Hardwicke to Anglesey complained that the Act of Union had increased rather than diminished demands upon him.[68] Some, such as the Bedfords, could afford every extravagance. Richmond tried to maintain these standards of offering "every delicacy and the choicest wines... in profusion."[69] But he found the financial burden intolerable, as his guests followed his own example by consuming large quantities of his best vintages. After 1810, therefore, he entertained less lavishly despite an admonition from the *Dublin Evening Post* that Townshend had been able to "drink down" the Irish aristocracy when it was much larger than it is now. Whitworth revived Dublin's morale by increasing the number of parties. This reinforced the prejudice that a great entertaining viceroy was a successful viceroy, and indeed Northumberland was despatched to Dublin in 1829 precisely because he loved to host parties and possessed the wherewithall to do it.[70]

Inevitably most viceroys demanded an increase in allowances and salary. In 1783 the salary was set at £20,000 per annum.[71] In 1800 this was considered more than sufficient for the post-Act of Union period. Hardwicke soon discovered that this was not so, and Addington promised to support an increase. Renewed warfare distracted the Prime Minister and a long and acrimonious correspondence followed. He departed Dublin without any additional compensation and applied for a sinecure sufficient to make up the loss. [72] Richmond renewed the petition and Perceval informed the King that viceregal expenses had risen to nearly £40,000 per year. At length his salary was raised to £30,000. By this time Richmond had contracted debts of £50,000 and vowed to remain in Ireland long enough to eliminate the deficit by a bout of abstemious living.[73] Still, the new "princely salary" rarely sufficed.

The age was dominated by private philanthropy; humanitarian impulses were mature but not yet attached to government. Viceroys were expected to support a long list of "respectable" charities ranging from Dublin's famous hospitals to private educational, scientific and cultural institutions. Many, such as the Royal Irish Academy, were relatively young and eager to accumulate endowments. Most charities were decidedly Protestant, such as the Fund for the Support of Clergyman's Widows. Some were exotic; even the Irish Musical Fund Society for the Relief of Distressed Musicians and their Families was a perennial beneficiary of viceregal largesse.[74] A contribution sufficed for many. Others asked that the viceroy patronise fund-raising events and use their attendance to stimulate attendance. In 1826 Lady Manners' Dublin Tabinet Ball featured Wellesley attending in state. Lady Manners cleverly heightened the effect by producing a canopy and throne chairs, and the Protestant press accused Wellesley of staging a sham coronation.[75]

Charities identified with the Catholic and Dissenting churches also appealed to the viceroy for assistance. Hardwicke, Bedford and Wellesley responded favourably. Bedford was especially generous in grants for the construction of Catholic chapels. Richmond on the other hand declared that he could not go beyond "authorised" charities. Such contributions carried political overtones, and newspapers competed in citing instances of viceregal generosity to favourite causes. [76]

Civic celebrations were intended to promote loyalty to the British Crown, or at least to reaffirm it among the Protestant interest. Royal birthdays called for fireworks in the Phoenix Park and a reception at the Lodge. Bells rang, and the royal standard was displayed in the Castle yard. In 1814 celebrations were expanded to incorporate the centenary of the House of Brunswick's service as Britain's reigning dynasty. Fireworks, a military review, laying the cornerstone for the new post office, and a grand state dinner opened three days of festivities. Dressed in Irish manufactures, the lords and ladies attended a ball on the closing day. [77] Church services and parades were scheduled each day.   Commemorating King William's birthday and Protestant victories at the Boyne caused some problems. Orange Lodge members predominated on these occasions and some viceroys participated in a rather fainthearted manner. After 1820 Dublin Castle divorced itself completely from these affairs. In the same period the growth of Catholic influence was gradually recognised. Bedford marked St. Patrick's Day with a party of "unparalleled splendour" in Dublin Castle. Wellesley revived this custom. Anglesey rode through Dublin wearing a large shamrock in his hat.[78]

Military displays were sponsored by certain viceroys. Richmond, a military man himself, busied himself with reviews of the yeomanry and militia in the Phoenix Park. He liked to breakfast at Pigeon House in the harbour and follow it with demonstrations of artillery fire.[79] Bedford and Wellesley preferred to go in state to the theatre. The spectacle, according to the papers, could be "quite overpowering". [80] The upper classes followed the viceroy in their carriages. The middle classes illuminated their homes with candles and draped the balconies with crepe. Lower classes cheered at the roadside. All these festivities underscored British power in Ireland as much as it did in India, even if the scale was less splendid.

Most viceroys looked on the prospect of tours to the provinces with undisguised horror. Visits to remote areas were as rare as they were important. The Castle bureaucracy depended upon unreliable agents for analyses of rural conditions. A viceroy on tour was not likely to meet many representatives of the "depressed classes," but visits to country houses and to remote municipalities offered an opportunity to test normal sources of information. Equally important was the chance to discuss patronage matters, to solicit support, and to flatter the faithful with an occasional knighthood.[81]

The Hardwicke papers contain a complete set of records on the

Earl's southwestern tour in the summer of 1802. After much deliberation as to the proper route, sifting of invitations, inquiries into the condition of roads and availability of horses and carriages, Hardwicke departed Dublin 30 August 1802. He carried with him copies of addresses from various municipal corporations and his proposed responses. After resting near Kilkenny, his wife, her retinue, carriages with supplies, and the military undersecretary Edward Littlehales (who wrote daily to the Civil Undersecretary in Dublin and handled each day's bundle of correspondence) moved towards Waterford in easy stages. In Waterford they were the guests of the Marquess of Waterford at his estate at Curragh-more. Hardwicke visited the town, made a good impression, and bolstered the town's economy by purchasing some Waterford decanters. [82]   On the way to Cork the journey made Lady Hardwicke ill. The roughness of the surface snapped the springs of the "*Irish* postchaise", crippling two horses and leaving a third on death's door. [83]   The host, Lord Shannon, was ill upon the arrival of the viceregal party but "rallied to help the Lord Lieutenant". Cork city spared no exertion on behalf of the guests. It hosted a "splendid ball," a military review, an oratorio, an inspection of the barracks, and a tour of the harbour. Hardwicke contributed £100 to local charities, which reportedly delighted the citizenry, who lined their streets with troops and cannons primed for a royal salute. [84]   After a pause at Bandon the party rose early and reached Killarney after a gruelling thirteen-hour ride over bad roads. The following day the party "embarked in several boats with bands of music," toured the lake and returned to Killarney "after much meandering and sightseeing." Starting back to Dublin, Hardwicke's party participated in a multitude of military exercises, trips to barracks, dinners, and meetings with the local nobility and gentry. Hardwicke endured horse races and only privately complained of the "very bad sport". [85] The party reached Dublin at the end of September. Lady Hardwicke was ill once more. The viceroy expressed his gratification at the loyal state of the country and betrayed in private his sense of relief that the trip was over. [86]

Before leaving Dublin every viceroy was charged with preparing arrangements for his successor. Every viceroy but two departed unpopular and cheers of good riddance accompanied him to the pier. Hopes for better times meant a warm reception for the next viceroy. Prior to the actual transfer of power a furious exchange of letters covered advice on household appointments, supplies, members of the household staff, and entertainment. The date for arriving was subject to intense debate; usually the incumbent pressed his successor to come as soon as possible after the appointment had been made public. [87] The sale of horses, carriages, and wine cellars was negotiated and letters of introduction were prepared for household officials fortunate enough to be retained.[88]

An ancient ritual marked the transfer of power. After a night spent on board ship the new viceroy stepped ashore at 3 p.m. to an artillery salute and proceeded immediately to the Castle. Weather conditions permitting, "a great display of beauty and fashion" might be seen in the streets. Occasionally the viceroy himself came to the pier. Talbot, accompanied by the Hussars, city officials, the nobility in their carriages and an ominously swollen crowd of citizens, all greeted Wellesley at Pigeon House. Anglesey, in contrast, found the city quite unprepared, for Wellesley had already departed. He arranged an "impromptu [dinner] of thirty covers to all the bigwigs". At the Castle a simple ceremony commemorated the transfer of power. The Privy Council convened to hear the new viceroy's patent and letter. He received the sword of state, took the oath of allegiance, was admitted to the Order of St. Patrick, and, rather incongruously, took his seat at the head of the table to hear his wine warrant read.[89] The retiring viceroy thereupon departed immediately, enduring the crowds still gathered in the streets. Bedford and Anglesey were wildly acclaimed. In Bedford's case the crowds surged forward, detached the horses, and dragged his carriage two miles to Pigeon House. Anglesey was cheered all the way to Dun Laoghaire by a sober, tearful crowd.[90]

What mark did the viceregal image leave on early nineteenth century Ireland? Only in part can a parallel be drawn between the practice of visual display in Ireland and in contemporary India. In India the panoply of power was supported by almost unlimited local independence. The Raj was real as well as theatrical. In Ireland the visible and outward sign of power was in some respects a substitute for the reality, and perhaps for this reason was cultivated so assiduously. In Ireland, moreover, there was disagreement as to whom all this splendour should be directed. For the most part Tory viceroys catered to the Irish upper classes, who no less than their social inferiors craved this display of authority. Bedford, Wellesley and then Anglesey manipulated power as if preparing a plebiscite. Unlike in India, elements of Irish society were beginning to dismiss the theatrical elements of viceregal power as frivolous and perhaps even unfortunate in a land so poor. But this was by no means a universal feeling in 1801, or even in 1830, though by the latter date it was clear that this particular aspect of the viceroy's activity was no longer of primary importance. If the dinners, the tours, the charities, and the civic ceremonial did not protect Ireland from lower class agitation by cowing the masses, they did encourage cohesion among the ruling caste, and made them believe their power was, as it had been in the eighteenth century, still secure. The ceremonial obscured on one hand the realities of brute force as it was practised in Ireland even after 1800, and on the other the rising, consuming power of the new popular movement which O'Connell mobilised under the banner of the Catholic Association.

1. Dublin *Evening Post*, 30 June 1814, p.2, cols. 4-5.

2. Peel to John Beckett, 4 September 1813, Peel MSS, 40285/137, summarised by Arthur Aspinall in "The Use of Irish Secret Service Money in Subsidising the Irish Press," *English Historical Review*, LVI (1941), 265.

3. Dublin *Evening Post*, 11 April 1807, p.2, col.4; 26 April, 1814, p.3, cols. 3-4; 28 June 1814, p.3, col.4; 18 December 1821, p.2, col.4.

4. R. B. McDowell, "The Irish Government and the Provincial Press," *Hermathena*, LIII, 146-47.

5. Dublin *Evening Post*, 11 November 1813, p.2, col.2.

6. Brian Inglis, *The Freedom of the Press in Ireland, 1784-1841* (London: Routledge and Kegan Paul, 1954), pp.184-85; Peel to Goulburn, 14 November 1823, Peel MSS, 40329/217.

7. Aspinall, "Secret Service Money," p.640.

8. Peel to Sidmouth, 24 December 1813, Peel MSS, 40285/166.

9. Inglis, *Freedom*, pp.147-49.

10. Aspinall, "Secret Service Money," p.640.

11. John Giffard to Hardwicke, Hardwicke MSS, 35728/128; Dublin *Evening Post*, 28 November 1805, in Inglis, *Freedom*, pp.113-42.

12. Wellesley to Hawkesbury, 13 March 1808; Arthur Wellesley to Richmond, 13 March 1808, printed in Wellington, *Ireland*, pp.361-62.

13. Parker, *Peel*, I, 115.

14. Peel to Gregory, 29 March 1816, Peel MSS, 40202/177.

15. Corbett to Gregory, 15 December 1815, Peel MSS, 40201/293.

16. Aspinall, "Secret Service Money," p.643.

17. Gregory to Peel, 16 April 1813, Peel MSS, 40196/27.

18. *Ibid*.

19. 2 *Hansard* V (1821), 1446-47.

20. Inglis, *Freedom*, p.115.

21. *Ibid*.

22. 1 *Hansard* XXV (13 April 1813),

23. Gregory to Peel, 8 May 1813, Peel MSS, 40196/146.

24. Peel to Gregory, 31 January 1817, Peel MSS, 40292/122.

25. Whitworth to Peel, 21 February 1817, Peel MSS, 40193/62.

26. 2 *Hansard* XV (21 April 1826), 542.

27. Shawe, "Sketch," printed in Aspinall, George IV, III, 299-311.

28. Goulburn to Peel, 29 January 1827, Peel MSS, 40332/254.

29. Unsigned memorandum, 1828, Peel MSS, 40307/165; Lamb to Lansdowne, 17 September 1827, Bowood MSS, printed in Arthur Aspinall, "The Irish Proclamation Fund, 1800-1846," *English Historical Review*, LVI (1941), 277.

30. Torrens, *Melbourne*, I, 250.

31. Philip Stanhope, Third Earl Stanhope and Lord Cardwell, eds., *The Memoirs of Sir Robert Peel* (2 vols.; London: John Murray, 1856), I, 231.

32. 2 *Hansard* XXV (2 July 1830), 922.

33. Peel, quoted in Madden, *Castle*, p.12.

34. Peel to Gregory, 13 May 1813, Parker, *Peel*, I, 115.

35. Dublin *Evening Post*, 11 April 1807, p.2, col.4.

36. *Annual Register*, XLVI (1804), 390.

37. *Ibid.*, LV (1813), 14.

38. Dublin *Evening Post*, 9 October 1813, p.3, col.1; 30 August 1814, p.3, col.1.

39. *Dublin Correspondent*, 6 April 1807, p.3, col.2; Dublin *Evening Post*, 26 March 1807, p.2, col.1; 23 April 1807, p.2, col.2; 25 April 1805, p.3, col.1; 21 September 1813, p.3, cols. 1-3.

40. Dublin *Evening Post*, 23 April 1807, p.2, col.2; 2 June 1807, p.3, col.2; 1 September 1807, p.3, cols. 3-4.

41. *Ibid.*, 9 January 1813, p.3, cols. 1-2; 19 August 1813, p.3, col.1; 21 August 1813, p.3, col.1.

42. *Ibid.*, 24 July 1817, p.3, col.1; The *Patriot*, 5 January 1822, p.3, col.3.

43. *Dublin Journal*, 5 December 1821, p.2, col.1.

44. Dublin *Evening Post*, 27 April 1822, p.3, col.4; 27 December 1821, p.2, col.4.

45. *Ibid.*, 16 May 1822, p.3, col.5.

46. Dublin *Evening Mail*, 31 October 1825, p.2, col.5.

47. *Ibid.*, 19 October 1825, p.3, col.3.

48. *Ibid.*

49. *Ibid.*, quoted in W. J. Fitzgerald, ed., *The Correspondence of Daniel O'Connell* (2 vols.; London: John Murray, 1888), I, 88.

50. Dublin *Evening Post*, 6 September 1814, p.2, col.4.

51. *Ibid.*, 25 May 1807, p.2, col.3.

52. *Ibid.*, 27 December 1821, p.2, cols. 3 and 4; also see Constantia Maxwell, *Dublin under the Georges* (Rev. ed.; London: Faber and Faber, 1956), p.94.

53. Forbes to Anglesey, 6 August 1827, Plas Newydd MSS, cited in Anglesey, *One-Leg*, p.185.

54. *The Patriot*, 5 January 1822, p.2, col.4.

55. Dublin *Evening Post*, 16 April 1814, p.3, col.3; 21 April 1814, p.3, col.2; 4 January 1823, p.3, col.5.

56. Plowden, *Ireland*, I, 107-109.

57. Goulburn to Peel, 18 December 1822, 21 December 1822, 1 January 1823, 16 January 1823, Peel MSS, 40328/300-307, 40329/1-3, 18; Dublin *Correspondent*, 17 December 1822, p.3, cols. 1-4; Dublin *Evening Post*, 4 January 1823, p.2, col.5; for some examples of the addresses to Wellesley see the Dublin *Correspondent*, 19, 22, 24, 28 December 1822.

58. Goulburn to Peel, 3 January 1823, Peel MSS, 40329/5-9, 37-40; Wellesley to Goulburn, 1, 22 January 1823, Kingston-on-Thames, Surrey Record Office, Goulburn MSS, acc. 319, 11/22; *Annual Register*, LXV (1823), 49-51; Wellesley, memorandum, 20 February 1823, Wellesley MSS, 37300/248-50.

59. Dublin *Evening Post*, 28 January 1823, p.3, col.4.

60. Wellesley's draft, 26 December 1822, Wellesley MSS, 37300/115-16; Goulburn to Peel, 1 January 1823, Peel MSS, 40329/1; Dublin *Evening Post*, 2 January 1823, p.3, col.4. The *Post* considered Wellesley's style "proverbially admirable... It... sunk, not only into memory, but into the heart of the country."

61. Shawe to Knighton, 13 June 1827, printed in Aspinall, ed., *George IV*, III, 252.

62. The *Patriot*, 28 February 1822, p.3, col.4.

63. Dublin *Evening Herald*, 18 May 1807, p.2, col.4; Faulkner's *Dublin Journal*, 3 February 1807, p.2, col.3.

64. Forbes to Anglesey, printed in Anglesey, *One-Leg*, p.186; Dublin *Correspondent*, 1 April 1807, p.3, col. 3; The *Patriot*, 9 April 1822, p.3, col.3.

65. O'Brien, *Dublin Castle*, p.95.

66. Faulkner's *Dublin Journal*, 31 March 1807, p.2, col.1; The *Patriot*, 8 January 1822, p.3, col.2.

67. Dublin *Correspondent*, 7 January 1807, p.2, col.3.

68. Hardwicke to Addington, 22 July 1802, Hardwicke MSS, 35708/230.

69. Dublin *Evening Herald*, 26 June 1807, p.2, col.2.

70. Dublin *Evening Post*, 9 April 1807, p.2, col.3.

71. John Fane, Tenth Earl of Westmoreland, to Pitt, Public Record Office MSS, 30/9/331, f.253; Richard Grenville-Temple, Earl Temple, to Rutland, 1784, BM Add. MSS, 34418/383; Beresford, *Correspondence*, I, 73; Johnston, *Great Britain*, p.20.

72. Hardwicke to Addington, 22 July 1802; Hardwicke to Charles Yorke, 7 November 1803, Hardwicke MSS, 35772/21-23, 248-51; Hardwicke to Pitt, n. d.; Hardwicke to Addington, 22 July 1802; Hardwicke to Charles Yorke, 7 November 1803, 16 November 1803, 9 January 1804, September 1804, Hardwicke MSS, 35708/226-44; Hardwicke to Pitt, 2 November 1804, Hardwicke MSS, 35709/152-53; Hardwicke to Charles Yorke, 25 March 1804, Hardwicke MSS, 35705/204.

73. 1 *Hansard* XVII (1810), 513-30; Richmond to Bathurst, 27 November 1812, *Bathurst MSS*, pp.220-21; Aspinall, ed., *Later Correspondence of George III*, V, 600. Wellesley took the

post partly to restore his finances and did so; Arbuthnot to Peel, 6 July 1827, cited in Aspinall, *Formation,* p.254; Cornwallis to Ross, 18 April, 22 April, 7 May 1801, Cornwallis, *Correspondence,* III, 357-59.

74. Shawe to Knighton, 6 June 1826, printed in Aspinall, ed., *George IV,* III, 151.

75. *New Monthly Magazine,* XVI, 544-544-51; XVII, 193-200.

76. Dublin *Correspondent,* 12 March 1807, p.3, col.4; Dublin *Evening Post,* 5 April 1814, p.3, col.3; Dublin *Journal,* 31 December 1821, p.3, col.4; Dublin *Evening Post,* 21 May 1822, p.3, col.1.

77. Dublin *Evening Post,* 28 July 1814, p.3, cols. 3-4.

78. *Ibid.,* 18 March 1828, cited in Anglesey, *One-Leg,* p.192.

79. Dublin *Evening Herald,* 1 June 1807, p.2, col.2; 3 June 1807, p.2, col.2.

80. Shawe to Knighton, 19 April 1826, printed in Aspinall, ed., *George IV,* III, 146.

81. Cornwallis to Portland, 1799, in Robert Stewart, *Memoir and Correspondence of Viscount Castlereagh* (12 vols.; London, 1848-53), II, 373, 430; George Townshend, Fourth Viscount Sydney to George McCartney, 19 August 1769, Northern Ireland Public Record Office MSS, DOD/572/1; Johnston, *Great-Britain,* p.20.

82. Littlehales to Marsden, 5 September 1802, Dublin, State Paper Office, Official Papers, Second Series, Carton 539, no.290/3.

83. *Ibid.,* 8 September 1802, 11 September 1802, Dublin, State Paper Office, Official Papers, Second Series, Carton 539, no. 290/3.

84. *Ibid.,* 15 September 1802, Dublin, State Paper Office, Official Papers, Second Series, Carton 539, 290/3.

85. *Ibid.,* 17 September 1802, Dublin, State Paper Office, Official Papers, Second Series, Carton 539, No.290/3.

86. Hardwicke, memorandum of itinerary, 1802, Hardwicke MSS, 35736/49-125; Plowden, *Ireland,* I, 151.

87. See as examples: Bedford to Richmond, 8 April 1807; Richmond to Whitworth, 12 June – 6 August 1813; Whitworth to Richmond, 11 June – 1 August 1813, Richmond MSS, 72/1617, 68/1085-87, 69/1088-1092, 68/1108-1114; Northumberland to Peel, 2 February 1829, Peel MSS, 40327/14; Dublin *Evening Herald,* 27 August 1813, p.3, col.2; Dublin *Evening Post,* 9 October 1817, p.2, col.4; *Ibid.,* 29 December 1821, p.3, cols. 1-2.

88. McDowell, *Irish Administration,* pp. 53-54; Dublin, State Paper Office, Irish Privy Council Minutes, quoted in Gash, *Peel,* p.130.

89. Anglesey to Lamb, 2 March 1828, Plas Newydd MSS, Anglesey, *One-Leg,* p.192.

90. Anglesey, *One-Leg,* pp.216-17; Dublin *Evening Post,* 23 April 1807, p.2, col.2.

William Henry Paget, Marquess of Anglesey
Lord Lieutenant
February 1828–January 1829

Chapter 6
Law and Order

While we acted on the forbearing system it was perfectly wise... to forbear thoroughly; and when we adopt the interfering system, for the very same reason it will... be equally wise to interfere effectually.

Peel to Whitworth, 8 June, 1814

THE IRISH VICEROYALTY originated in the conquest of portions of Ireland by English arms, a conquest stoutly resisted from time to time. Gradually demonstrations of force gave way to instruments of social control familiar to England. Landlords staffed the county magistracy and government by due process prevailed in times of relative tranquility. Each spring, and sometimes more frequently, the parish vestry brought together the landed gentry, the established clergy, and the stalwart if sometimes impecunious Protestant tenantry. The vestry levied the annual cess, enforced local regulations, voted church supplies, raised recruits for the army, and implemented legislative directives. These "little parliaments" generally excluded Catholics and therefore reflected only a minority interest in most areas.

MILITARY RESOURCES

The army remained important. Ostensibly it protected Ireland from foreign intrusion; in fact it also assisted county authorities against indigenous discontent. Peel noted that without the army "the whole framework of civilised society would be threatened with dissolution," so great was popular antipathy to civilian authorities.[1] All this reserved to the viceroy an important role in Irish affairs. He was ultimately responsible for the army. He also directed the activities of the Irish militia. And as the head of the civil administration the viceroy controlled the normal executive and judicial apparatus.

Prior to 1800 the viceroy's relationship remained ill-defined, and this generated bitter controversy after the Act of Union. During the eighteenth century the Crown issued instructions through the Secretary of State for the Southern Department and the Lord Lieutenant, or through the Secretary of State for War and the Chief Secretary, who relayed instructions to the Lord Lieutenant. Through the commander-in-chief the viceroy could advise the King, but he made all appointments and arrangements personally.[2] From every point of view this system was unsatisfactory. Viceroys and Commanders-in-Chief competed for control of Irish military patronage and the army itself. This led to several bitter confrontations, and they increased in intensity as the Act of Union approached. Viceroys complained that their office would decay if deprived of control over military patronage. Army authorities alleged that viceregal patronage policies undermined the army's efficiency.[3] In part because the Commander-in-Chief and the viceroy clashed so bitterly between 1795 and 1797 Earl Cornwallis was given both offices in 1798. Thus combined, the two offices tended to take on more the military character. In 1799 the Civilian Undersecretary, Edward Cooke, went so far as to declare that Cornwallis had come to Ireland "as a military man to take command of the government" and that "he had nothing to do with the civil government."[4] Cornwallis was indeed identified with military affairs, and in 1798 Ireland was convulsed by rebellion. But the precedent was ominous, and after the Act of Union the offices of Lord Lieutenant and Commander-in-Chief were once more separated.[5]

In 1801 the contest resumed, but conditions became more complex. The Duke of York, brother to the King and Commander-in-Chief in Britain, interpreted the Act of Union to mean that his authority now extended to Ireland in the same fashion as it stood in Britain. Hardwicke and the trembling new Commander-in-Chief of the Irish Forces, General Meadows, hastily consulted each other. Hardwicke surrendered some prerogatives to Meadows in an effort to bolster Meadows' position and to parry York's demands.[6] York would accept nothing less than a full viceregal surrender, and Pelham rushed to assist the Duke. Patronage was the central consideration. Hardwicke was burdened by his lengthy "union engagements" list and complained to the Prime Minister that if the Duke of York's pretensions were upheld the whole network of promises made to secure approval of the Act of Union would be placed in jeopardy.[7] York in turn complained to the

King of Hardwicke's stubbornness.[8] York won the first round, and Hardwicke had to be content with control over minor offices and non-binding recommendations for the major ones.[9] But York's defects as Commander-in-Chief were notorious and when a mistress assumed responsibility for allocating some military patronage Parliament's patience was exhausted. These developments removed him as a contender on the Irish military patronage scene. This permitted the viceroy and the Irish Commander-in-Chief to battle between themselves. In this second theatre the viceroy enjoyed the advantage. Irish Commanders-in-Chief often verged on incompetence and Hardwicke took advantage of this to assume the offensive. He upbraided his brother Charles Yorke as Secretary for War for denying him intelligence on military plans for Ireland.[10] He intervened in Irish military matters, such as when he demanded improvements in living conditions in the barracks and payment to soldiers in solid currency. He protected his control over the Irish militia by undercutting the Duke of York's plans to raise regular troops from the Irish militia. Hardwicke advanced other proposals for more efficient use of the militia.[11] All this political skirmishing was eventually overtaken by more unfortunate events. Champions of Irish independence, led by Robert Emmet, staged an abortive uprising on 22 July 1803. The rising itself was tragicomic in scale and strategy, but it revealed fully Ireland's defective military situation. Samuel Marsden, the incumbent Military Undersecretary and purveyor of secret funds. apparently received warnings of the revolt but said nothing to Hardwicke until hours before Emmet's band attacked Dublin Castle. Hardwicke warned the Commander-in-Chief, who continued with plans to dine out and who neglected to shift troops from Phoenix Park to the city centre. Hardwicke ordered some modest countermeasures. Meanwhile, unknown to the Viceroy, the Army Ordnance had removed every cartridge from the Castle. Emmet's accomplices were subdued in a brief skirmish in which neither side covered itself with glory.

The shots died away. A battle of words followed. In Parliament Hardwicke was criticised for being unprepared. The ministry tried to cover its embarrassment by urging Parliament to grant the Viceroy extraordinary powers to suppress the rebellion.[12] But all this did not protect Hardwicke from some savage accusations. He responded that he had not been in the least surprised, that the insurrection had been easily suppressed, and that the incumbent Commander-in-Chief, General James Fox, was to blame for any shortcomings. Lady Hardwicke wrote to her friends that Fox was "infirm in mind and body" and a "stupid soul" protected by the Duke of York, who was "always jealous of his own authority". In an extraordinary betrayal of previous protestations, Hardwicke declared that he did not have jurisdiction over "the independent commander of the forces". All this augured disaster if a more serious uprising should visit Ireland.[13]

Either Hardwicke or Fox had to go. Fox was at length exiled to a Mediterranean command.[14] At a critical moment Hardwicke failed to demand that the office vacated by Fox be given to him. He asked Cornwallis to intervene so that the "undefined situation of Lord Lieutenant and Commander of the Forces could be treated by temperate men."[15] Instead, Whitehall despatched Sir William Shaw Cathcart, who negotiated an agreement which enhanced Hardwicke's jurisdiction but denied him the office itself.[16] Hardwicke's correspondence betrays no further problems.

In 1807 Richmond renewed efforts to be Commander-in-Chief as well as viceroy. He scheduled additional dress reviews and parades in Phoenix Park. He took the initiative in restoring discipline after an embryonic revolt among Irish units early in 1808. The revolt, according to Richmond, reflected intolerable conditions in the barracks. When the Commander-in-Chief resigned, Richmond secured the succession.[17] He was a military man himself, and he favoured rigorous disciplinary measures in the army. Indeed, he viewed the army as a regular instrument for law and order in Ireland.[18] The Catholic Committee, he once observed, was a para-military force to be crushed if necessary by the cavalry.[19]

During these years of war the militia played a subordinate role. In Ireland the militia was subject to regulations "so numerous, so complicated, and so much at variance with each other" as to obscure completely the parameters of viceregal authority.[20] Recruiting procedures were unsatisfactory: use of the ballot, purchasing substitutes, and reliance on parish bounties were all calculated to produce a large and unreliable corps for domestic service.[21] Catholics began to enter the lowest ranks late in the eighteenth century, but the upper ranks were reserved to gentlemen who in peacetime treated their appointments as social marks of approbation.

Observers divided sharply on the usefulness of the militia. Poorly trained and sometimes sullen troops, expensive to maintain and unreliable as guardians of the peace, were used only when the exigencies of war denuded Ireland of regular forces. Not surprisingly, news of the Peace of Amiens in 1801 prompted Pelham to urge on Hardwicke the advisability of dismantling the militia.[22] Recruitment was curtailed and the viceroy's jurisdiction contracted.[23] Hardwicke resisted rapid demobilisation, fearful of exacerbating Ireland's unemployment problem and of encouraging rebellious elements to renew their agitation. But in April 1802 he moved to revise and consolidate militia regulations and to reduce them to conformity to English legislation. Whitehall and Parliament showed little interest in this.[24] When war resumed in 1804 the militia was still unreformed, and an active market in the sale of commissions raised Hardwicke's ire.[25] Bounties failed to supply sufficient troops for the regular army, and the militia's responsibilities in Ireland necessarily increased again. The militia was directed to protect mail coaches, man the coastal defences, and ferret out distilleries. Ireland depended upon the militia as never before. Until 1814 both the militia and the army were employed on the Irish countryside.

At war's end Parliament agitated for reductions in both the army and the militia. The militia's virtual disbandment excited little opposition. Whitworth feared, like Hardwicke before him, that militiamen "would experience difficulty in procuring employment" and might react violently when mixed with those of the lower orders who were already "prone to licentious habits and insubordination to the laws." [26] Whitworth's arguments against reducing the size of the army were more substantial. At first he maintained that Ireland demanded a "strong and active policy and a commanding military establishment" of 40,000 troops.[27] Later, when warned that the army's role in domestic policing duties was one factor contributing to its low morale, Whitworth changed his mind and even encouraged some reductions.[28] In 1816 the Liverpool ministry placed a ceiling of 25,000 on troop strength in Ireland. Whitworth protested, and then acquiesced. After 1817 the army was again reduced in size.[29] By then new instruments of law and order were taking shape. They would carry Dublin Castle through the turbulent years of Catholic Emancipation.[30]

CIVIL AUTHORITIES

The army and the militia were both extraordinary devices for maintaining law and order. That they were employed so frequently underscores the seriousness of Ireland's problems in the early nineteenth century. But their use also betrayed the total inadequacy of "ordinary" instruments. Dublin Castle struggled against the excesses and incompetence of local authorities. Irate M.P.s denounced the entire system and provided numerous examples of the miscarriage of justice. The lower classes mastered the techniques of civil disobedience and a new breed of leader fanned Catholics' resentment. In all of this Viceroys vacilated between conciliation and coercion.

The ordinary mechanisms of law and order combined British precedents and Irish irregularities. At the base were the magistrates, drawn from the smaller landlords, wealthy Protestant tenants, some clergy of the Established Church, and in later years an occasional "responsible" Catholic. Commissions were traditionally awarded with little thought as to qualifications; patronage considerations were frequently decisive. Magistrates' powers were broad and loosely defined, but they did not include, unlike in England, responsibility for raising the militia. Above them were the sheriffs. They appointed the grand juries which laid county taxes. Their political influence was considerable; the recommendations often influenced allocation of local patronage, and at elections their role was sometimes notorious. Viceroys appointed them, and this often disturbed Parliament. Nonetheless, this patronage constituted viceroys' most effective method of controlling county officials.[31]

Central to local government was the parish vestry. The vestry system reflected the medieval practice of legitimatising local government by marrying it to the Established Church. In Ireland it served as a principal agency of social control, especially in rural areas, by combatting illegal distillation, supervising certain humanitarian functions, enforcing sabbatarian regulations, and even maintaining roads and public buildings. The Established clergy presided, and the vestry's functions were intimately identified with the Church of Ireland itself. This identification certainly helped to undermine the vestry's effectiveness in its efforts to govern those parishes which were heavily Catholic. Frequently the vestries compounded problems by ignoring their responsibilities or by allocating funds for the benefit of the small Protestant community alone. Parliament was shocked to uncover instances of disbursements for church expenses in parishes which had no church, or for church wardens and sextons who had never been appointed.[32] Many viceroys were aware of this widespread if relatively minor corruption, and therefore relied heavily on powerful county families to exercise some control over these "little parliaments".[33]

Viceroys also exercised direct control in certain instances. They possessed power to pardon, and use it to ameliorate the rather harsh sentences often meted out by the courts. Under terms of the Irish Convention Act of 1793 and subsequent martial law and insurrection acts viceroys could assume direct jurisdiction over disturbed regions. Recourse to these powers often prompted allegations of dictatorship by landlords who resented any assault on their local prerogatives. The records suggest, however, that such extraordinary prerogatives, when exercised by viceroys, often improved the tone of Irish local government. Local government in Ireland was a weak reed indeed, and perhaps the viceroys of the period resorted to extreme measures too infrequently. Certainly few of them felt comfortable in summoning these reserve powers. Hardwicke vowed in public and in private to rely on ordinary instruments of law and order when the insurrection of 1797-98 eventually subsided. As peace returned, however, Hardwicke began to hear of abuses attached to local authorities.[34] Thus when war with France resumed and caches of treasonable correspondence surfaced in Ireland Hardwicke repaired to the Privy Council to obtain limited authority to proclaim martial law. He did not request power to suspend habeas corpus.[35]

In the wake of Emmet's rebellion Hardwicke was roundly criticised for failing to use all the reserve powers at his disposal. Hardwicke responded that the insurrection had been suppressed easily enough without using them.[36] But the opposition introduced a motion in parliament to censure Hardwicke. It was defeated and the King somewhat unenthusiastically complimented Hardwicke on his conduct.[37] Hardwicke was thereupon voted additional powers.[38] Some of them, the viceroy observed, posed grave dangers if abused and he himself refused to countenance use of some of the severer provisions.[39] He would not, for instance, tolerate a long series of executions as mandated by the new legislation.[40] He circumvented parliament's intentions by declaring that the new powers had only a "prospective operation"; Emmet's accomplices could not be tried under them. London acquiesced.[41] Mass executions were avoided, and in those cases where capital punishment could not be avoided Hardwicke tried to ensure that some element of dignity and humanity be attached to the proceedings.[42] Hardwicke departed Ireland convinced that his conciliatory tone had contributed to peace after 1803. Even Henry Grattan, the great Irish nationalist and reliable critic of Britain's Irish policies, commended Hardwicke and Lord Redesdale. Had they been in office earlier, Grattan observed, the rebellion of 1797-98 would not have occurred.[43]

Bedford took Hardwicke's conciliatory policies a step further. Extraordinary powers, he believed, generated an extraordinary response, and imaginative government agents exaggerated symptoms of unrest when they prepared their voluminous reports.[44] His tenure was too brief to test his theory adequately. But even before he departed Dublin "threshers" were mounting a campaign of resistance to tithes, and agitation was severe enough to prompt the Grenville ministry to launch an investigation into the tithe problem. Bedford came under increasing pressure to apply the insurrection acts.[45] He refused.[46] Many landlords reacted angrily as Bedford appeared to be more interested in remaining popular with Catholics.[47] At length the landlords were mollified and Bedford permitted an insurrection bill to be drawn up. A generation would pass before another viceroy would dare to attempt to rule Ireland without recourse to extraordinary devices.

To Richmond harsh measures were essential. Critics claimed that he even found them agreeable. In the summer of 1807 Parliament approved an insurrection act designed to meet an outbreak of violence in rural parts of Munster and Connaught. Landlords responded enthusiastically; Dublin newspapers filled their pages with commendatory resolutions. Nevertheless, agitation continued to spread. Tipperary reported conditions worse than those of the great insurrection. Richmond advertised his determination to apply strong measures. Liverpool warned Richmond that conditions must "really exist" to warrant applying the acts lest the opposition in parliament be given ammunition sufficient to block passage of such legislation in the future.[48] Protection of life and property, Liverpool observed, was indeed the viceroy's primary responsibility, but liberty must not be sacrificed completely.[49] In Richmond's case this was advice well worth repeating, for his measures tended to be harsh. On another occasion Arthur Wellesley reminded Richmond of Bedford's forebearance and the "universal approbation" he derived because of it.[50] But Richmond also listened to contrary advice from landlords and local officials.[51] In 1809 the cabinet demanded from Richmond prior notice of every application of the Insurrection Act. Wellesley recorded perceptively the dangers involved in this arrangement. Richmond would receive valuable support now but in time it "might be construed into a virtual annihilation of the general authority before entrusted to the Lord Lieutenant to carry on the government of Ireland."[52]

Richmond also relied on the 1793 Convention Act, which if strictly construed virtually forbade assembly without prior authorisation. Richmond's administration quickly became identified with a generous resort to police powers. Nonetheless, in 1813 as in 1807, "the same spirit of outrage and tendency to unlawful combination still existed".[53] In Richmond's defence it should be recorded that many appreciated his personal qualities; in addition, the period covered the dark days when Napoleon's power waxed strongest in Europe.[54] And Richmond was not alone in failing to distinguish treason from reaction to oppression and economic privation. Like others he tended to accept alarmist reports at face value and allowed subordinates too free a hand. He purchased six years of tranquility while Catholic Ireland laid the groundwork for a new wave of agitation.

Whitworth was less sensitive to alarmist reports from the countryside. In late 1813 he refused to support renewal of the Insurrection Act. "It is not good," he lectured Sidmouth, "to get into the habit of suspending the constitution, and it weakens the effect of such suspension."[55] To Peel he expressed similar sentiments; only "irresistible necessity" should warrant application of police powers at the beginning of his government.[56] He was not sanguine, however, and even told Peel that a little revolt might not be unwelcome.[57] In June 1814 Whitworth took a harder line. On Peel's advice he outlawed the Catholic board founded by O'Connell and his associates.[58] Peel's philosophy made sense to Whitworth: "forebear thoroughly" when forebearing; "interfere effectually" when interfering.[59] The insurrection acts were applied to Tipperary in September 1814 and a tranquil interval followed.[60] No extraordinary measures were necessary in 1816.[61]

Peel accustomed Talbot to those principles of law and order which seemed to work successfully under Whitworth. But when Charles Grant replaced Peel he demanded that the Insurrection Act not be used. If Talbot was unhappy about this, Sidmouth was definitely alarmed, for he saw ominous implications (including a French invasion) in almost every turn of events.[62] Grant argued that the grievances of Irish peasants would not be removed by repressing the agitation resulting from them. But Talbot inclined to Sidmouth's point of view.[63]   In 1821 a widespread potato failure excited serious unrest in many rural areas. Grant and Talbot between them could not fashion an effective policy. Sidmouth took alarm. Talbot agreed that "a formidable and deep-seated conspiracy had been organised" in Ireland. Whitehall decided to despatch a new team to Dublin.

In December 1821 Wellesley found that "a general insurrection prevailed in the south of Ireland". Civil power had "ceased to have any authority and was incapable of affording protection". Priests had "lost all influence with the people". An entirely new system of law enforcement was called for.[64] Wellesley surveyed the Irish scene with his mind's eye set on India: the times called for a new philosophy as well as renewed vigor. Wellesley resented Protestants' monopoly of local and Castle offices; it aggravated Catholics' grievances and circumscribed viceregal power. He was also determined to fashion policy. Central to his approach was a conviction that only radical concessions to Catholics would bring peace to Ireland. But he also believed that this should be coupled with a suppression of lawlessness sufficient to convince Ireland that concessions did not result from pressure. Wellesley appreciated the need for substantial tithe and land reform and realised that this would not come quickly. If Protestants could be induced to see that politicised Catholics manipulated the Catholic tenantry to promote their own electoral ambitions, perhaps Protestants would eventually concede the needed economic reforms.

To educate the world to his point of view Wellesley began his administration by forwarding to London frequent, detailed and perceptive reports on the condition of Ireland.[65]   Wellesley's arguments in favour of timely concessions went unheeded; but Parliament inclined towards an insurrection act calculated to strengthen Wellesley's executive powers. Like Hardwicke and Whitworth, Wellesley at first shied away from soliciting permission from the legislature to use such drastic measures.[66] But even liberals urged them on Wellesley; his own despatches convinced them that he would use them wisely.[67] Peel and Goulburn pledged the ministry to limit the new powers to six months. The provisions of the act were unparalleled in their severity: magistrates could search without warrant; those violating a night-time curfew in proclaimed districts were subject to transportation. Even more severe punishments were reserved for those taking secret oaths and producing seditious publications; those suspected of

123

conspiracy could be retained without bail until August 1822. Importation of arms was restricted for seven years.[68]

While Parliament deliberated in early 1822 Ireland's unrest spread rapidly.[69] Limerick, Cork and Tipperary were convulsed by "banditti" even as Wellesley reached Dublin Wellesley feared that open rebellion would follow unless the Catholic clergy opposed it. Resistance to tithe payments spread to once peaceful areas. "Obedience to the law," Wellesley declared, was fundamental to "the happiness and prosperity of the people, whose condition must ever be miserable, while it shall be more safe to violate, than to obey the law." He managed in 1822 to ease the crisis by promoting Catholics' claims against an entrenched Protestant bureaucracy. He dismissed secret informers, whom he suspected were animated largely by private grudges. He gave increased weight to reports from local law officials, preferred transportation to capital punishment, and disciplined some overzealous magistrates. These measures retained for Wellesley a modicum of popularity. They did not end the unrest.[70]

In July Wellesley asked to have his emergency powers extended beyond August to the following April, and then to January 1823.[71] Goulburn wanted these powers made permanent; by 1825 Wellesley was inclined to support Goulburn on this point. He supplied additional reports on Ireland, but Peel resisted making the insurrection acts permanent. Wellesley was defeated; nonetheless he had relied on emergency powers for far more than half of his administration. During that period he succeeded in stimulating Catholics' expectations and in alarming Protestants. Rural agitation gradually subsided, but Daniel O'Connell can claim credit here, as even Wellesley ruefully admitted. Insurrection acts, with all the power they represented, counted for nothing against Protestants whose power was woven into the nation's legal, economic and social fabric. Nor did they relieve hunger or rectify tithe iniquities. Coercion might suppress symptoms; it never addressed causes.[72]

In one area these sombre observations can be qualified. Peel and Whitworth launched some important reforms in Ireland's arsenal of law enforcement instruments after 1814. At that time one observer claimed that the bench of magistrates was "filled by brewsters, maltsters, distillers and blackrent landlords." [73] This perhaps was so, but they constituted a loyal Protestant interest, and to suggest that reforms were necessary was offensive. It would be "very wounding to the feelings of many loyal good men,"

Saurin once observed, "to lose their seats on the bench, although they were the chief mischief makers."[74] Peel agreed and turned instead to the county constabulary. Under terms of legislation extracted from parliament in 1814 ("Peace Preservation Act") the Lord Lieutenant could appoint salaried constables in disturbed areas if the resident gentry's law enforcement functions proved inadequate to the needs. These reforms were not seriously tested until the tithe agitation of 1821-22.[75]

Early in 1822 Peel and Wellesley turned their attention to additional reforms. Parliament was invited to approve new legislation transferring from local authorities to the viceroy the right to choose Ireland's 4,500 constables and sub-constables.[76] Irish M.P.s, aware of the loss of patronage involved, opposed this reform, and parliament thereupon conceded to the viceroy only the power to appoint a few principal officials in each county.[77] Equally pressing was the need to improve the calibre of magistrates. Frequently magistrates declined to prosecute suspects out of fear of retaliation. Many were clearly incompetent and owed their positions to the venality of certain sheriffs. A complete revision of the magistracy lists was called for. As before, vested interests in large part frustrated this reform. But, as Wellesley noted, even the prospect of changing the magistracy system had a salutary effect on magistrates' behaviour.[78] This, coupled with several other changes which the viceroy could effect without resort to Parliament, considerably increased popular confidence in Irish justice.[79] In 1824 Wellesley reported to Liverpool that "every measure, insurrection act, police, tithe bill, revisions of the magistracy, petty sessions, better administration of the law, has succeeded beyond my most sanguine hopes."[80]

Wellesley could not foresee that the emergence of the Catholic emancipation issue in its most acute form would fundamentally alter the Irish legal and political landscape. A tightly disciplined popular movement, the threat of civil disobedience on a massive scale, could not be suppressed by traditional methods. Wellesley discovered this after 1824, and when he left Ireland many early reforms had been obscured. When Anglesey reached Dublin an ominous peace had settled over the country. In Ireland, however, peace was defined in its own way, as Anglesey wryly observed: "It begins, all is perfectly quiet here! Then the first two acts recorded are first, an atrocious murder, and secondly, a violent riot by seven persons who beat the police and terribly injured one of them!!!" Anglesey urged London to sponsor a large programme of public works, but this enlightened approach was rejected. Like his predecessors, Anglesey was soon reduced to issuing proclamations against seditious meetings and appealing for more troops. [81] Wellington despatched eight regiments and promised to commit "all the resources of the empire" against illegal assemblies. Anglesey was reluctant to pit troops against O'Connell's popular movement. Wellington was displeased: "Lord Anglesey and Lord Francis Leveson Gower have no notion how much they increase my difficulties with the King," he lamented to Peel, "by their unwillingness to carry in to execution the measures necessary to show that the government will preserve the peace of the country." [82]

Shortly thereafter Northumberland arrived equipped with even stronger police powers. He, like Anglesey, saw the futility of applying force against Daniel O'Connell's mass movement; he perceived the danger of widespread violence to be greatly exaggerated; indeed, in O'Connell's hands Ireland became ominously tranquil. Northumberland was fortunate; Catholic Emancipation soon followed. The next chapter in the history of Irish violence would start even as Northumberland surrendered his seals late in 1830. [83]

For three decades following the Act of Union viceregal powers in the area of law and order grew enormously. The insurrection acts were made almost permanent, and in attempting to counter O'Connell's Catholic Association the Irish Convention Act of 1793 was interpreted liberally. Two developments, however, weakened viceroys' powers. The ancient infrastructure of local government had deteriorated. The courts were overwhelmed by litigation resulting from tithe agitation, civil disturbance, and the assault on rackrents. The vestry system had collapsed in many areas. At the same time London exercised a steadily growing direction over the application of the viceroys' vast policy powers. The tension which resulted from conflicting objectives was nowhere demonstrated more clearly than in the Catholic Emancipation crisis.

1.1 *Hansard*, XXXII (22 February 1816), 928; H. W. Davies, "Catholic Emancipation," in *Cambridge Modern History* (John Edward Acton, Baron Acton, et. al., eds.; 1934 ed.) Cambridge: Cambridge University Press, X, 637-38.

2. Johnston, *Great Britain*, p.14.

3. *Ibid.*, pp.55-56.

4. Edward Cooke to Auckland, n. d.. [January 1799], Auckland, *Journals*, IV, 83-84.

5. Cornwallis, *Correspondence*, II, 357-58.

6. Hardwicke to Addington, 27 March 1801, Hardwicke MSS, 35707/5-6; Hardwicke to Portland, 11 June 1801, Hardwicke MSS, 35707/36-39.

7. MacDonagh, *Viceroy's Post-Bag*, pp.69-72.

8. Frederic, Duke of York, to George III, 20 August 1801, printed in Aspinall, ed., *Later Correspondence of George III*, III, 595-96.

9. Memorandum, n. d., Hardwicke MSS, 35771/89-97; Hardwicke to Abbot, 15 July 1801, Hardwicke MSS, 35771/31; Hardwicke to Charles Yorke, 20 August 1801, Hardwicke MSS, 35771/45; Colchester, *Diary*, quoted, in O'Brien, *Dublin Castle*, pp.85-89.

10. Hardwicke to Charles Yorke, 25 March, 13 June, 23 April 1804, Hardwicke MSS, 35705/204, 35706/59, 35705/264.

11. *Ibid.*, 29 March 1804, Hardwicke MSS, 35705/212.

12. Cabinet minute, 8 November 1803, Hardwicke MSS, 35704/98; Hardwicke to Charles Yorke, February 1804, Hardwicke MSS, 35705/39.

13. Pellew, *Sidmouth*, II, 207-11.

14. Redesdale to Abbot, 2 August 1803, Colchester, *Diary*, I, 436-37; Charles Lindsay to Samuel Marsden, 2 December 1803, Dublin, State Paper Office, Official Papers, Second Series, 325/160/5.

15. Hardwicke to Abbot, 8 August 1803, Colchester, *Diary*, I, 437.

16. Redesdale to Addington, 19 August 1803, Pellew, *Sidmouth*, II, 214; Addington to Hardwicke, 23 August, 1803, Pellew, *Sidmouth*, II, 215-16; *Annual Register*, *XLVI (1804)*, 22, 23.

17. Dublin *Evening Post*, 4 June 1807, p.3, col.1; Arthur Wellesley to Richmond, 21 March 1808, Richmond to Arthur Wellesley, 17 March, 19 March 1808, printed in Wellington, *Ireland*, pp.377-79; Arthur Wellesley to Littlehales, 19 February 1809, in in Wellington, *Ireland*, pp.580-81; Arthur Wellesley to Richmond, 28 March 1809, Richmond MSS, 58/62.

18. Richmond to Hawkesbury, 5 August 1808, Liverpool MSS, 38568/173.

19. Richmond to Peel, 13 March 1813, Parker, *Peel*, I, 79.

20. Hardwicke MSS, 35771, in Henry W. W. McAnally, *The Irish Militia, 1793-1818: a Social and Military Study* (Dublin: Clonmore and Reynolds, 1949), pp.173-74.

21. Hardwicke to Pelham, January 1802, in McAnally, *Militia*, pp.165-66.

22. Pelham to Hardwicke, October 1801, Hardwicke MSS, 35711/193.

23. Wickham to Castlereagh, November 1802, Castle Despatches, IV, 23/3/33 and 14/11/02, in McAnally, *Militia*, p.172.

24. *Annual Register*, 1804, p.71 (note); Hardwicke to Charles Yorke, 17 September 1803, Hardwicke MSS, 35775.

25. Clements Papers, in McAnally, *Militia*, p.188.

26. Whitworth to Sidmouth, 26 March 1816, Home Office MSS, 100/169.

27. Whitworth to Peel, 20 April 1814, Peel MSS, 40188, cited in Broeker, *Rural Disorder*, p.63; Whitworth to Sidmouth, 20 April 1814, Peel MSS, 40188, cited in Broeker, *Rural Disorder*, p.63.

28. Whitworth to Sidney, 19 January 1816, 20 February 1816, Public Record Office, Home Office MSS, 100/189; Peel to Whitworth, 18, 19, 20, 21 March 1816; Peel to Littlehales, 25, 26 March 1816; Peel to Gregory, 26 March 1816, Parker, *Peel*, I, 215-18; Whitworth to Sidmouth, 7 April 1816, Public Record Office, Home Office MSS, 100/189.

29. Broeker, *Rural Disorder*, p.98.

30. Wellesley to Peel, 23 June 1822, Peel MSS, 40324, cited in Broeker, *Rural Disorder*, p.122.

31. Hardwicke to Redesdale, 11 July 1803, Hardwicke MSS, 35772/205.

32. Dennis Browne to Peel, 6 March 1815, Peel MSS, 40217.

33. Hardwicke to Charles Yorke, 5 July 1803, Hardwicke MSS, 35772/210-11.

34. *Ibid.*

35. *Annual Register*, XLV (1803), 316.

36. Croker to Abbot, 25 July 1803, printed in Colchester, *Diary*, I, 434-36; Hardwicke to Abbot, 8 August 1803, printed in Colchester, *Diary*, I, 437; Warren-Buckeley to Hardwicke, 24 January 1804, MacDonagh, *Viceroy's Post-Bag*, p.448.

37. *Parliamentary History*, XXXVI, 1703-12 (11 August 1803); Pelham to George III, 26 July 1803, printed in Aspinall, ed., *Later Correspondence of George III*, IV, 144.

38. Charles Yorke to Hardwicke, 12 September 1803, Hardwicke MSS, 357 0/60; Hardwicke to Abbot, 8 August 1803, Colchester, *Diary*, I, 437.

39. *Annual Register*, XLV (1803), 300; XLVI (1804), 145.

40. *Ibid.*, XLVI (1804), 6.

41. Hardwicke to Abbot, 8 August 1803, Colchester, *Diary*, I, 437.

42. Hardwicke to Charles Yorke, 10 September 1803, Hardwicke MSS, 35770/50-57; Charles Yorke to Hardwicke, 12 August 1803, Hardwicke MSS, 35702/326.

43. Stephen L. Gwynn, *Henry Grattan and his Times* (Westport, Conn.: Greenwood Press, 1971), p.367.

44. Bedford to George John Spencer, Second Earl Spencer, 23 December 1806, Dublin, State Paper Office, IV, 16/2, cited in McDowell, *Public Opinion*, pp.51-52.

45. *Annual Register*, XLVIII (1806), 263; Buckingham to Grenville, 18 December 1806.

46. Bedford to Grenville, 19 December 1806; Grenville to Bedford, 29 December 1806, *Fortescue MSS*, VIII, 474-79, 480, 486-88.

47. Dublin *Correspondent*, 8 January 1807, p.1, col. 1.

48. Liverpool to Richmond, 8 October 1807, Richmond MSS, 59/162, 70/1343.

49. Liverpool to Richmond, 1 October 1807, Richmond MSS, 70/1344.

50. Arthur Wellesley to Richmond, 1 October 1807, printed in Wellington, *Ireland*, p.135.

51. Dublin *Correspondent*, 13 January 1808, p.1, col.3.

52. Arthur Wellesley to Sir Charles Saxton, 12 February 1809, printed in Wellington, *Ireland*, pp.570-71.

53. Dublin *Evening Post*, 2 October 1813, p.3, cols. 3-5.

54. *Annual Register*, LVIII (1816), 405-406.

55. Whitworth to Sidmouth, 13 December 1813, Public Record Office, Home Office MSS, 100/175.

56. Whitworth to Peel, 27 November 1813, Peel MSS, 40187, cited in Broeker, *Rural Disorder*, p.50.

57. *Ibid.*, 18 November 1813, Peel MSS, 40187.

58. *Annual Register*, LVI (1814), 217; Parker, *Peel*, I, 138.

59. Peel to Whitworth, 8 June 1814, Parker, *Peel*, I, 140.

60. Dublin *Evening Post*, 15 September 1814, p.3, col.3.

61. Report to Sidmouth, 5 June 1816, Public Record Office, Home Office MSS, 100/189; Broeker, *Rural Disorder*, p.95; Peel to Whitworth, 30 March 1816; Peel to Gregory, 2 April 1816, Parker, *Peel*, I, 219; Peel to Sidmouth, 17 August 1816, Parker, *Peel*, I, 288-89; *Annual Register*, XVIII (1816), 402-17.

62. Sidmouth to Peel, 1820, State Paper Office, IV, 13, 18, in McDowell, *Public Opinion*, pp.51-52.

63. "Extract of a Despatch from Earl Talbot to... Sidmouth," 1 December 1821, Wellesley MSS, 37298/94.

64. Shawe, "Sketch of Measures," printed in Aspinall, ed., *George IV*, III, 300.

65. Wellesley, drafts, 3, 11, 19, 27, 31 January 1822, National Library of Ireland MSS, 322; Wellesley to Sidmouth, n. d., Wellesley MSS, 37298/1-30; Wellesley to Peel, 3 January 1825, Wellesley MSS, 37303/29; Wellesley to Peel, 1 May 1822, National Library of Ireland MSS, 322.

66. Goulburn to Peel, 18 January 1822,

Peel MSS, 40328/7.

67. Peel to Goulburn, 24 January 1822, Peel MSS, 40328/13; Peel to Wellesley, 5 February 1822, Wellesley MSS, 37298/ 152; 2 *Hansard*, VI (1822), 104-50, 163-219.

68. *Statutes of the United Kingdom of Great Britain and Ireland*, 3 *George IV* 1822 (London, 1822), pp. 1-12, 15-23.

69. Col. Thornton to Lt. Col. Snell, in Goulburn MSS, acc. 319, 11/22; Wellesley to Peel, 31 January 1822, Wellesley MSS, 37298/123-24; Wellesley to Sidmouth, 3 January 1822, Wellesley MSS, 37298/7-12; The *Patriot*, 8 January 1822, p.2, col.4; Wellesley to Peel, 21 January 1822, Public Record Office, Home Office MSS 100/123; The *Patriot*, 21 February 1822, p.3, col.4.

70. Peel to Wellesley, 12 April 1822, Peel MSS, 40324; *Annual Register*, LXV (1823), pp.50-56 of the appendix. Goulburn to Wellesley, 25 March 1824, Wellesley MSS, 37302/237; Goulburn to Peel, 16 April 1824, Peel MSS, 40330/ 39-42.

71. Wellesley to Peel, 28 January 1825, Peel MSS, 37303.

72. Robert Peel, *Speeches... Delivered in the House of Commons* (4 vols.; London, 1853), I, 318; Wellesley to Peel, 28 January, 30 January 1825, Wellesley. MSS, 37307.

73. Thomas Flynn to Peel, 30 April 1816, Peel MSS, 40253.

74. William Saurin to Peel, 4 April 1816, Peel MSS, 40211.

75. Gash, *Peel*, pp.178-81; Parker, *Peel*, I, 140-49; Broeker, *Rural Disorder*, p.23.

76. Broeker, *Rural Disorder*, p.104; Peel to Wellesley, 12 April 1822, Wellesley MSS, 37299/54.

77. Wellesley to Goulburn, 16 June 1822, Goulburn MSS, Acc. 319, 11/22; *Annual Register*, LXIV (1822), 43-48; Broeker, *Rural Disorder*, pp.144-47; Wellesley to Liverpool, 22 November 1824, printed in C. D. Yonge, *The Life and Administration of Robert Banks Jenkinson, the Second Earl of Liverpool* (3 vols.; London, 1868), III, 312-13.

78. Whitworth to Sidmouth, 21 April 1814, Public Record Office, Home Office MSS, 100/177; McDowell, *Public Opinion*, p.70; Peel to Whitworth, 10 April 1816, printed in Parker, *Peel*, I, 223; Wellesley to Peel, 31 January 1822, National Library of Ireland, Wellesley MSS, 322; Wellesley to Peel, 29 January 1823, Public Record Office, Home Office MSS, 100/208; Broeker, *Rural Disorder*, p.151; McDowell, *Public Opinion*, p.81.

79. Lamb to Lansdowne, 3 August 1827, cited in Aspinall, *Formation*, pp.287-88.

80. Wellesley to Liverpool, 22 November 1824, cited in Yonge, *Liverpool*, III, 312-13.

81. Anglesey to Lamb, March 1828, quoted in Anglesey, *One-Leg*, p.190; Peel to Anglesey, 28 September 1828; Anglesey to Peel, 2 October 1828, Peel MSS, 40326/105, 139.

82. Anglesey to Wellington, 6 October 1828; Wellington to Anglesey, 10 October 1828, Wellington, *Despatches*, V, 112, 121; Anglesey to Lamb, 28 June 1828, Plas Newydd MSS, cited in Anglesey, *One-Leg*, p.200; Wellington to Peel, 5 November 1828, printed in Wellington, *Despatches*, V, 214; *Annual Register*, LXXI (1829), 8-9.

83. Northumberland to Peel, 14 July 1829, Peel MSS, 40327/34-38.

The R^t Honble. the Earl of NORTHUMBERLAND Lord Lieut.of
IRELAND 1764.

Hugh Percy, Duke of Northumberland
Lord Lieutenant
January 1829–December 1830

Chapter 7
Protestants and Catholics and the Viceregal System

No doubt the Duke of Richmond means well but much mischief is done by this system of clerical barter and so extensive a line of exchange; it sets every jobber to work, and draws down ridicule on the Church of Ireland by exhibiting a set of clerical jockeys in the Castle year whenever a government preferment becomes vacant...   *Warburton to Stuart, 2 April 1810*

CENTRAL TO ANY study of the governance of Ireland is the religious factor. Pitt hoped that the fusion of the British and Irish legislatures would ease denominational tensions in Ireland. In the larger forum, he theorised, the Irish Protestant classes would gain sufficient security to persuade them that Catholics too could share the advantages of full citizenship. This did not happen. The King's conscience and Protestant "ultras" resisted concessions to Catholics. Catholics in turn came to champion repeal of the Act of Union. A complicating factor was the role of the Church of Ireland, established by law but religious home to only one fifth of the nation's inhabitants. The Church was a great landlord and in addition received enormous revenues from a tithe on tillage. Church rents and the vexatious tithe identified it with the nation's economic and social problems.

British administration in Ireland rested on Dublin Castle, and to a lesser but still significant degree on the Church of Ireland. The tendency to identify Catholicism with Irish nationalism reinforced the official character of the established Church. The bishops and clergy also performed a wide range of civil functions in the early nineteenth century, and in parts of rural Ireland where landlords preferred the life of an absentee their services were crucial. Nonetheless, the Church of Ireland was too weak to contribute in a meaningful way to the stability of British rule. Successive viceroys were painfully aware of this, even when they reinforced the Church's problems by promoting unwholesome ecclesiastical patronage policies. The erastian system in retrospect benefited neither Church nor state.

CHURCH REFORM

The Church of Ireland was on Whitehall's mind when Hardwicke's instructions were framed in 1800: tithes; Catholic pressure for access to vestry meetings and graveyards; clerical residence; pastoral effectiveness; and the status of the Presbyterian communion were all adverted to. Hardwicke was enjoined to participate in Church functions.[1] The same instructions also made it clear that the Church of Ireland had long since surrendered much of its autonomy as the price for protection against Dissent and Catholicism.[2] During the reign of Charles I, Archbishop Laud and the viceroy Earl Strafford had injected viceregal influence into the ecclesiastical situation.[3] Later, when indifference cooled theological passions, Irish ecclesiastics became in effect officers of state: George Stone as Archbishop of Armagh from 1747 to 1765 virtually ruled Ireland for extended periods. His predecessor Hoadly was so political in his orientation that he "did not seem to have printed anything, even the customary sermon or two."[4] Not surprisingly, the eighteenth century Church failed in its mission to proselytise and indeed cast scorn on demonstrations of religious "enthusiasm". From time to time civil and ecclesiastical authorities upbraided each other for discouraging needed reforms within the Church. Often, however, other matters predominated: ecclesiastical patronage and tithes.

Ecclesiastical appointments had long been identified with larger political interests. Before the Reformation the papacy matched wits with the Normans and tried to blunt the Celtic tendency towards ecclesiastical autonomy. After 1535 viceroys laboured to reconcile the Irish Church to the principles of the English Reformation, although without much success. Under Charles I Strafford revamped the bench of bishops to promote Laud's "high church" policies and to counter Puritanism.[5] Finally the Hanoverians determined to nominate Englishmen to Ireland's highest ecclesiastical positions. This policy prompted some of Jonathan Swift's most ascerbic commentary. "The misfortune of having bishops perpetually from England" undermined morale among the Irish faithful, or so Swift alleged in 1725.[6] The Church of Ireland assumed a character more and more alien to the nation and more and more subservient to the state. Inevitably Church offices and properties were manipulated for political ends, and patronage irregularities assumed scandalous proportions.

One article of the Act of Union was designed to unite the English and Irish churches in "doctrine, worship, discipline and government". This formula was intended to eliminate nationality considerations in ecclesiastical appointments, restore confidence among Irish Anglicans by grafting the beleaguered minority establishment to England's healthy stock, and to expose Irish dioceses to English reformers. And indeed, the impact was dramatic, but entirely unanticipated. "Union engagements" included some thirty pledges to grant important Church positions to government supporters. This undermined chances to base many promotions on merit. Within the Church itself revulsion against patronage scandals associated with "Union engagements" finally prompted demands for reform. The King aided this impulse by placing in the Irish primacy a man whose high standards and independent views were destined to vex and challenge Castle policies for twenty years.

The debate between Church and Castle over patronage policies began in earnest in 1800. Hardwicke and the new Primate, William Stuart, arrived in Ireland almost simultaneously. Stuart was one of the numerous progeny of George III's onetime intimate friend, Lord Bute. He was also, until 1800, bishop of the small see of Saint David's in Wales. Pitt wanted the primacy placed at his disposal; no opportunity should be missed to relieve the pressure of "union engagements". But the King replied that the appointment was "essential to the quiet of the Irish Established Church."[7] Stuart's shy exterior camouflaged a strong commitment to ecclesiastical reform, as Hardwicke realised in implementing "union engagements".[8] At immediate issue was the vacant bishopric of Kilmore. Hardwicke was hard pressed to cope with the clamour of those whose support had helped to extinguish the Irish parliament.[9] The Ulster diocese of Kilmore, with its ample revenues and properties, was vacant. At London's instigation Hardwicke nominated George de la Poer Beresford, Bishop of Clonfert and son of John Beresford, whose political influence had earned him the sobriquet "King of Ireland". Stuart investigated Bishop Beresford's background and on 27 November 1801 declared him to be a "profligate" character. Moreover, Stuart alleged, two other bishops in Ulster were "reported to be the most profligate men in Europe" and the Church in Ulster would not likely survive the appointment of a third.[10] Hardwicke was shocked, but he feared the Beresford family's anger more than the

Primate's threat to resign, "extraordinary and unprecedented" as this would be.[11]   Bishop Beresford entered Kilmore. Stuart declined to resign but retired to Armagh to brood over the King's failure to support him.[12]

Dublin Castle was wonderfully alarmed: Stuart had broken with a tradition of ecclesiastical support for the viceroy's measures. His spirit of independence was bound to cheer Catholics and to quicken the spirit of criticism within the Church. For two years Stuart remained aloof. In 1803 Hardwicke was pressed by powerful Irish families, not excluding the Beresfords, to favour each with the vacancy at Clogher, one of Ireland's wealthiest dioceses.[13]   Stuart broke his silence, condemned the nominees and their families, and raised a sympathetic response in England. Through Lord Hawkesbury Pitt agreed that too little attention had been paid "to the purity and respectability" of the bench.[14] Hardwicke was also pleased to see that Whitehall was now aware of the pernicious consequences of "union engagements".[15] Lay magnates must be persuaded that the "bench is not to be taken by storm".[16]   Burying old differences, Hardwicke urged Stuart to abandon his isolation and he pledged to refer to the Primate all cases of ecclesiastical preferment where no candidate held an irrefutable claim.[17]

A spirit of contrived amity prevailed thereafter. Bedford tried to gratify Stuart by pledging his administration to Church reform under Stuart's leadership. Richmond dedicated himself to observe more stringent standards in dispensing ecclesiastical preferment. No commitments would be made until the office was "actually vacant," a far cry from the prevailing practice to pledge major offices far into the future.[18]   No plans would be made to use a vacancy on the bench as on occasion to translate a large number of bishops from one see to another. Due respect would be shown for merit rather than political clout.[19] At first Richmond frequently consulted Stuart and avoided unedifying ecclesiastical promotions.[20] By 1810, however, Richmond found political pressures unbearable. In Dublin some "Union engagements" remained unsatisfied. In London the ministry was weak and it urged Richmond to conciliate as many Irish M.P.s as possible. Richmond thereupon devised a series of promotions and translations involving a dozen ecclesiastical preferments. London acquiesced. Stuart got wind of Richmond's plan from various bishops, and he advised Richmond that their language was couched in terms "which I do not think proper to repeat but which is strongly expressive of their feelings. Indeed," Stuart added, "it is a very disagreeable duty to state to your Grace what I must shortly state to the public, that in my opinion, the Church establishment cannot subsist under its present management." [21] Stuart then lashed out at one of the nominees, attaching to him a "history of fraud and absenteeism."

Richmond was stunned. He pleaded ignorance of the foibles of his nominees. He eventually recovered enough to attribute his imperfect knowledge to Stuart's solitary habits; he had not resided in Dublin three days in three years, and during all that time it was impossible "to attend the Parliamentary interest" without causing some problems for the Church. Stuart was not to be mollified:

I have asked, and certainly asked in vain, that the Church should not be degraded and ruined by placing in one of the most important sees in Ireland [Waterford] a man confessedly of bad character and whose positive guilt I have declared myself ready to prove. I ask that the patronage of the Crown should not be bartered, but freely given as the patronage of the Crown is given by English ministers. How far bartering preferment in the gift of the Crown is constitutional is for Parliament to decide; but this practice... is prejudicial to the morals, the character, and even the happiness of the clergy. [22]

When Peel became Chief Secretary in 1812 Richmond was glad to surrender almost all responsibility for distribution of ecclesiastical patronage. Whitworth also acquiesced. Peel's correspondence reflects a high level of conscientiousness in matching qualified clerics with vacant preferment. His ability to scold aristocrats and censor bishops without exciting hostility supplied many of Richmond's earlier deficiencies. But when Peel surrendered his responsibilities much remained to be done. Talbot intended no criticism of Peel (and Whitworth) in observing in 1818 that "the whole system of Church preferment as conducted, or rather as is wished it be conducted here, is disgraceful." [23]

Wellesley took a personal but largely unsympathetic interest in the Church. He approved Peel's "reformist tone".[24] Indeed, he went further in his opposition to importing Englishmen as bishops, and in time to influence the succession to the primacy at Armagh and the archdiocese of Cashel. Both of these became vacant in 1822, when Stuart accidentally poisoned himself and Charles Broderick of Cashel succumbed to his ailments. Wellesley lobbied successfully to place an Irishman in the primacy. London opposed this, then relented, but insisted all the while that an Englishman be sent to Cashel. Stuart could rest satisfied that there now existed a group of episcopal reformers prepared to carry on his own work. To be sure, there remained much to do. In 1822 one ecclesiastic unable to secure an attractive place by legitimate methods threatened to make public a chronicle listing abuses in Church patronage during the previous forty years. Goulburn admitted that the manuscript reflected "infinite discredit on the Church and much on the government". Goulburn resisted the author's bid for a lucrative preferment but paid £300 for the scandalous history.[25]

Ironically, Wellesley himself tested the strength of the reform movement most seriously of all. His brother Gerald wanted to be a bishop; three brothers had gained peerages by virtue of accomplishments in other fields and a fourth would soon do so. In 1807 Arthur Wellesley had tried and failed to make Gerald a bishop.[26] Now the Marquess was prepared to tie a bid to a declaration that as viceroy he could make whatever appointments he wished.[27] Liverpool wrote a long letter disputing vigorously Wellesley's pretensions and his brother's fitness for the bench. Wellesley and Wellington fell silent.[28] Liverpool's warnings as to the dangers posed to the Church by unconscionable patronage politics were soon fulfilled. After 1830 the Whigs disendowed the more lucrative benefices. This reduced sharply the amount of ecclesiastical patronage available to the viceroy. The era of "radical" reform within the Church had now begun.

TITHES

When not distracted by patronage matters, viceroys were invited to weigh the need for structural reform and spiritual renewal in the Church of Ireland. Until 1830 the most important single issue was tithes. On the basis of pronouncements ratified by Church councils in the twelfth century the tithe was defined as a tax on the renewal annual produce of the land. After the Reformation the Established Church gradually pre-empted tithe rights. In the confusion, many tithes fell into the hands of laymen or the Crown.[29] After 1660 the Crown moved to restore to the Church tithe income which had come into its own hands, and to press landlords to follow suit. As agriculture expanded ecclesiastical revenues advanced steadily, so much so that in 1735 the Irish House of Commons by a patently illegal device removed pasture lands from tithe jurisdiction. This reflected Protestant landlords' resentment against an ecclesiastical institution distinguished more by its wealth than its zeal. Nonetheless, by 1800 a rapidly expanding rural population and the resulting increase in tillage swelled tithe revenues once more. But now peasants, pushed to a subsistence level by shrinkage of their tenant holdings, joined many landlords in condemning the tithe.

And indeed the situation was serious. The tithe was difficult to collect and uneven in its levy. Proctors assessed the value of crops, sometimes established arbitrary amounts, and retained for themselves everything above what the clergy had agreed beforehand was their due. From county to county different items were subject to tithe. Because the clergy could not dispose easily of tithes paid in kind, commutation to a money payment often took place, and the tithe was discounted at varying rates. But worst of all, as more peasants crowded the land and as rackrents rose, tenant resistance intensified. Sometimes it was discreetly encouraged by landlords themselves.

Many observers were amazed that such a tax could survive. But nothing proved sufficient to undercut Church arguments that the tithe was an inalienable property right. The Irish administration was reluctant to address so volatile an issue. Few viceroys were equipped to master the complexities of the tithe; fewer believed any viable alternatives to the existing system could be found. Hardwicke's correspondence refers rarely to the subject. Bedford was drawn into a short but intensive study when tithe resistance spread in 1806.[30] He seems to have been prepared to recommend some dramatic reforms, including conversion of tithes to a tax on landlords.[31] Richmond, too, attempted to grapple with the problem. He was soon dismayed by its complexity and was dissuaded from further work when agitation subsided. Until agricultural prices declined after 1815 successive viceroys could afford to ignore the tithe issue.

By the time Wellesley reached Dublin tithes had emerged as a central issue. Wellesley's determination to refurbish his reputation as a decisive reformer prompted him to study the Irish tithe problem even prior to his appointment.[32] Talbot's final days as viceroy were marred by several savage riots. Wellesley immediately consulted knowledgeable Irish observers as to what should be done. By late February 1822 Wellesley was ready with a reform plan of his own. The initiative was timely, because in London the ministry had concluded reluctantly that only an investigatory commission would blunt demands for immediate and radical tithe reform. Goulburn was forced to pledge the ministry to submit substantive reform legislation the following year and to offer immediately some interim palliatives.[33] Wellesley himself did not resume work on the tithe issue until autumn. Meanwhile Goulburn proposed that the clergy be encouraged to set tithe rates for a twenty-one year period. This would at least eliminate the tithe "proctors" who set the assessment each year and against whom the tenants directed much of their anger. Goulburn refused to contemplate the use of force against those clergy who refused to co-operate; nonetheless, Church leaders rose in unison to defend the sanctity of private property. And many Irish land-lords, rather belatedly alarmed at the assault on private property which tithe reform seemed to imply, began to condemn the Liverpool ministry.[34]

All of this intimidated Goulburn and Peel, and Wellington and Wellesley-Pole warned their brother in Dublin that no tithe reform plan would work.[35] But Wellesley's discussions with Irish observers furnished ample evidence that without reform the countryside might remain in a state of perpetual agitation. His considered plan, therefore, called for a compulsory, permanent and uniform commutation to a money payment assessed on landowners rather than on tenants. Commutation agreements would be valid for twenty-one years, the rates being revised every seven years to reflect the average annual value of agricultural production during the preceding seven years. The vestries would serve as a forum for negotiating settlements; compulsory government arbitration would be supplied if necessary.[36]

In retrospect Wellesley's plan was entirely appropriate to Ireland's requirements.[37] It was pragmatic, fair, compulsory. But Liverpool shied away from the prospect of compulsion and the Protestant clergy and laity, as already noted, considered it entirely prejudicial to their interests. In 1823 Goulburn introduced a tithe bill which reflected most of Wellesley's proposals, but stripped of the provision for compulsion. As enacted it proved inadequate, as did a slightly stronger measure approved in 1824. For several years dramatic progress in establishing commutation agreements in Ireland prompted predictions that the tithe problem would gradually disappear. Wellesley himself took a large measure of credit for this interval of rural peace which marked the closing years of his administration.[38] He was entitled to do so, for his detailed analyses, fruitful interviews with suspicious churchmen, and active interest in seeing tithe agreement concluded contributed substantially to the success of the 1823 and 1824 measures. Studies of the period have tended to discount his contributions in this area, in part because when tithe agitation flared again the lack of compulsory arbitration provisions meant that the earlier measures had never been applied in the most distressed districts. Finally in 1838 the tithe problem would be settled by converting the tithe to a tax on landlords' properties. Compulsion was introduced. Wellesley's proposals were vindicated.

CLERICAL ABSENTEEISM AND NEGLECT

No less controversial was the debate on proposals to increase the pastoral effectiveness of the established Church. Archbishop Stuart was not alone in describing the Church as one of the most anomalous ecclesiastical institutions in the world. In many respects the problems of the Church reflected centuries of war, unrest, religious controversy, and simple neglect. From time to time viceroys undertook to purge the Church of abuses. Strafford was one of these; his assessment in the 1630s of what was wrong with the Church of Ireland was echoed by many observers for two centuries. The "patient," he observed, "suffered from the effects of an unreverenced clergy, the lay appropriation of ecclesiastical property, ruined churches, and absentee vicars."[39] After 1660 Charles II urged his viceroys to superintend the recovery of the established Church. Too often government interference raised the clergy's political and not its pastoral effectiveness. In 1715 Archbishop King observed that "the diligence, piety, humility and prudent management of the clergy when they had nothing else to trust proved much stronger motives to gain the people than the favour of the government which put the clergy on other methods and made them odious to the people."[40] Perhaps this attitude explains the tendency of many viceroys during the eighteenth century simply to ignore the Church. By 1800 the need for reform was greater than ever, because voices of protest were much stronger.

The Act of Union provided a suitable occasion for taking a new look at the Church of Ireland. Most obvious to observers was the misapplication of revenues: many benefices received enormous incomes, and yet the Church could not generate sufficient revenues to build new churches and clerical residences, to improve schools, and to increase salaries in certain deprived parishes. One reason given for this institutional poverty was the failure of beneficial clergymen to contribute their first year's income to the Board of First Fruits. The legal obligation was unclear because no effort had been made to reassess the value of Irish benefices since the Reformation. Many bishops and clergy therefore satisfied the law by contributing the sum appropriate three hundred years earlier. Others paid nothing at all. Over the years churches and glebe houses had been allowed to decay. By 1800 hundreds of parishes (and unions of parishes) never saw a Protestant clergyman.

This scandalous condition led George III to urge Hardwicke to enforce clerical residence more vigorously.[41] The viceroy duly obliged, but without facilities for residence and preaching, and without a congregation to listen, clergymen could not be forced to reside in these neglected jurisdictions. Unless Parliament took the initiative, therefore, little could be accomplished.[42] Many churchmen, including the reforming element, feared that this would lead to radical changes and even to secularisation of ecclesiastical properties.[43] Hardwicke was reluctant to deal with Stuart more frequently than was absolutely necessary, and was glad enough to leave Ireland before the question of Irish Church reform attracted wider attention.

But problems of such magnitude could not be postponed indefinitely. The Church inadvertently accelerated the pace by applying to the united parliament for funds to build churches and glebe houses. Parliament responded with a grant and with an investigation of the Church of Ireland's finances, clerical residence, and pastoral effectiveness.[44] The bishops were permitted to supervise the inquiry, and carried out their responsibilities so inefficiently that a second inquiry followed. Stuart took charge of this one.[45] Despite the archbishop's best efforts the reports obscured many anomalies. A modest Church reform law was enacted in 1808.[50] Conservatives within and without the Church rejoiced that a more thorough-going assault had been parried. A few perceptive bishops agreed with Thomas O'Beirne, Bishop of Meath, that piecemeal reform would never do: "whether our ruin shall be gradual, or accomplished at one blow, is the only difference."[47]

Until 1820 the Church of Ireland busied itself with such in-house reforms still possible in the face of clerical resistance, widespread episcopal indifference, and Dublin Castle's refusal to involve itself in this sensitive area. Leading churchmen sounded

140

the alarm periodically against "that torrent" of reform "which would destroy the landmarks of all property" and bring on "revolutionary confiscation".[48] Wellesley threatened to support reforms but reserved his efforts for the tithe question. The Church of Ireland was therefore left exposed to the prospect of radical reform at some future date.

It came soon: by the Church Reform Act of 1834 the state took charge of ecclesiastical revenues, sharply reduced the number of dioceses, revamped clerical incomes, enforced constant residence and removed the Church of Ireland from areas where it had few adherents.

CATHOLIC RELIEF

The erastian system bound together the Church of Ireland and Dublin Castle. During most of the eighteenth century this alliance kept in check the Roman Catholic Church. By 1800, however, Catholicism had assumed the initiative, inured as it was to hardships and persecution, wed to poverty when its resources were confiscated, and sustained by a devout clergy drawn from the peasantry themselves. As the ruling caste lost its stomach for perpetual repression the penal codes weakened. After 1800 Dublin Castle could no longer avoid facing the question of how to handle renascent Catholicism, and how far the entrenched Protestant interest would permit this to go.

Hardwicke adopted a modestly conciliatory policy. He urged London to admit Catholics to full political rights. He moved slowly, making no effort to undermine Protestant influence in the militia and yeomanry, or in local government. He refused to recognise the Catholic hierarchy's pretensions but he did enlighten Pitt as to his conversations with prominent Catholic laymen. In the wake of Emmet's rebellion perhaps this was as much as the ascendancy could tolerate. After returning to England he strongly supported Catholic emancipation and urged Parliament to approve the necessary concessions. His advice was ignored. Bedford's sympathy towards Catholics reflected the attitude of the entire Grenville ministry. Grenville proposed to admit Catholics to the militia and to permit them to form separate units.[49] Bedford feared that this might alarm Protestants and promote "a premature discussion" of Catholic claims. Grenville persisted nonetheless, and Bedford was instructed to consult prominent Catholics and to begin recruiting immediately. Response to this invitation encouraged Grenville to prepare a bill to permit Catholics to hold commissions. In Ireland Catholics petititioned in favour of the bill and Grenville advised Bedford to discourage such demonstrations of support. Bedford advised Grenville that this would simply stimulate increased Catholic exertions. Now that the bill had been prepared, Bedford proceeded to take an uncompromising line, despite Grenville's attempts to hold him back. And when the King saw fit to resist the bill, Bedford proclaimed his intention to resign on the grounds that withholding concessions to Catholics would make Ireland impossible to govern. Despite Grenville's attempts at moderation, the ministry collapsed. Bedford retired into obscurity; it proved to be the end of his brief career of public service.[50]

Richmond was far from sympathetic to Catholics. He constantly urged the cabinet to refuse all concessions, and in September 1809 he refused to remain in Dublin without "a direct explanation that the religious laws of Ireland are not to be altered."[51] The strategy succeeded. In May 1812, when Perceval was assassinated by a disappointed office-seeker, Richmond reacted with alarm to rumours that the cabinet might be reconstructed on a platform of Catholic relief. Richmond penned a series of letters designed to meet each new rumour with a devastating rebuke. On 22 June the Chief Secretary, Wellesley-Pole, announced his own conversion to the Catholic cause and resigned. Richmond warned that concessions would bring rebellion. The Marquess Wellesley and Canning failed in their attempt to form a ministry and Liverpool launched his lengthy tenure as prime minister on the basis of treating the Catholic issue as an "open question".[52]

Richmond responded by urging his beliefs even more forcefully. He recommended disenfranchisement of the forty shilling freeholders, even at the risk of a Catholic revolt. Liverpool opposed this politely. In March 1813 the House of Commons passed a resolution urging the ministry to consider granting relief to Catholics. Richmond promptly predicted revolt in Ireland. "We shall probably have a little fighting," he told Peel, "but that is not of much consequence. We shall lose a few valuable lives, and hang a good many that richly deserve it."[53] Such insensitivity was also reflected in Richmond's Castle policies. In 1807, when the Portland ministry reduced the annual grant to the Catholic seminary at Maynooth, Richmond exasperbated affairs by nominating for the Privy Council a vitriolic Orange partisan,

142

Patrick Duigenan. Canning and other pro-Catholic leaders who had accepted the Maynooth reduction in order to help bring harmony to the Cabinet were deeply angered.[54] Richmond was warned to be more circumspect. In 1810 the viceroy determined to harrass a committee organised to press Catholic claims in Parliament "with or without Cabinet approval". His efforts to identify and capture alleged subversive agents failed.[55] The next year he forbade Lord Fingall and the Catholic committee from sponsoring a public meeting. His castle staff supported this initiative, and Fingall acquiesced. But the cabinet "was so much shaken by the unexpected zeal and independence of their colleagues in Dublin" that Richmond was again strongly admonished. Richmond therefore permitted a meeting in 1812. But he advised Peel "most strongly nothing be granted to them, for nothing that could be given would satisfy them".[56] In a sense Richmond was vindicated: his own intransigence encouraged Catholics to follow the more militant line espoused by Daniel O'Connell.

In Catholics' eyes Whitworth inevitably benefited by any comparison with Richmond. The *Dublin Post* observed that while Whitworth could not concede Catholics more liberties than his predecessor he could distribute existing rights more equitably.[57] Whitworth's mild temperament suggested that he would pursue this policy, even though O'Connell's Board, "a combination of vice and folly," alarmed him. He acted only when London authorised him to do so, and after intense lobbying secured indirect sanction from the Cabinet for his policies.[58] The Board was suppressed and because of subsiding interest in the Catholic issue Whitworth closed his viceregal tenure on a peaceful note. He observed, nonetheless, that eventually Parliament must succumb to Catholic pressure.

Catholics' quiescence continued under Talbot; the presence of the pro-Catholic Grant was one reason. Of course Wellesley's appointment was widely applauded in Catholic circles. Four decades earlier he had been among the first to invite Catholics to join the Volunteer corps. In 1809 he joined the Perceval ministry after insisting that the ministry keep open the Catholic issue. He strongly supported concessions in 1812 and attempted to forge a ministry based on that principle.[59] Despite this, the terms under which he accepted office in 1821 insured that he could do relatively little to meet Catholics' expectations: Wellesley vowed to support the laws, not to change them.[60] For Catholics, nonetheless, even-handed justice was a considerable improvement, and many Protestants reacted with alarm. Wellesley tried to interpose between Catholic extremists and Protestant enthusiasts a third group of Protestants willing to make concessions to Catholics' claims.[61] It failed. While justifying ultra-Protestants' worst fears, Wellesley's reforms fell far short of Catholics' expectations. Every viceregal gesture was amplified by "a community of information and gossip".[62] O'Connell took the lead in making Wellesley's life uncomfortable. He relayed reports of illegal societies to the Castle and offered to protect the viceroy against the Protestant party. Wellesley's refusals only excited more suspicion.[63]

Wellesley soon had to face something more concrete than simply a climate of suspicion. In 1823 O'Connell launched Ireland's first political mass movement based on adequate financial resources, an efficient local organisation, and a simple, attractive ideology. Earlier than most other observers, Wellesley measured the true significance of the new movement. In June 1823 he asked London for powers to suppress it. Peel replied that parliament would not support special legislation against so insignificant a body and held that existing powers were quite sufficient. Wellesley decided simply to monitor the new Catholic Association.[64] His long reports were invaluable to London for in them he "was finally able to separate the activities of the agrarian secret societies from those of the Association". This in turn enabled Dublin Castle and the Cabinet "to drop their military preparations and concentrate on less spectacular methods of breaking the power of O'Connell and his organisation". At the same time Wellesley satisfied himself that O'Connell had so adroitly constructed the Catholic Association that it violated no existing legislation.[65]

In October 1824 Peel began to see the wisdom of new legislative powers. The growth of receipts from the "Catholic rent" was ominous. O'Connell's speech praising Bolivar as the type of hero Ireland required embarrassed even Canning. Wellesley gallantly declared the next move to be up to London; he "had not shrunk from vigorous measures"; let others who held "a different view of the danger" plan the next move. Goulburn and Peel were not humoured at Wellesley's ploy; "on this as on all other occasions of difficulty Wellesley was always the first to impute the difficulty to others".[66] Peel asked Wellesley to submit a proposal for parliament's consideration. Plunket did so but Wellesley, with an eye to Catholic reaction, refused to recommend it formally. Peel was angered at Wellesley's apparent unwillingness to share the blame if the bill proved unpopular.[67] Wellesley pledged to be more co-operative but called for a full inquiry first. Peel insisted that no time be wasted.[68] On 10 February 1825 he introduced legislation to suppress the Association. It was approved quickly. Wellesley now had his "Law Against Unlawful Societies".

Wellesley refused to use the law. He contended that legal proceedings had come too late. A Protestant jury had already embarrassed Wellesley and Plunket by denying O'Connell's Bolivar speech was treasonous. Such juries, Wellesley was certain, would use the new law to embarrass him further. Wellesley proclaimed to Plunket a policy of "firmness, calmness, perseverance, and (for the present) steady inaction". In Parliament a new bid to relieve Catholics of their disabilities failed; Wellesley waxed eloquent and fatalistic, looking "with a humble but steadfast confidence" to his "final reward".[69] When Sheil chastised the Duke of York for his ultra-Protestantism, Wellesley resisted London's demands to prosecute Sheil for libel. Peel's unhappiness was complete; Wellesley's government was satisfied to remain "a quiet spectator of the increasing evil," too much afraid of failure.[70] Plunket admitted the truth of this, but also urged Canning to persuade the cabinet that prosecution would simply strengthen O'Connell's mass movement.[71] Indeed, Wellesley suggested that he initiate private contacts with O'Connell, a device which Goulburn held would make an illegal society legal.[72]

All the while the Catholic Association advanced from triumph to triumph. After passage of the "Unlawful Societies Act" O'Connell simply altered the technicalities and resumed its legislation. Wellesley was glad enough to demonstrate a sympathy for the Catholic cause by declaring that O'Connell's clever tactics made prosecution impossible.

Wellesley's policy towards the Orange Lodges was equally difficult. On 1 July 1822 O'Connell complained that Wellesley was willing to use the insurrection acts only against Catholics; would the viceroy interdict celebrations commemorating King William's birthday? Wellesley did not, but he vowed to cancel the November festivities commemorating Guy Fawkes. Peel objected.[73] The Castle's legal advisors supported Wellesley and Wellesley thereupon prohibited decoration of King William's statue.[74] Some Orange Lodge enthusiasts responded with the famous "Bottle Riot" when Wellesley went in state to the theatre in December. Goulburn saw Wellesley the Monday following this Friday evening episode. He told Peel that Wellesley remained "in a state of great excitation, announcing in the most direct and explicit terms" that this was "part of a systematic plan to murder him."[75] Wellesley's overreaction made him look ludicrous in London, but in Dublin Orange Lodges suffered a loss of membership. They moderated their celebrations.

Almost as notorious were Wellesley's confrontations with an Irish clergyman named Harcourt Lees, a baronet with vigorous anti-Catholic instincts. He pamphleteered for three years against Wellesley and his pro-Catholic sentiments and at length confronted the viceroy at a Dublin ball. On this occasion "the most noble and puissant Marquis shot his fine and indignant eyes into the soul" of the clergyman. Harcourt Lees, "blending the grin of an ostler with the acrimony of a divine," treated Wellesley with "jocular disdain". Dublin buzzed for weeks. Harcourt Lees went on to write ever more vituperative pamphlets.

How significant was Wellesley's role in the last stages of the Catholic emancipation process? Few historians have been generous with their compliments. But one of the most knowledgeable observers has written that "while Fitzwilliam and Bedford accomplished nothing but retained their popularity, Wellesley, a more able man, accomplished a good deal at the expense of his popularity.... He perhaps understood that the one solid benefit he could offer Catholics was to eliminate Orange influence at the Castle".[76] By cultivating what he called the "respectable" Catholic interest he introduced a check on Orangeism.

Anglesey attempted to carry on these policies but his enthusiasm for the Catholics' cause cost him a good deal. He managed to become embroiled simultaneously in arguments with Catholics and Protestants, and rising pressure to relieve Catholics of their disabilities distracted guidance from London. The Irish poet Thomas Moore likened Anglesey to a man riding several horses in the circus ring:

> If once my Lord his graceful balance loses
> Or fails to keep each foot where each horse chooses,
> If Peel but gives one extra touch of whip
> To Papist's tail or Protestant's ear tip
> That instant ends their glorious horsemanship.
> Off bolt the several steeds, for mischief free
> And down, between them, plumps Lord Anglesey.[77]

Neither Wellington nor Peel saw fit to warn Anglesey that the Tories planned to introduce Catholic emancipation legislation.

Anglesey busied himself sending London urgent missives favouring concessions, while the Prime Minister resolved not to hint at their change of heart.[78] They complained instead of Anglesey's reluctance to suppress rural agitation, a move which they were certain would reinsure Protestants.[79] Anglesey at length adopted a harder line, but his recall had already been decided on.[80] Thus it was that Northumberland presided when the Catholic Emancipation Act was enacted. His own sympathies were deeply anti-Catholic, but he kept his own counsel.[81] To him was given the dubious honour of reporting to London that O'Connell had organised a new movement to agitate for repeal of the Act of Union.[82] A new age of mass unrest was about to begin.

1. "Copy of the Private Instructions to His Excellency the Earl of Hardwicke, Ld. Lt. of Ireland," enclosed in a letter, Portland to Hardwicke, n. d. [April 1801], Hardwicke MSS, 37507/332-35.

2. J. C. Beckett, "The Government and the Church of Ireland under William III and Anne," *Irish Historical Studies*, II (March 1941), 302.

3. H. P. Kearney, *Strafford in Ireland, 1633-1641* (Manchester: *Manchester University Press, 1959)*, p.113.

4. C. L. Falkiner, "Correspondence of Archbishop Stone and the Duke of Newcastle," *English Historical Review*, XX, 508-42, 735-63.

5. Kearney, *Strafford*, pp.106, 114-15.

6. Hugh Boulter, *Letters... to Several Ministers of State in England, and Some Others, Containing an Account of the Most Interesting Transactions which have Passed in Ireland from 1724 to 1738* (2 vols.; Dublin, 1770), *passim*.

7. George III to Pitt, 19 July 1800, printed in Aspinall, ed., *Later Correspondence of George III*, III, 379.

8. Cornwallis to the Bishop of Litchfield and Coventry, 22 December 1800, Kent Record Office MSS, printed in Aspinall, ed., *Later Correspondence of George III*, III, 436.

9. Hardwicke to Lady Londonderry, 7 November 1801, Hardwicke MSS, 35753/182.

10. William Stuart, Archbishop of Armagh, to Addington, 27 November 1801, Hardwicke MSS, 35771/152.

11. Hardwicke to Addington, 22 December 1801, Hardwicke MSS, 35771/154.

12. Stuart to Addington, 14 January 1802, printed in Aspinall, ed., *Later Correspondence of George III*, IV, 12-13; Hardwicke to Addington, 29 December 1801, Hardwicke MSS, 35771/166; Lindsay to Hardwicke, 5 January 1802, printed in MacDonagh, *Viceroy's Post-Bag*, p.112.

13. Hardwicke to George le Poer Beresford, 27 December 1803; Hardwicke to Addington, 29 December 1803, Hardwicke MSS, 35746/12, 34; Addington to Hardwicke, January 1804; Beresford to Addington, January 1804; Hardwicke to Addington, January 1804,

quoted in MacDonagh, *Viceroy's Post-Bag*, pp.129-30. Lindsay to Hardwicke, 18 December 1803, Hardwicke MSS, 35744/230.

14. Hawkesbury to Hardwicke, 20 May 1804, in MacDonagh, *Viceroy's Post-Bag*, pp.136-37.

15. Hardwicke to Lady Londonderry, 7 November 1804, Hardwicke MSS, 35753/182, printed in Aspinall and Smith, eds., *English Historical Documents*, XI, 264.

16. Hardwicke to Nepean, 9 June 1804, printed in MacDonagh, *Viceroy's Post-Bag*, p.142.

17. *Ibid.*; Stuart to Hardwicke, 28 September 1804, Hardwicke MSS, 35752/264.

18. Arthur Wellesley to Wellesley Pole, 17 March 1808, in Wellington, *Ireland*, p.367.

19. Arthur Wellesley to Richmond, 22, 26, 28, 29 June, 22, 24 July 1807, printed in Wellington, *Ireland*, pp. 93, 97, 98, 123, 127, 128.

20. Liverpool to Richmond, 14 July 1809; Dundas to Richmond, 17 July 1809; Egremont to Richmond, 19 July 1809; Richmond to Egremont, 31 July 1809, Richmond MSS, 71/1385, 1367, 69/1245, 1254.

21. Warburton to Stuart, 2 April 1810, Richmond MSS, 63/600.

22. Stuart to Richmond, 25 April 1810, Richmond MSS, 63/902.

23. Talbot to Peel, 6 May 1818, Peel MSS, 40194/250.

24. Liverpool to Charles Arbuthnot, 20 May 1822, printed in Arthur Aspinall, ed., *The Correspondence of Charles Arbuthnot* (Camden Third Series, Vol. LXV; London: Royal Historical Society Society, 1941), p.30.

25. Goulburn to Wellesley, 11 May 1824, Wellesley MSS, 37302/261-62.

26. Arthur Wellesley to Richmond, 5 July 1807, printed in Wellington, *Ireland*, p.107; the original is in Richmond MSS, 58/32.

27. Liverpool to Wellesley, 19 August 1826; Wellington to Wellesley, 20, 21 August 1826; Wellington to Liverpool, 30 August 1826, 1 September 1826, Wellesley MSS, 37304/181-206.

28. Liverpool to Wellesley, 19 August

1826, Liverpool MSS, 37304, 177-78.

29. Kearney, *Strafford*, p.103.

30. Bedford to Grenville, 14 January 1807, 26 February 1807, *Fortescue MSS*, IX, 9-14, 59-61.

31. Grenville to Bedford, 11 March 1807; Bedford to Spencer, 14 March 1807; Grenville to Bedford, 11 March 1807, *Fortescue MSS*, IX, 68-72, 9-12, 82-97.

32. Shawe, "Sketch," printed in Aspinall, ed. *George IV*, III, 309.

33. Goulburn to Wellesley, 13 February 1822, Wellesley MSS, 37298/200; *Ibid.*, 9 July 1822, Wellesley MSS, 37299/278; *Ibid.*, 5, 14 March 1822, Wellesley MSS, 37298/207-208.

34. Goulburn to Wellesley, 14, 23, 29 March 1822, Wellesley MSS, 37298/207-208, 209, 210; Wellesley to Goulburn, 23 February 1822, 5 July 1822, Goulburn MSS, Acc. 308, 11/22; 2 *Hansard*, VII (1822), 1029-37; "Draft of a Tithe Bill with Marginal Comments," c.15 April 1822, Elrington to Peel, 22 April 1822, Peel MSS, 40327/50-61; Thomas O'Beirne, "memorandum," n. d. [1822], Wellesley MSS, 37298/288-90; William Magee to Wellesley, 9 March 1822, Wellesley MSS, 37298/295-97.

35. "Extract of a Letter from Lt.Col. Shawe to the Marquess Wellesley," 26 February 1822, Wellesley MSS, 37298/269-71.

36. Goulburn to Wellesley, 15 June 1822, Wellesley to Peel, 21 November 1822, Wellesley MSS, 37299/213-14; 37300/69.

37. Wellesley, memorandum on tithes, n.'d., Wellesley MSS, 37302/1-40.

38. Wellesley, memoranda, February 1828, Wellesley MSS, 37305/302-13.

39. C. V. Jourdan, "The Rule of Charles I," in Walter Allison Phillips, *History of the Church of Ireland from the Earliest Times to the Present Day* (3 vols.; London: Oxford University Press, 1933), III, 12-13.

40. William King, Archbishop of Dublin, to Dr. Charlott, 1 April 1715, quoted in Charles S. King, *A Great Archbishop of Dublin: William King, D.D., 1650-1729* (London: Longmans and Co., 1906), p.220.

41. George III to Hardwicke, 8 May 1801, Hardwicke MSS, 35349/75.

42. Hardwicke to William Knox, 23 October 1802, Hardwicke MSS, 35776/68-70.

43. Knox to Hardwicke, 25 October 1802, Hardwicke MSS, 35734/158; Stuart to Charles Brodrick, Archbishop of Cashel, 8 April 1803, National Library of Ireland, Brodrick MSS, 8869/3.

44. 1 *Hansard*, VI (1806), 154.

45. See returns for Derry, Clogher and Down, submitted 7, 8 January 1806, 28 April 1806, in Dublin, State Paper Office, Official Papers (Second Series), I, 1790-1810, 529/208/2, 3, and 6; Elliot to Grenville, 11 April 1806, *Fortescue MSS*, 89-90; Bedford to Grenville, 2 May 1806, Grenville to Bedford, 6 May 1806, *Fortescue MSS*, VIII, 128-29, 135-36.

46. Stuart to Brodrick, 24 March 1808, Brodrick MSS, 8869/5; 1 *Hansard*, XI (1808), 67; Auckland to Grenville, 3 May 1808, *Fortescue MSS*, IX, 199.

47. O'Beirne to Arthur Wellesley, 16 May 1808, printed in Wellington, *Ireland*, p.438.

48. Beresford to Wellesley, 14 February 1823, National Library of Ireland, Beresford MSS, 38; Gash, *Peel*, p.140.

49. Colchester, diary, 20 February 1801, printed in Colchester, *Diary*, I, 241; Higgins to Marsden, 24 June 1801, Dublin, Public Record Office, Rebellion Papers, 620/18/14; Hardwicke to Pitt, November and December 1804, Hardwicke MSS, 35708; Plowden, *Ireland*, II, 503-504.

50. Grenville to Elliot, 8 August 1806, *Fortescue MSS*, VIII, 261-62; Grenville to Bedford, 11 August 1806; Bedford to Grenville, 13 September 1806, *Fortescue MSS*, VIII, 270, 328-29; Buckingham to Grenville, 11 December 1806, *Fortescue MSS*, VIII, 463-67; Grenville to Bedford, 29 December 1806, *Fortescue MSS*, VIII, 486-88; Bedford to Grenville, 19 December 1806, encl. Viscount Dillon to Grenville, 6 December 1806; Grenville to Elliot, 2 December 1806; Grenville to Bedford, 29 December 1806, *Fortescue MSS*, VIII, 479-81, 486-88; Grenville to Bedford, 12 February 1807, *Fortescue MSS*, IX, 36-37; Bedford to Grenville, 7 March 1807, *Fortescue MSS*, IX, 65-67; Ibid., 17 March 1807, *Fortescue*

MSS, IX, 99; Grenville to Bedford, 26 March 1807, *Fortescue MSS*, IX, 128; Lauderdale to Grenville, 2 May 1808, *Fortescue MSS*, IX, 197-98.

51. Richmond to Bathurst, 21 February 1811, Richmond MSS, 61/337.

52. Wellesley Pole to Richmond, 12 March 1812; Richmond to Wellesley Pole, 12, 13 March 1812, 15 May 1812, Richmond MSS, 67/1041, 66/952, 66/953, 68/1076; Richmond to Wellesley Pole, 26 June 1812, Richmond MSS, 68/1059; Richmond to Bathurst, 28 June 1812, *Bathurst MSS*, pp.182-83; Richmond to Wellesley Pole, 8 July 1812, Richmond MSS, 68/1058.

53. Richmond to Bathurst, 9 July 1812, *Bathurst MSS*, pp.185-86; Richmond to Peel, 9 August 1812, Parker, Peel, I, 71; Bathurst to Richmond, 15 September 1812, Richmond MSS, 70/1301.

54. Canning to Richmond, 27 May 1808, Richmond MSS, 59/147; Arthur Wellesley to Richmond, 12 May 1808, Wellington, *Ireland*, p.419; Gregory, *Letter-Box*, p.40. Duigenan was a constant source of anxiety to the government; his raspy voice and indiscretions gave almost universal offence. Even Saurin in, 1812 made an attempt to dismiss Duigenan; Peel thought this would be most cruel and urged Saurin to lend Duigenan a hand "in buckling on his cumbrous armour for another encounter." Peel to Saurin, 2 October 1812, Parker, *Peel*, I, 45-46.

55. Wellesley Pole to Ryder, 30 June 1810, in Westbrook Hay MSS, cited in Dennis Gray, *Perceval*, p.412; Richmond Bathurst, 13 February 1811, *Bathurst MSS*, p.154.

56. Richmond to Wellesley Pole, 8 March 1811, Wellesley Pole to Ryder, 16 April 1811, Westbrook Mss., Gray, y, *Perceval*, p.418; Ryder to Richmond, 1 January 1812, Richmond MSS, 60/276; Wellesley to Richmond, 29 June 1812, Richmond MSS, 60/277.

57. Dublin *Evening Post*, 2 February 1813, p.2, col.2; 16 March 1813, p.2, col.2; 11 September 1813, p.3, cols. 3-5.

58. Parker, *Peel*, I, 104; Gash, *Peel*, pp.160-61; Peel to Whitworth, 16 June 1814, Parker, *Peel*, I, 158-59; Gregory, *Letter-Box*, p.107; Madden, *Castle and Country*, pp.7-8; Dublin *Patriot*, 8 January 1822, p.3, col.1.

59. 1 *Hansard*, XXI (1812), 434-46.

60. The *Patriot*, 16 April 1822, p.2, cols. 304.

61. James A. Reynolds, *The Catholic Emancipation Crisis in Ireland, 1823-1829* (New Haven: Yale University Press, 1954), pp.108-109.

62. Gregory to Peel, 10 November 1824, Peel MSS, 40330/175; Goulburn to Wellesley, 11 March 1826, Wellesley MSS, 37304.

63. *Ibid*.

64. Peel to Wellesley, 29 June 1823, Peel MSS, 40330/175; Goulburn to Wellesley, 11 March 1826, Wellesley MSS, 37301/154-56; Wellesley to Peel, 22 June 1823, National Library of Ireland, Wellesley MSS, 322; Wellesley to Peel, 2 November 1823, Wellesley MSS, 37301/302; Goulburn to Wellesley, 26 March 1824, Wellesley MSS, 37302/240.

65. Shawe to Liverpool, 6 December 1824, Peel MSS, 40304, cited in Broeker, *Rural Disorder*, pp.164-65; Joy to Wellesley, 12 May 1823, Wellesley MSS, 37301/57-58; Peel to Wellesley, 16 May 1823, Wellesley to Peel, 12 July 1823, Peel MSS, 40324/156-59, 40611/54-67; Wellesley to Peel, 30 November 1824, Wellesley MSS, 37303/9-15; see "W. B. Burney's Account for Attending the Catholic Association," Dublin, State Paper Office, Official Papers, II, 588/672/10. Gurney's transcription totalled 51,746 pages for the period September 1826 through September 1827.

66. Peel to Goulburn, 2 November 1824, Peel MSS, 40330/161-62; Goulburn to Peel, 9 November 1824, Peel MSS, 40330/173.

67. Peel to Goulburn, 22 November 1824, Peel MSS, 40330/173.

68. Peel to Wellesley, 11 December 1824, Wellesley MSS, 37303/47.

69. Wellesley to Plunket, 22 May 1825, Plunket, ed., *Plunket*, II, 207.

70. Peel to Wellesley, 24 November 1826, Wellesley MSS, 37304/244; Peel, memorandum for the cabinet on the Catholic question, 31 March 1828, Peel MSS, 40340/4-9,

71. Plunket to Canning, 18 December 1825, in Plunket, ed., *Plunket*, II,

224-26.

72. Goulburn to Peel, 31 December 1825, Peel MSS, 40331/281.

73. Dublin *Evening Post*, 13 July 1822, p.3, cols. 3-4.

74. Goulburn to Plunket, 14 October 1822, Liverpool MSS, 38103/60; Peel to Wellesley, 2 November 1822, Wellesley MSS, 37300/1.

75. Goulburn to Peel, 21 December 1822, Peel MSS, 40328/302-304.

76. Senior, *Orangeism*, p.197.

77. Thomas Moore, "Thoughts on the Present Government of Ireland, 1828,"

Poetical Works of Thomas Moore, Collected by Himself (1841), VIII, 272.

78. Anglesey to Peel, 16 July 1828, Peel MSS, 40325/119.

79. Anglesey to Peel, 18 August 1828, Parker, *Peel*, II, 61; Anglesey to Leveson Gower, 2 July 1828, Parker, Peel, I, 51; Stanhope and Cardwell, eds., *Memories of Peel*, pp.203-204.

80. Anglesey, *One-Leg*, p.208.

81. Northumberland to Peel, 1829, Peel MSS, 40327/70, quoted in Gash, *Peel*, p.157.

82. Daniel Madden, *Ireland*, I, 56-57.

EPILOGUE

I have been of opinion that the office of Lord Lieutenant might be altogether abolished and the business conducted by a minister resident here. I am not of that opinion now: exclusive of the amount of money spent and influence produced in Dublin by the maintenance there of a sort of regal authority and show, I think it is of vital consequence to have there an executive officer, ready to act upon his own responsibility, if necessary, and charged with the distribution of local patronage, the receipt of local applications, and forming an efficient check upon the underlings in authority.

Stanley to Earl Grey, 10 March 1831

BY 1830 BRITISH administration in Ireland had undergone substantial changes. The central executive in London had acquired important new powers. The bureaucracy at Dublin Castle had been reformed. In 1830 the Whigs broke the Tories' ascendancy, and in doing so themselves evolved into a more responsive party mechanism. Patronage activities had declined. New instruments of law and order were in place. Irish viceroys had surrendered substantial parts of their own power to facilitate these reforms and on occasion had even quickened the pace of change. In all this nothing was more surprising than the survival of the viceregal system itself. The terms of the Act of Union had hinted strongly at its demise. Every viceroy was led to believe that he might be the last of the line. Yet it survived for almost another full century, amid an extended debate as to its usefulness.

This debate began in 1800. Pelham's logic was disturbingly compelling: either the Act of Union made Ireland an integral part of the United Kingdom or the Act itself was a sham. If integrated, the kingdom could not justify a separate executive in Dublin. As he had been, the King and his officials chose to ignore Pelham's logic.[1] But Hardwicke prepared a detailed and convincing *apologia* for the viceregal system. He dismissed Pelham's fears that a powerful local system would obstruct London's superintending authority: with the Irish legislature extinguished the Lord Lieutenant would look only to London for counsel. He reminded his readers how frequently Ireland's vested interests secured favours by exploiting English ignorance of Irish

153

conditions, and how efficient a local administration could be. Ireland was a troubled land; the peace was guaranteed by 60,000 men under arms (Hardwicke's estimate). The alternative to this "wholesome and general English discipline" was "the sport of local party and cabal".[2]

Hardwicke's arguments and a general disinclination to contemplate drastic changes protected the Irish viceroyalty, but the loss of patronage prerogatives undercut successive viceroys' decisive role in Irish affairs. This prompted suggestions that responsibility for Irish government be concentrated in the office of the Irish Chief Secretary, who would at once enjoy access to Parliament and wield extraordinary powers such as those granted to colonial governors. Charles Abbot favoured this proposal, and urged as well that the Chief Secretary be elevated to the cabinet. Supported by a permanent Irish office in London, control of Ireland's military establishment, and residence in Dublin when Parliament was not in session, the Chief Secretary would indeed be a formidable political figure.[3]

Abbot's proposal received scant attention. The mediocre quality of some contemporary Chief Secretaries and antipathy to constitutional manipulation were in part responsible. Abbot could take comfort, however, in the thought that others were prepared to support related proposals. In 1804 Cornwallis wondered how long Ireland could be governed without making the Chief Secretary supreme in Irish affairs.[4] In 1806 Grenville contemplated putting some member of the Irish administration into the Cabinet, but could devise no formula likely to meet Ireland's need for strong personal rule and the requirements of ministerial unity all at once.[5] After 1810 the whole question was shelved for a decade.[6]

By 1820 Peel's performance as Chief Secretary suggested to many that Abbot's proposal be re-examined. An Irish M.P., Henry Parnell, reopened the question of the usefulness of the Lord Lieutenancy.[7] Parnell and his friend Joseph Hume were indefatigable foes of fiscal extravagance. In June 1823 Hume delivered a long speech contending that the corpus of viceregal powers could be wielded with equal effectiveness from London. He observed that the viceroy no longer possessed an independent military authority, an effective voice in formulating policy, or autonomy in finance. The office was therefore not only superfluous; it actually impeded Irish administration. The viceroy could "not appropriate a shilling" without Parliament's sanction, and the Privy Council's duties were so trifling "that all records since 1810 were kept in one book".[8] Hume cited Wellesley as an example of a viceroy frustrated in his best efforts by London's intervention.[9] He urged that the viceroy and the Chief Secretary be replaced by a secretary of state for Ireland and a Lord Lieutenant in each county.

Hume's thoughtful observations inevitably prompted a response. Conservatives and some liberals constructed a defence of the traditional system. Goulburn observed in an unusually frank moment that the viceroyalty was Ireland's "last vestige of dignity", the Irish "would look upon... the abolition... as the last scene of their degradation".[10] Peel adverted to the viceroys' role in the distribution of ecclesiastical and civil patronage in sustaining the morale of Ireland's ruling classes. Canning feared abolition "would destroy the last link which bound the two countries together". [11]

But four years later, in July 1827, Canning himself apparently underwent a change of heart. An Irish M.P., David Spring Rice, allegedly persuaded Canning that the Irish viceroyalty was no longer necessary. But Canning died one month later, ending speculation that he would abolish the office before Christmas.[12] William Lamb observed nonetheless that the office might well expire with Wellesley. [13] But Peel and Wellington were pre-occupied with the Catholic Emancipation crisis and did nothing. In 1830 Hume prepared to take a stronger line. Abandoning his earlier emphasis on economy (some Irish nationalists resented the inference that Ireland was not worth the expenditure), Hume now maintained that the viceroyalty endangered private liberties by cultivating class distinctions, by sustaining Protestant hegemony, and by encouraging an arbitrary conduct "inconsistent with all principles of freedom". The office violated the Act of Union and subjected Ireland to a "continued state of vaccilation" while Dublin and London competed for control of Irish policy. Landlords fled Ireland to escape "the annoyances of the mobs and bristle of state parties" excited by the viceroy's presence. Justice was warped by the Castle's influence, and taxes required to sustain the system necessarily oppressed the lower classes.[14] In supporting Hume, Spring Rice observed that Dublin was now closer than was Edinburgh; he "valued a single steam-boat more than a whole wilderness of Lord Lieutenants"; the viceroyalty had come to be simply "the mimic splendour of the viceregal throne".[15] Viscount Althorp concluded the attack by observing that the viceregal system gave Ireland all the trappings and none of the advantages of monarchical government.[16]   Whigs hinted that they would abolish it if they came to power.

The Whigs replaced Wellington's Tory ministry in November 1830. At first it did appear that Anglesey would be the last viceroy. Earl Grey installed Edward Stanley as Chief Secretary and gave him Cabinet rank. Anglesey protested that he too should be included.[17]   He was denied his wish on the grounds that his residence in Dublin meant that "a key which can only open [Cabinet] boxes never within your reach would...[be] an idle honour if any".[18]   All this did not lead to the abolition of Anglesey's office, perhaps because of a change of heart by Edward Stanley. Stanley concluded that it was of vital consequence "to have in Ireland an executive officer, ready to act upon his own responsibility, if necessary..."[19]   Stanley's view prevailed among the Whigs and the great reform movement did not touch the ancient Irish executive.

The remainder of the century saw occasional efforts to remove the viceroy. Peel's nominee as viceroy from 1841 to 1846 was Lord de Grey, "a self-confident peer with ultra-Protestant connections". He squabbled so vigorously with the Chief Secretary over education policies that Peel admitted in a speech that he was weighing the merits of abolishing the office.[20] But Peel could not determine how the Chief Secretary could govern in Ireland when he resided in London, or have a voice in the Cabinet when he visited Dublin.[21]   In 1846 Earl Russell and the Whigs introduced a bill to replace the viceroy, Chief Secretary and Undersecretary by three secretaries of state and three undersecretaries. It was approved by a substantial margin in the House of Commons, but later dropped because what were considered to be more important matters intruded.[22]

During the 1850s and 1860s a resident Irish executive was justified as necessary to cope with a revival of Irish nationalist agitation.[23] Some enthusiasts proposed despatching the Queen on an occasional visit or the Prince of Wales as a surrogate ruler, but no one wished to identify the Crown so closely with Irish politics. Instead between 1830 and 1868 five viceroys were granted Cabinet rank.[24] Gladstone hailed one of them, Earl Spencer, as a "working viceroy", but most of them devoted more and more time to formal functions. Lord Houghton discovered how painful this could be; when Gladstone first introduced a home rule bill his receptions were surrendered to "soldiers, policemen, knights and nobodies".[25] But pretensions died hard. In 1902 the Chief

Secretary and viceroy battled for supremacy on a sensitive land reform issue. Lord Dudley as viceroy signed some instructions for the estates commissioners. Thereupon the Chief Secretary directed the viceroy to implement them on the promise that as minister responsible to parliament for Irish affairs he was pre-eminent in this instance. Dudley recoiled at the prospect of being held sub- ordinate to his Chief Secretary. The Prime Minister, Arthur Balfour, was invited to arbitrate. He alluded to the "practical paradox" involved; the viceroy's "legal and social status remained what it had been", but "his political position was quite altered". He was in fact a "constitutional monarch". The Chief Secretary had triumphed. In 1906 Lord Aberdeen conceded the validity of Balfour's verdict but requested recognition as "a partner in the Irish government in respect to his formal functions". As the man on the spot, he advised, he was often better qualified to judge developments correctly. [26]

After Aberdeen, vestiges of ancient forms in the Irish adminis- tration quickly melted away. During the First World War viceroy Winborne complained that London provided him no information regarding the war; after much agitation he managed to gain only a "partial insight". [27] Traditional social functions disappeared during the war, and the Easter rebellion of 1916 persuaded many prominent Irishmen that they "did not care to expose themselves to the risk attendant on a stay at the viceregal lodge".[28] When the Dail superseded the Irish representation at Westminster and accepted the Free State, the new Irish Prime Minister, Michael Collins, appeared in the Castle yard. Viscount FitzAlan, the last viceroy, was introduced to the Free State Government, entered his automobile, and sped away.

The viceregal system in Ireland came to an end more than fifty years ago, and more than a century separates the present era from the subject of this study. The unprepossessing cluster of buildings, turrets and courtyards known as Dublin Castle still stands guard over Trinity College, the ancient Irish parliament, and the Liffey. It is not an impressive place; there is no sense of space or grandeur or confidence. Indeed, the Castle is secretive and defensive. Britain's efforts to govern Ireland and to integrate that island into the British polity prompted numerous exercises in administra- tive experimentation.

One dimension of administrative change has been treated in this book: the erosion of the ancient viceregal autonomy in favour of a more centralised but often more enlightened administrative apparatus located in London. This process failed to obliterate Ireland's separate identity, and the very survival of an anachronistic viceregal system until the emergence of the Free State implies how viable the concept of Irish autonomy continued to be even after the extinction of the Dublin Parliament.

Few will lament the disappearance of the ancient administrative system which called Dublin Castle its home. This system was burdened with centuries of unhappy memories for many Irishmen. Power was often exercised arbitrarily. A sense of crisis prevailed even in times of tranquility, and no amount of administrative reform and regularity sufficed to extinguish it. The viceroys exploited an ancient fascination for status and the symbols of authority. Police and patronage powers constituted the foundations of social control; the first demeaned Britain's indigenous institutions of law and order and the second undermined the Irish administrative apparatus. And yet not all was bad. During the period of this study a concerted effort was made to raise the tone of Irish administration, if only to make it more palatable to a nation recently deprived of its own legislature. Men of good battled against entrenched bigots and placemen, and they made vital gains. They averted the devastation of a full-fledged rebellion and they set in place the foundations of a system of government and social policy not yet completely extinguished.

For the moment, from 1800 to 1830, a monumental factor was also a negative one. The survival of a separate Irish government in the wake of the Act of Union could not have been predicted at the beginning of the nineteenth century. The Act of Union certainly anticipated the complete integration of Ireland into the United Kingdom, much as Scotland had been subsumed a century earlier. This did not happen. Viceregal administration, ancient and in many respects anachronistic, survived a crucial period of political integration and kept alive the idea that Dublin was a legitimate capital in its own right, and that Ireland was not simply another "English county".

1. George III to Addington, 1801, printed in O'Brien, *Dublin Castle*, p.85.

2. "Remarks on Lord Pelham's Famous Paper of Consideration to Marsden, October 1801," Hardwicke MSS, 37507/168-74. Hardwicke to Yorke, 19 October 1803, Hardwicke MSS, 35772/243-46.

3. Abbot to Addington, April 1801, Hardwicke MSS, 35707/24-28.

4. Cornwallis to Ross, 18 October 1804, Cornwallis, *Correspondence*, III, 519.

5. *Fortescue MSS*, VII, 351; VIII, 1, cited in Aspinal, "Cabinet Council," p.162.

6. *Hansard*, XVII (1810), 527.

7. *Hansard*, I (1820), 465.

8. *Ibid.*, IX (1823), 1215-18.

9. *Ibid.*, IX (1823), 1215-18.

10. *Ibid.*, 1226-30, 1236-37.

11. *Ibid.*, 1232-35.

12. Arbuthnot to Peel, 6 July 1827, Peel MSS, 40340/156-59; Lamb to Wellesley, 7 June 1827, Wellesley MSS, 37305/122.

13. Lamb to Lansdowne, 11 November 1827, printed in Torrens, *Melbourne*, I, 259.

14. *Hansard*, XXIV (1830), 557-62.

15. *Ibid.*, 566-68.

16. McDowell, *Irish Administration*, p.66.

17. Edward Stanley to Grey, 10 March 1831, Howick MSS, cited in Aspinall, "Cabinet Council," p.161.

18. Holland to Anglesey, 29 June 1831, Plas Newydd MSS, printed in Aspinall, "Cabinet Council," p.162.

19. Stanley to Grey, 10 March 1831, Howick MSS, printed in Aspinall, "Cabinet Council," p.161.

20. McDowell, *Public Opinion*, pp.204-205.

21. *Hansard*, LIV (1844), 856.

22. *Ibid.*, CXLVI (1847), 1048 ff.; CLXIX (1847), 712.

23. National Library of Ireland, Larcom MSS, 7504, cited in McDowell, *Irish Administration*, pp.68-70.

24. Charles Trevelyan to William Ewart Gladstone, 20 August 1883, British Museum Add. MSS 40310, in McDowell, *Irish Administration*, pp.60-61.

25. McDowell, *Irish Administration*, p.55.

26. John Campbell Hamilton-Gordon. Seventh Earl of Aberdeen, to Henry Campbell-Bannerman, 28 December 1906, British Museum Add. MSS, 41210; McDowell, *Irish Administration*, p.62.

27. Great Britain, Parliament, House of Commons, *Royal Commission on Rebellion in Ireland: Minutes of Evidence* (1916), p.34.

28. Anon., "Last Days of Dublin Castle," p.157; *Blackwood's Magazine*, August 1922.

BIBLIOGRAPHY

MANUSCRIPT SOURCES

The principal depositories for material used in this study are the Public Record Office, London, the Public Record Office, Dublin, the British Museum, the National Library of Ireland, and private collections listed below.

Beresford MSS
The papers and typescript copies of correspondence of George de la Poer Beresford, Archbishop of Armagh, preserved in the library of the Representative Church Body of the Church of Ireland, Dublin.

Canning MSS
The papers of George Canning, in the possession of the Earl of Harewood and housed in the Sheepscar Library, Leeds.

Goulburn MSS
The papers of Henry Goulburn as Irish Chief Secretary, 1821-1827, preserved in the Surrey Record Office, Kingston on Thames.

Hardwicke MSS
The papers of Philip Yorke, Third Earl Hardwicke, catalogued and housed in the British Museum. This collection offers remarkable insights into "union engagements" patronage activities from 1801 to 1805.

Liverpool MSS
The papers of Robert Banks Jenkinson, Second Earl Liverpool, preserved in the British Museum.

Monteagle MSS
The papers of Thomas Spring Rice, First Baron Monteagle, housed in the National Library of Ireland, Dublin.

Newport MSS
The papers of Sir John Newport, Bart., preserved in the National Library of Ireland.

Peel MSS
The papers of Sir Robert Peel, Second Baronet. This collection is especially valuable for the light it sheds on patronage matters between 1812 and 1818, and for the relationship between Whitehall and Dublin Castle during the 1820s.

Perceval MSS
A small collection of papers belonging to Spencer Perceval, Prime Minister 1809-1812, and preserved in the British Museum.

Richmond MSS
A portion of the papers of Charles Lennox, Fourth Duke of Richmond, covering his tenure as Lord Lieutenant, 1807-1813.

Sidmouth MSS
The papers of Henry Addington, First Viscount Sidmouth, as Prime Minister and Home Secretary. They have been catalogued recently and are housed in the Devon Record Office, Exeter.

Wellesley MSS
The papers of Richard Colley Wesley, Marquess Wellesley. This voluminous

collection includes originals and copies of Wellesley's official and private correspondence as Lord Lieutenant, 1821-1827, as well as many letters from his friends and political associates.

UNPUBLISHED DISSERTATIONS

Brashares, Richard A. "The Political Career of the Marquess Wellesley in England and Ireland." Duke University: Ph.D. Dissertation, 1968.

Burke, G. F. "The Viceroyalty of Lord William Fitzwilliam: A Crisis in Anglo-American Political History." American University: Ph.D. Dissertation, 1968.

Empey, C. A. "The Butler Lordship in Ireland." Trinity College, University of Dublin: Ph.D. Dissertation, 1970.

Frame, R. F. "The Dublin Government and Gaelic Ireland, 1272-1361: The Making of War and the Making of Peace in the Irish Lordship." Trinity College, University of Dublin: Ph.D. Dissertation, 1971.

CONTEMPORARY PRINTED MATERIAL

Barrett, Alexander. *Essay on Conciliation, or Review of the Vice-Royalty of Marquis Wellesley.* Dublin, 1823.

Blessington, Charles J. Gardiner, Earl of. *A Letter to the Marquess Wellesley on the State of Ireland. By a Representative Peer.* Dublin 1822.

Boulter, Hugh. *Letters... to Several Ministers of State in England and Some Others Containing an Account of the Most Interesting Transactions Which Have Passed in Ireland from 1724 to 1738.* 2 vols. Dublin, 1770.

Bowdler, John. *Reform or Ruin: Take Your Choice.* Third ed. Dublin, 1798.

Lodge, John. *Peerage of Ireland.* Ed. Mervyn Archdall. Dublin, 1789.

Madden, Daniel O. *The Castle and the Country.* Dublin, 1850.

Ireland and its Rulers: Since 1829. London, 1843-44.

Magee, John. *The Trial of John Magee for Publishing an Historical Review of the Duke of Richmond's Administration in Ireland.* Dublin, 1813.

Morgan, John H. "How Ireland is Governed." *Nineteenth Century* (September 1913), pp.568-79.

Norbury, John Toler, First Earl of. *Report of the Charge of the Lord Chief Justice on the Trial of C. B. Johnston and T. J. Haydn, for a Libel Against... Richard Marquess Wellesley, Lord Lieutenant of Ireland.* Dublin, 1825.

Sisson, Jonathan. *Second Letter to the Right Hon. Earl Grey, on the Necessity of an Appointment of a Board, or Council at Dublin, for the Internal Interests of Ireland.* London, 1832.

Stock, Joseph. *A Narrative of What Passed at Killala.* London, 1800.

Wakefield, Edward. *An Account of Ireland: Statistical and Political.* 2 vols. London, 1812.

MEMOIRS, DIARIES, CORRESPONDENCE AND BIOGRAPHIES

Alison, Sir Archibald, Bart. *Lives of Lord Castlereagh and Sir Charles Stewart, the Second and Third Marquesses of Londonderry.* 3 vols. Edinburgh:

W. Blackwood and Son, 1861.

Anglesey, George Charles Henry Victor Paget, Marquess of. *One Leg: the Life and Letters of Henry William Paget, First Marquess of Anglesey, K.G., 1768-1854.* London: Reprint Society, 1963.

Ashley, Anthony E. M. *The Life and Correspondence of Henry John Temple, Viscount Palmerston.* 2 vols. London, 1879.

Aspinall, Arthur, *Lord Brougham and the Whig Party.* Manchester: Manchester University Press, 1927.

Aspinall, Arthur, ed. *Correspondence of Charles Arbuthnot.* London: Royal Historical Society (Camden Third Series, Volume 65), 1941.

———*Correspondence of George III.* Cambridge: Cambridge University Press, 1962 ff.

———*Correspondence of George, Prince of Wales, 1770-1812.* New York: Oxford University Press, 1963.

———*Later Correspondence of George III.* Cambridge: Cambridge University Press, 1962 ff.

———*The Letters of King George IV, 1812-1830.* 3 vols. Cambridge: University Press, 1938.

Bagot, Josceline, ed. *George Canning and His Friends.* 2 vols. London: J. Murray, 1909.

Bamford, Francis, and Arthur Wellesley, Seventh Duke of Wellington. *The Journal of Mrs. Arbuthnot.* 2 vols. London: Macmillan, 1950.

Barnes, Donald G. *George III and William Pitt.* Stanford: Stanford University Press, 1939.

Beresford, William, ed. *Correspondence of the Right Honourable John Beresford.* 2 vols. London: Woodfall and Kinder, 1854.

Brougham, Henry. *Life and Times.* 3 vols. New York: Harper and Row, 1871. *Works.* 11 vols. London: R. Griffin and Co., 1855-1861.

Buckingham and Chandos, Richard Plantagenet Temple-Nugent-Brydges-Chandos-Grenville, Duke of. *Memoirs of the Courts and Cabinets of George III.* 2 vols. London: Hurst and Blackett, 1853-55.

Colchester, Charles Abbot, First Baron. *Diary and Correspondence.* 3 vols. London: J. Murray, 1861.

Curtis, Edmund. "Richard Duke of York as Viceroy of Ireland, 1447-1460." *Journal of the Royal Society of Antiquaries of Ireland,* Vol. LXII (1932), 158-86.

Falkiner, Caesar Litton. "Correspondence of Archbishop Stone and the Duke of Newcastle." *English Historical Review,* Vol. XX, pp.508-42, 735-63.

Fitzgerald, W. J., ed. *The Correspondence of Daniel O'Connell.* 2 vols. London: John Murray, 1888.

Gash, Norman. *Mr. Secretary Peel: The Life of Sir Robert Peel to 1830.* Cambridge: Harvard University Press, 1961.

Granville, Castalia Rosalind Gower, Countess of, ed. *The Private Correspondence of Lord Granville Leveson Gower.* 2 vols: London: John Murray, 1916.

Gray, Dennis. *Spencer Perceval: The Evangelical Prime Minister.* Manchester: Manchester University Press, 1963.

Great Britain. Historical Manuscripts Commission. *Report on the Manuscripts of J. B. Fortescue, Esq., Preserved at Dropmore.* 10 vols. London: Her Majesty's Stationery Office, 1892 ff.

———Report on the Manuscripts of Henry Seymore. Third Earl Bathurst, Preserved at Cirencester Park. Francis Lawrance Berkley, ed. London: His Majesty's Stationery Office, 1923.

Gregory, Augusta Isabella, Lady, ed. *Mr. Gregory's Letter-Box, 1813-1830.* London: Smith, Elder and Co., 1898.

Greville, Charles C. F. *A Journal of the Reigns of King George IV and King William IV.* 2 vols. ed. Richard Henry Stoddard. New York: Scribners, Armstrong, 1875.

Gwynn, Stephen L. *Henry Grattan and His Times.* Westport, Conn.: Greenwich Press, 1971.

Harcourt, Leveson Vernon, ed. *The Diaries and Correspondence of the Rt. Honourable George Rose.* 2 vols. London: R. Bentley, 1860.

Hogge, George, ed. *The Journal and Correspondence of William Eden, Lord Auckland.* 4 vols. London, 1861-62.

Jennings, Louis, J., ed. *The Correspondence and Diaries of John Wilson Croker.* 3 vols. London: John Murray, 1885.

Kearney, H. F. *Strafford in Ireland, 1633-41.* Manchester: Manchester University Press, 1959.

King, Charles S. *A Great Archbishop of Dublin: William King, D.D., 1650-1729.* London: Longmans and Co., 1906.

MacDonagh, Michael. *The Viceroy's Post-Bag: Correspondence hitherto Unpublished of the Earl of Hardwicke, First Lord Lieutenant of Ireland after the Union.* London: John Murray, 1904.

McDowell, Robert B., ed. "Some Fitzgibbon Letters from the Sneyd Muniments in the John Rylands Library." *John Rylands Library, Manchester, Bulletin,* Vol. XXXIV (1952), pp. 296-311.

Malmesbury, James Harris, First Earl. *Diaries and Correspondence.* 4 vols. London: R. Bentley, 1844.

Parker, Sir Charles S., ed. *Sir Robert Peel.* 3 vols. London: John Murray, 1891.

Pellew, George, ed. *The Life and Correspondence of the Right Honourable Henry Addington, First Viscount Sidmouth.* 3 vols. London: John Murray, 1847.

Plunket, David, ed. *The Life, Letters and Speeches of Lord Plunket.* 2 vols. London: Smith, Elder and Co., 1867.

Ross, Charles, ed. *The Correspondence of Charles, First Marquess Cornwallis.* 3 vols. London: J. Murray, 1859.

Russell, John Russell, First Earl, ed. *Memoirs and Correspondence of Charles James Fox.* 4 vols. London: Richard Bentley, 1853-57.

Rutland, Charles, Seventh Duke of, ed. *Correspondence between the Right Honourable William Pitt and Charles, Duke of Rutland, Lord Lieutenant of Ireland, 1781-1787.* London: A. Spottiswoode, 1842.

Somerville, Edith Anna Cenone. *An Incorruptible Irishman: Being an Account of Chief Justice Charles Kendal Bushe.* London: J. Nicholson and Watson, 1932.

Stanhope, Philip Stanhope, Fifth Earl, and Edward T. Cardwell, Viscount Cardwell, eds. *The Memoirs of Sir Robert Peel.* 2 vols. London: John Murray, 1856.

Torrens, William M. *Melbourne.* 2 vols. London: Macmillan, 1878.

Walpole, Sir Spencer. *Life of Spencer Perceval.* 2 vols. London: Hurst and

Blackett, 1874.

Wellington, Arthur Wellesley, First Duke of. Vol. 5 of *Supplementary Despatches and Memoranda*. 15 vols. London: John Murray, 1852-72.

_____*Despatches Correspondence and Memorabilia*. 8 vols. London: J. Murray, 1867-80.

Yonge, C. D. *Life and Administration of Lord Liverpool*. 3 vols. London, 1868.

Ziegler, Philip. *Addington*. New York: John Day Co., 1965.

SECONDARY SOURCES

Anon. "The Last Days of Dublin Castle". *Blackwood's Magazine* (August 1922), pp.137-90.

Aspinall, Arthur. "The Cabinet Council, 1783-1835". The Raleigh Lectures on History (Separate from Proceedings of the British Academy). *Proceedings of the British Academy*, XXXVIII (1952).

_____"George IV and Sir William Knighton." *English Historical Review*. Vol. LV (1940).

_____"The Irish Proclamation Fund, 1800-1846." *English Historical Review*. Vol. LVI (1941).

_____"The Use of Irish Secret Service Money in Subsidising the Irish Press". *English Historical Review*. Vol. LVI (1941).

_____*Politics and the Press, 1780-1850*. London: Home and Van Thaal, 1949.

Aspinall, Arthur, ed. "The Formation of Canning's Ministry, February to August, 1827." London: Royal Historical Society (*Camden Third Series*, Vol. LIX), 1937.

Beckett, J. C. "Anglo-Irish Constitutional Relations in the Later Eighteenth Century." *Irish Historical Studies*. Vol. XIV, pp.20-38.

_____"The Government and the Church of Ireland under William III and Anne," *Irish Historical Studies*. Vol. II (March 1941).

_____*The Making of Modern Ireland, 1603-1923*. London: Faber and Faber, 1966.

Black, R. D. C. *Economic Thought and the Irish Question, 1817-1870*. Cambridge: Cambridge University Press, 1960.

Bolton, G. C. *The Passing of the Act of Union*. London: Oxford University Press, 1966.

Brock, William Ranulf. *Lord Liverpool and Liberal Toryism, 1820-1827*. Cambridge: Cambridge University Press, 1941.

Broeker, Galen. *Rural Disorder and Police Reform in Ireland, 1812-1836*. London: Routledge and Kegan Paul, 1970.

Bryce, James. "England and Ireland". *Century Magazine* (June 1883), pp. 249-64.

Butterfield, Herbert. *George III, Lord North, and the People, 1719-1780*. London: Beel, 1949.

Chart, D. A. *Ireland from the Union to Catholic Emancipation*. London: J. M. Dent and Sons, 1910.

Clarke, M. V. *Fourteenth Century Studies*. Oxford: At the Clarendon Press, 1937.

Curtis, Lewis Perry. *Coercion and Conciliation in Ireland, 1880-1892*.

Princeton: Princetón University Press, 1963.

Davies, H. W. "Catholic Emancipation". John Edward Acton, Baron Acton, et al., eds. *Cambridge: Modern History.* Cambridge, Cambridge University Press, 1934.

Falkiner, Caesar Litton. *Studies in Irish History and Biography.* London: Longmans, Green and Co., 1902.

Gilbert, Sir John Thomas. *History of the Viceroys of Ireland.* Dublin: J. Duffy, 1865.

Gwynn, Dennis. *The Struggle for Catholic Emancipation, 1750-1829.* London: Longmans and Co., 1928.

Hamilton, William B. "Constitutional and Political Reflections on the Dismissal of Lord Grenville's Ministry." *Canadian Historical Association Report* (1964), pp.89-104.

Harlow, V. T. *The Founding of the Second British Empire* 2 vols. London: Longmans, Green and Co., 1952 and 1964.

Hughes, J. L. J. "The Chief Secretaries in Ireland". *Irish Historical Studies,* VIII, 59-72.

Johnston, Edith M. *Great Britain and Ireland, 1760-1800: A Stády in Political Administration.* Edinburgh: Oliver and Boyd, 1963.

Judd, G. P. *Members of Parliament, 1734-1832.* New Haven: Yale University Press, 1955.

Kiernan, T. J. *The Financial Administration of Ireland to 1817.* London: P. S. King, 1930.

O'Connell, Maurice R. *Irish Politics and Social Conflict in the Age of the American Revolution.* Philadelphia: University of Philadelphia Press, 1965.

O'Hegarty, Patrick Sarsfield. *A History of Ireland under the Union, 1801-1922.* London: Methuen, 1952.

O'Mahoney, Charles. *The Viceroys of Ireland.* London: John Long, 1912.

Otway-Ruthven, Jocelyn. "The Chief Governors of Medieval Ireland." *Journal of the Royal Society of Antiquaries of Ireland.* Vol. XCV (1965), pp. 227-36.

——— *A History of Medieval Ireland.* London: Ernest Benn, 1968.

Phillips, Walter Allison, ed. *History of the Church of Ireland from the Earliest Times to the Present Day.* 3 vols. London: Oxford University Press, 1933.

Plowden, Francis. *History of Ireland, 1801-1810.* Dublin, 1811.

Reynolds, James A. *The Catholic Emancipation Crisis in Ireland. 1823-1829.* New Haven: Yale University Press, 1954.

Rose, John Holland. *Pitt and Napoleon: Essays and Letters.* London: C. Bell and Sons, 1912.

Senior, Hereward. *Orangeism in Ireland and Britain, 1795-1836.* London: Routledge and Kegan Paul, 1966.

White, Terence de Vere. "Mahaffy, the Anglo-Irish Ascendancy and the Vice-Regal Lodge." F. X. Martin, ed. *Leaders and Men of the Easter Rising.* London: Methuen, 1967.

Wood, H. "The Office of Chief Governor of Ireland, 1172-1509." *Proceedings of the Royal Irish Academy.* Vol. XXXVI, Section C, pp.206-38.

Wyse, Thomas. *Historical Sketch of the Late Catholic Association of Ireland.* 2 vols. London, 1829.

Annual Register. London: W. Ottridge and Son, 1791-1813; and Baldwin, Cradock and Joy, 1814-1836.

Aspinall, Arthur, and E. Anthony Smith, eds. *English Historical Documents, 1783-1832.* London: Eyre and Spottiswoode, 1959.

Burke, John Bernard. *A Genealogical and Heraldic Dictionary of the Peerage and Baronetage.* 97th Edition. London: Burke's Peerage, 1939.

Curtis, Edmund and R. B. McDowell, eds. *Irish Historical Documents, 1172-1922.* New York: Barnes and Noble, 1943.

Gilbert, John Thomas, ed. *Documents Relating to Ireland, 1795-1804.* Dublin: J. Dollard, 1893.

Great Britain. *The Parliamentary Debates from the Year 1803 to the Present Time.* First Series. London: T. C. Hansard, 1820.

_____ Second Series. London: T. C. Hansard, 1830.

LeFevre, George John Shaw. *Peel and O'Connell: A Review of Irish Policy of Parliament from the Act of Union to the Death of Sir Robert Peel.* London: Kegan Paul, Trench, 1887.

McAnally, Henry W. W. *The Irish Militia, 1793-1816: A Social and Military Study.* Dublin: Clonmore and Reynolds, 1949.

McCracken, J. L. "The Conflict between the Irish Administration and Parliament, 1753-6." *Irish Historical Studies,* Vol. III, pp. 159-79.

McDowell, Robert B. *The Irish Administration, 1801-1914.* London: Routledge and K. Paul, 1964.

_____ "The Irish Executive in the Nineteenth Century." *Irish Historical Studies.* Vol. IX (1954-55), pp. 264-80.

_____ "The Irish Government and the Provincial Press." *Hermathena.* Vol. LIII (1939).

_____ *Irish Public Opinion, 1750-1800.* London: Faber and Faber, 1944.

_____ *Public Opinion and Government Policy in Ireland, 1801-1846.* London: Faber and Faber, 1952.

Martin, Robert M. *Ireland before and after the Union with Great Britain.* Third Edition. London: J. B. Nichols, 1848.

Maxwell, Constantia. *County and Town under the Georges.* Revised Edition. Dundalk: Dundalk Press, 1949.

_____ *Dublin under the Georges, 1714-1830.* Revised Edition. London: Faber and Faber, 1956.

_____ Mitchell, Austin. *The Whigs in Opposition, 1815-1830.* Oxford: At the Clarendon Press, 1967.

_____ Mulvey, Helen F. "Nineteenth Century Ireland, 1801-1914." *Irish Historical Studies.* Vol. XVII (March, 1970), pp. 1-31.

O'Brien, Richard Barry. *Dublin Castle and the Irish People.* London: K. Paul, Trench, Trubner, 1909.

INDEX

Abbot, Charles (subsequently Baron Colchester), 54, 64,
  urges making Chief Secretary Irish Chief Executive, 154.
Absenteeism, among M.P.s, 29.
Act of Union, 6, 7, 9, 10, 20, 46,
  patronage used to secure passage of, 10, 24,
  delimits Viceregal powers, 25,
  effect on patronage policies, 25,
  impact on communication between Dublin and London, 41,
  reference to Church of Ireland, 133.
  fails to extinguish Ireland's identity, 158.
Addington, Henry, see Sidmouth, Henry Addington, Viscount.
Anglesey, Henry Paget, Marquess of, 27, 28, 45,
  recalled by Wellington, 29,
  biographical material, 33,
  opposition to appointment as viceroy, 33,
  complains about Wellington, 43,
  relationships with Cabinet, 43,
  animosity towards Gregory, 71,
  reduces household staff, 72,
  religious policies assessed, 146,
  supports Catholic claims, 147,
  reasons for recall, 147.
Aristocracy, in Ireland, 8.
Armagh, Archbishopric of, vacancy in, 137.
Army,
  role in Ireland, 114,
  Lord Lieutenant and Commander-in-Chief contest jurisdiction over, 115.
Audiences, granted by viceroys, 104.
Balfour, Arthur,
  Arbiter as Prime Minister between Chief Secretary and Lord Lieutenant, 157.
Bandon, visit by Hardwicke, 107.
Bedford, John Russell, Duke of, 27, 42, 146,
  career before 1806, 30,
  relationship to Castle bureaucracy, 71,
  favours certain newspapers, 98,
  reluctance to use insurrection acts, 121,
  attempts to mollify Archbishop Stuart, 134,
  tithe reform efforts, 137.
Beresford, George de la Poer,
  condemned by Archbishop Stuart, 133.
Beresford, John, opposes patronage reforms, 133.
"Bolivar Speech," attempt to prosecute Daniel O'Connell for, 144.
"Bottle Incident," 102.
Buckingham, George, Marquis of, 72.
Bushe, Charles Kendall, as Solicitor General, 1805-1822, 68.
Canning, George, 33, 54,
  attempts to remove Wellesley in 1827, 29,
  relationship to Wellesley, 43,

supports Dougherty as Solicitor General, 69,
  patronage policies, 84,
  embarrassed by O'Connell, 144,
  defends viceregal system, 155,
  allegedly contemplates abolition of Lord Lieutenant's office, 155.
Cashel, Archbishopric of, 135.
Castle, see Dublin Castle.
"Castle Press," 10.
Castlereagh, Robert Stewart, Viscount, 54,
  expands powers of Chief Secretary's office, 48,
  performance as Chief Secretary, 47.
Cathcart, Sir William Shaw, 117.
Catherine the Great, falsely connected to Earl Whitworth, 32.
Catholic Association, Wellesley's reaction to, 68,
  growth of, 126,
  Wellesley assesses in 1823-24, 144,
  legislation designed to suppress in 1825, 145.
Catholic Committee, opposed by Richmond, 1810-1812, 143.
Catholic Emancipation, 7, 8.
Catholics, persecution in 1690s, 7.
Ceremony, justification for viceroys' use of, 108.
Chancellorship of the Exchequer, extinguished by Liverpool, 67.
Charities, 105,
  supported by governments, 101.
Charles I (of England), 132.
Charles X (of France), Coronation of, 34.
Chester, Rev. Charles, aspirations for bishopric, 73.
Chief Secretary to the Lord Lieutenant,
  subordinate to the viceroy in the eighteenth cen century, 47-8
  proposed as chief executive for Ireland, 154,
  evidence of office's slight prestige, 55,
  relationship to viceroy a "practical paradox", 56, 157.
Church of Ireland, 20,
  legal position, 20,
  Lord Lieutenant's obligations towards, 132,
  before the Act of Union, 132-3,
  referred to in the Act of Union, 133,
  condition in the seventeenth century, 139,
  legislation of 1808, 140.
Church Reform Act of 1834, 132.
Churches, appeals for assistance from, 105.
Civic celebrations, 106.
Civil Departments, Composition of, 65.
Clare, John Fitzgibbon, Earl of,
  resents Anglicization of the Irish adminis- tration, 64,
  opposition to Hardwicke, 65,
  patronage disputes with Hardwicke, 85.
Clerical residence,

169

172